ON FREUD'S
"MOURNING AND MELANCHOLIA"

CONTEMPORARY FREUD
Turning Points and Critical Issues

General Editor: Leticia Glocer Fiorini

IPA Publications Committee

Leticia Glocer Fiorini (Buenos Aires), Chair; Salman Akhtar (Philadelphia); Thierry Bokanowski (Paris); Alessandra Lemma (London); Sergio Lewkowicz (Porto Alegre); Mary Kay O'Neil (Montreal); Piers Pendred (London), Ex-officio as Director General; Cesare Sacerdoti (London), Ex-officio as Publications Director

On Freud's "Analysis Terminable and Interminable"
    edited by Joseph Sandler

Freud's "On Narcissism: An Introduction"
    edited by Joseph Sandler, Ethel Spector Person, Peter Fonagy

On Freud's "Observations on Transference-Love"
    edited by Ethel Spector Person, Aiban Hagelin, Peter Fonagy

On Freud's "Creative Writers and Day-Dreaming"
    edited by Ethel Spector Person, Peter Fonagy, Sérvulo Augusto Figueira

On Freud's "A Child Is Being Beaten"
    edited by Ethel Spector Person

On Freud's "Group Psychology and the Analysis of the Ego"
    edited by Ethel Spector Person

On Freud's "The Future of an Illusion"
    edited by Mary Kay O'Neil, Salman Akhtar

On Freud's "Splitting of the Ego in the Process of Defence
    edited by Thierry Bokanowski, Sergio Leukowicz

ON FREUD'S
"MOURNING AND MELANCHOLIA"

Edited by
Leticia Glocer Fiorini, Thierry Bokanowski,
Sergio Lewkowicz

Foreword by
Ethel Spector Person

CONTEMPORARY FREUD
Turning Points and Critical Issues

KARNAC

Part I: Grateful acknowledgement is made to Sigmund Freud Copyrights, Ltd; the Institute of Psycho-Analysis, London; the Hogarth Press; and Basic Books, a member of Perseus Books Group, for permission to reprint "Mourning and Melancholia" as published in *The Complete Edition of the Psychological Works of Sigmund Freud, Vol. 14*, trans. and ed. James Strachey. All rights reserved 1957. Reproduced by arrangement with Paterson Marsh Ltd., London. And in *The Collected Papers of Sigmund Freud, Vol. 4*, authorized translation under the supervision of Joan Riviere, published by Basic Books, Inc., a member of Perseus Book Group, by arrangement with the Hogarth Press, Ltd. and the Institute of Psycho-Analysis, London. Reprinted by permission of BASIC BOOKS, a member of Perseus Book Group.

Chapter 6: To the Institute of Psychoanalysis T. H. Ogden, "A New Reading of the Origins of Object-Relations Theory", reprinted from *International Journal of Psychoanalysis, 83* (2002): 767–782; copyright © Institute of Psychoanalysis, London, 2002. Reprinted by permission of the International Journal of Psychoanalysis.

Chapter 9: To Thomson Publishing Services, and to Routledge, a member of Taylor & Francis Group, for J. M. Quinodoz, "Teaching Freud's 'Mourning and Melancholia'" based on the content of "Papers on Metapsychology written between 1915 and 1917; Introductory Lectures on Psycho-Analysis (1916-1917)", pp. 135–155 in *Reading Freud: A Chronological Exploration of Freud's Writings* (London & New York: Routledge, 2004). By permission of the publisher.

First published in 2007 by
The International Psychoanalytical Association

This edition published in 2009 by
Karnac Books
118 Finchley Road
London NW3 5HT

Copyright © 2007, 2009 by The International Psychoanalytical Association

British Library Cataloguing in Publication Data

A C.I.P. for this book is available from the British Library

ISBN: 978-1-85575-744-8

10 9 8 7 6 5 4 3 2 1

Edited, designed, and produced by Communication Crafts

Printed in Great Britain

www.karnacbooks.com

CONTENTS

PART II
Discussion of "Mourning and Melancholia"

CONTEMPORARY FREUD

IPA Publications Committee

The Publications Committee of the International Psychoanalytical Association has decided to continue editing and publishing the Contemporary Freud series, which had been discontinued since 2001. This significant series was founded by Robert Wallerstein and first edited by Joseph Sandler, Ethel Spector Person, and Peter Fonagy, and its important contributions have greatly interested psychoanalysts of different latitudes. That is why it was with great pleasure that we invited Ethel Spector Person to write the Foreword for this volume with which the series is reinitiated.

The objective of this series is to approach Freud's work from a present and contemporary point of view. On the one hand, this means highlighting the fundamental contributions of his work that constitute the axes of psychoanalytic theory and practice. On the other, it implies the possibility of getting to know and spreading the ideas of present psychoanalysts about Freud's *oeuvre*, both where they coincide and where they differ.

This series considers at least two lines of development: a contemporary reading of Freud that reclaims his contributions and a clarification of the logical and epistemic perspectives from which he is read today. Both propositions have been taken into account in this project.

Freud's theory has branched out, and this has led to a theoretical, technical, and clinical pluralism that has to be worked through. It has therefore become necessary to avoid a snug and uncritical coexistence of concepts in order to consider systems of increasing complexities that take into account both the convergences and the divergences of the categories at play.

Consequently, this project has involved an additional task—that is, gathering psychoanalysts from different geographical regions representing, in addition, different theoretical stances, in order to be able to show their polyphony. This also means an extra effort for the reader that has to do with distinguishing and discriminating, establishing relations or contradictions that each reader will have to eventually work through. Martin Bergmann's Introduction enlightens this work to greater depth.

Being able to listen to other theoretical viewpoints is also a way of exercising our listening capacities in the clinical field. This means that the listening should support a space of freedom that would allow us to hear what is new and original.

We have chosen "Mourning and Melancholia" to reinitiate the series for the following reasons:

1. The processes of mourning and their differences—whether substantial or not—from melancholia are part of the life of every person and of the way in which he/she goes through the vital stages, separations and losses, real or imaginary.

2. The twentieth century and the beginnings of the twenty-first are strongly demarcated by traumatic social and political events. Social catastrophes, wars, genocides, State violence, terrorism, and so on, are phenomena that affect large groups and lead to the rupture of social ties and to an essential reflection about the processes of collective mourning related to them. This presupposes distinguishing which of Freud's contributions on this subject can be amplified and deepened.

3. This work is considered as the root of the object relations theories and the starting point of intersubjectivity in psychoanalysis.

Two themes run, among others, throughout this volume: the relations between psychic and social reality, and relations with others, both in apparently individual and in collective mourning.

In this spirit we have brought together authors deeply rooted in the Freudian tradition and others who have developed theories that had not been explicitly taken into account in Freud's work. This volume encompasses the metapsychology of mourning as well as its creative outcome in some subjects: mourning related to social catastrophes as well as individual mourning connected with unresolved, problematic primary relations; mourning in adolescence; and also a proposal concerning the teaching of "Mourning and Melancholia".

In this way, our purpose has been to go beyond a unique, uniform line of thought in order to sustain differences, which each reader might process creatively, and surpass as well.

Leticia Glocer Fiorini
Series Editor

ACKNOWLEDGEMENTS

We are pleased to reinitiate this series with the support of Cláudio Laks Eizirik, President of the International Psychoanalytical Association.

EDITORS AND CONTRIBUTORS

Carlos Mario Aslan is a Member and Training Analyst, Argentine Psychoanalytic Association (APA); former Editor, *Revista de Psicoanálisis* (APA). He was President of the Argentine Psychoanalytic Association, 1979–81; Vice-President of the International Psychoanalytical Association, 1983–85 and 1985–1987; Chair, Latin-American Program Committee, IPAC Madrid 1983, and Amsterdam 1993. He has published papers and chapters in books—mainly in Spanish, but also in English, French, and Italian—on the mourning process, pluralism, psychic structure, psychosomatics, etc.

Martin S. Bergmann is clinical professor of psychology, New York University Post-Doctorate Program in Psychoanalysis and Psychotherapy. He is an Honorary Member of the American Psychoanalytic Association and is Training and Supervising Analyst of the New York Freud Society. He has received the Sigourney Award and the Award of Psychoanalytic Education. His books include: *Understanding Dissidence and Controversy in the History of Psychoanalysis; The Hartmann Era; In the Shadow of Moloch; The Anatomy of Loving; Generations of the Holocaust;* and *The Evolution of Psychoanalytic Technique.*

Thierry Bokanowski is a training and supervising analyst of the Paris Psychoanalytical Society (SPP) and a member of the International

Psychoanalytical Association; a former secretary of the executive committee of the Paris Psychoanalytical Institute; and former editor of the *Revue Française de Psychanalyse*, he is the current President of the Scientific Committee of the Paris Psychoanalytical Society. He has published several papers in various psychoanalytic journals, including the *International Journal of Psychoanalysis*. His books include *Sándor Ferenczi*, and *De la pratique analytique*, translated under the title *The Practice of Psychoanalysis*.

Roosevelt M. S. Cassorla lives in Campinas, Brazil. He currently works as Full Professor at the Psychiatry and Psychological Medicine Department, Medical Sciences Faculty, State University of Campinas (UNICAMP), and as Professor of the Postgraduation Course of Mental Health as a visitor. He is a Titular Member, Training Analyst and Professor of the Institute of The Brazilian Psychoanalytic Society of São Paulo (SBPSP). He has edited three books on suicide and death and is author of 42 chapters on psychoanalysis and medical psychology subjects. His most recent papers refers to analytic technique and borderline configurations.

Leticia Glocer Fiorini is a training psychoanalyst of the Argentine Psychoanalytic Association. She is the current chair of the Publications Committee of the International Psychoanalytical Association and of the Publications Committee of the Argentine Psychoanalytic Association, and is a former member of the Editorial Board of the *Revista de Psicoanálisis* (1998–2002, Buenos Aires). She won the Celes Cárcamo Prize (APA, 1993) for her paper: "The feminine position: A heterogeneous construction". She is the author of *The Feminine and the Complex Thought* and editor of *The Other in the Intersubjective Field* and *Time, History and Structure. A Psychoanalytical Approach*. Among other contributions in psychoanalytic journals, she has also published in collected papers: "Assisted Fertilization, New Problems" in *Prevention in Mental Health*; "The Sexed Body and the Real: Its Meaning in Transsexualism" in *Masculine Scenarios*; "Psychoanalysis and Gender, Convergences and Divergences" in *Psychoanalysis and Gender Relations*; and "The Bodies of Present-Day Maternity" in *Motherhood in the Twenty-first Century*.

Florence Guignard was born in Geneva; she started her analytic training at the Swiss Society, moved to Paris in 1970, was elected Full Member of the Paris Society in 1979 and as Training Analyst in 1982.

As a Member of the COCAP of IPA, she created two Associations for Child Psychoanalysis, one French (APE, 1983), one European (SEPEA, 1993). She is the Head of the Editorial Board of *l'Année Psychanalytique Internationale* (a publication in French of the IJP). She has published many papers and two books: *Au vif de l'infantile*, and *Épître à l'objet*, both translated into Italian, Spanish, and Portuguese.

Sergio Lewkowicz is currently the Scientific Director of the Porto Alegre Psychoanalytical Society; Psychiatrist and Training and Supervising Analyst for the Porto Alegre Psychoanalytical Society; Professor and Supervisor for Psychoanalytical Psychotherapy in the Psychiatry Department, Medical School of the Federal University of Rio Grande do Sul; Member of the IPA Publications Committee; Member of the Programme Committee of the 43rd Congress of the IPA in New Orleans (2004); former President of the Society of Psychiatry of Rio Grande do Sul; former Editor of the Psychiatry Journal of Rio Grande do Sul. He has published papers on psychoanalytic technique and is the co-editor of *Truth, Reality and the Psychoanalyst* and editor of *Psychoanalysis and Sexuality: Tribute to the 100th Anniversary of the Three Essays on Sexual Theory*.

María Cristina Melgar is a medical doctor, psychiatrist, and psychoanalyst; she is a full member with training function at the Argentine Psychoanalytical Association, where she was Chair of the Department of Psychosis and of the Culture Board, member of the Directive Board and advisor for the Scientific Department. She was head of area at the J. T. Borda Psychiatric Hospital and professor at UBA and Del Salvador universities, as well as Director of *EOS, Journal of Art and Psychoanalysis*. She is the author of several books, among them *Images of Madness*; *Love Enamouredness Passion*; and *Art and Madness, Art and Psychoanalysis: From the Psychoanalytic Method to the Meeting with the Enigmatic in Visual Arts*, and of many published papers. She participated in the inaugural plenary of IPA first Interdisciplinary Symposium and has submitted at other IPA congresses her developments on the metapsychology of non-clinical psychoanalytic experiences. She is deeply interested in the creative side of trauma, of passionate madness, and of experiences of loss that lead to the construction of the new, and her works focus on this contribution to the evolution of the theory of technique and method, on psychoanalytic thought and on discovery itself.

Thomas H. Ogden is the Director of the Center for the Advanced Study of the Psychoses, a Supervising and Personal Analyst at the Psychoanalytic Institute of Northern California, and a member of the Faculty of the San Francisco Psychoanalytic Institute. He is the author of *This Art of Psychoanalysis: Dreaming Undreamt Dreams and Interrupted Cries; Conversations at the Frontier of Dreaming; Reverie and Interpretation: Sensing Something Human; Subjects of Analysis;* and *The Primitive Edge of Experience.* He was awarded the 2004 *International Journal of Psychoanalysis* Prize for the most important paper of the year.

María Lucila Pelento is Professor of Philosophy, a medical doctor and a Psychoanalyst; she is a member of the Argentine Psychoanalytical Association. She is co-founder of *Referencia Buenos Aires,* specializing in the theory and practice with children and adolescents. She was granted the Hayman Award 2004 and a Konex Award 2006 (Humanities). She has also conducted research on various effects of State-terrorism in Argentina—e.g., mourning for missing people; consequences of kidnapping and restitution of children on their sense of identity and belonging; creation of new social myths; disruptions of social links and marks on the body and on other surfaces; investigation of people affected by AMIA bombing; coordination of practices carried out with young people deprived of freedom and currently with victims of social exclusion.

Ethel Spector Person is Professor of Clinical Psychiatry at the College of Physicians and Surgeons, Columbia University, and a Training and Supervising Analyst at the Columbia University Center for Psychoanalytical Training and Research, where she was the Director from 1981 until 1991. Her books include *Feeling Strong: The Achievement of Authentic Power; The Sexual Century: Selected Papers on Sex and Gender; By Force of Fantasy: How We Make Our Lives;* and *Dreams of Love and Fateful Encounters: The Power of Romantic Love.* With Catherine Stimpson she co-edited *Women: Sex and Sexuality,* which was given an Award for Excellence in the field of education by Chicago Women Publishing. With Arnold Cooper and Otto Kernberg she co-edited *Psychoanalysis: The Second Century;* and with Arnold Cooper and Glen Gabbard she edited the APPI *Textbook of Psychoanalysis.* She has been active in the American Psychoanalytic Association, where she served both as a Fellow to the Board on Professional Standards and as an elected Councilor to the Executive Council. She was a Vice-President of the International Psychoanalytical Association from 1995 to 1999. Among other awards, she is the recipient of the Sigmund Freud Award from the American Society of Psychoanalytic Physicians; the Section III Recognition Award for her work in women's psychology from Division 39 of The American Psychological Association; and the Award for Distinguished and Meritorious Service to the IPA, 2000. In 2003, she was named the National Woman Psychoanalytic Scholar by the American Psychoanalytic Association. She is at work on a book: *Ah, I Remember It Well: Memories as the Building Blocks of Our Self-Identity*.

Jean-Michel Quinodoz is a psychoanalyst in private practice in Geneva. He is a Training Analyst of the Swiss Psychoanalytical Society and Honorary Member of the British Psychoanalytical Society. He was Editor for Europe of *The International Journal of Psychoanalysis* (1994–2003), and he is currently Editor-in-chief of *the New Annuals* published in French, Italian, German and Russian by *The International Journal of Psychoanalysis*. He has written more than 80 psychoanalytic articles published in various languages and is the author of *The Taming of Solitude: Separation Anxiety in Psychoanalysis*; *Dreams That Turn Over a Page*; and *Reading Freud: Chronological Exploration of Freud's Writings*.

Priscilla Roth is a Training Analyst and Supervisor of the British Psychoanalytical Society, where she is currently the Chair of the Education Committee. She has been a Principal Child Psychotherapist at the Tavistock Institute, London, and a lecturer in psychoanalytic theory at University College, London. She has taught extensively in Britain and abroad and is the author of a number of psychoanalytic papers and the editor of *On Bearing Unbearable States of Mind: The Collected Papers of Ruth Malcolm*, and, with Richard Rusbridger, *Encounters with Melanie Klein: The Collected Papers of Elizabeth Spillius*. She maintains a full-time psychoanalytic practice in London.

Vamık D. Volkan is Doctor of Medical Science *honoris causa*, University of Kuopio, Finland; Professor Emeritus of Psychiatry, University of Virginia, Charlottesville, VA; Senior Erik Erikson Scholar, Erikson Institute for Education and Research of the Austen Riggs Center, Stockbridge, MA; and Training and Supervising Analyst Emeritus, Washington Psychoanalytic Institute, Washington, DC.

PREFACE

We are honoured to present this new book, restarting the continuity of the Contemporary Freud Series and updating, with discussions and new developments, the seminal work of Sigmund Freud.

We chose "Mourning and Melancholia" (1917e [1915]), as it is a landmark in the understanding of the normal and psychopathological aspects of the mourning and depressive processes in human beings. It also marks a turning point in the importance being accorded to the object origins of object relations theories.

"Mourning and Melancholia" marks a pivot in the Freudian itinerary. In this work bridges between the first and the second topographic theories of the psychic apparatus are introduced, the critical instance of the ego is enlightened, identification as a result of object loss acquires relevance and distinctions, and relations between the real and the imaginary are worked through. It is a complex paper from which multiple paths are derived.

Our first task as editors of this book was to identify themes that could be developed from "Mourning and Melancholia". After a long and fruitful discussion we defined nine topics: the nine chapters of this book. The next step was to look for authors who had studied and published the most on the topics we had selected. In this context, we also took into account regional and institutional balances.

The different points of view we chose were an invitation to an enriching debate, in order to put into motion the ideas that had been proposed. Through the Introduction and the various chapters of this book it becomes evident how the Freudian text is inspiring and provocative, leading to new insights.

As the editors of this title, our aim has been to go beyond a final and definitive synthesis in order to focus on further developments and other views concerning this subject as well as to recover the huge richness of Freudian proposals.

Lastly, we would also like to thank the Publications Committee for the suggestions we received and all the persons who collaborated in this project.

Leticia Glocer Fiorini
Thierry Bokanowski
Sergio Lewkowicz

FOREWORD

Ethel Spector Person

It was a great pleasure to learn that the IPA "Contemporary Freud: Turning Points and Critical Issues" series is being revived. The original series was, of course, born at the suggestion of Robert Wallerstein, who appointed an IPA Committee on Publications under the Chairmanship of Joseph Sandler. Wallerstein had the keen perception that the analytic world was disjointed to some degree, in part due to the differences in language, but also in theory making, and he thought of the proposed series as a means to circulate new insights and ideas that were independently emerging in the three different regions.

The proposal grew out of the desire to provide the IPA membership with a new modality for an intellectual exchange among the European, Latin American, and North American psychoanalysts. It was through Joseph Sandler's organizational skills that Wallerstein's idea came to fruition and through the collaborative efforts of Drs Wallerstein and Sandler that "Contemporary Freud: Turning Points and Critical Issues" was born.

It was my great pleasure to work with both Joseph Sandler and Peter Fonagy in launching this series. The key idea was to provide a medium by which different ideas and different emphases within

three different regions—and even within one region—could be dis-
seminated among the larger psychoanalytic world.

My belief is that the series did, in fact, live up to its mandate,
which was to highlight different perspectives throughout the
three regions so as to allow us to understand more clearly and in
greater depth the important ideas, as well as the congruencies and
divergences, in different analytic perspectives. This project proved
successful in bringing together different groups and in disseminat-
ing some key insights and discoveries among the different regions.

For me personally, I feel enriched by the enduring friendships
that I was fortunate enough to make with people I met from Latin
America and from Europe. I am very happy that this series, which has
had too long an intermission, has now been revived. It is generally
true, however, that an intermission sometimes provides us with the
time to grow and to rethink our priorities. I am confident that the
rebirth of the series will prove to be an extremely creative one.

It is a good omen that the first volume in this revived series
starts with an introduction by Martin Bergmann, one of the most
renowned psychoanalysts in the United States, and that the series
itself resumes with "Mourning and Melancholia". Both melancholia
and mourning are triggered by the same thing—that is, by loss.
The distinction often made is that mourning occurs after the death
of a loved one, while in melancholia the object of love does not
qualify as irretrievably lost. Melancholia is about a loss that is
sometimes retrievable. What the IPA lost for a long stretch of time
was the Freud series. Thus, the title seems a fitting introduction to
the rebirth of this series, being an antidote to the "mourning and
melancholia" that some of us may have felt in losing the continuity
of the series. This vital resurrection bodes well for the ongoing
interchange among all our regions, each with its specific, and
sometimes unique, contributions.

ON FREUD'S
"MOURNING AND MELANCHOLIA"

Introduction

Martin S. Bergmann

On my bookshelves are six monographs published by the International Psychoanalytical Association, dealing with six seminal essays by Freud. I now have the privilege of introducing the seventh. Freud's paper "Mourning and Melancholia" (1917e [1915]) has always been regarded as one of his most illustrious. It is clearly written, well reasoned, and a pleasure to read. But as this monograph will demonstrate, it has given rise to significant controversy.

Before I introduce this monograph, a few words about the series as a whole are in order. These monographs, while very interesting, do not read easily, and the monograph I am introducing may also share their fate. A significant paper by Freud is assigned to a wide variety of analysts, and each of them is asked to comment. The result is interesting, but the reader has to carry a greater burden. The difficulty may be due to the fact that the curse of the biblical Tower of Babel may already have fallen on us: our language has become so confounded that we can no longer communicate easily. But it is also possible that what these monographs attempt is a complex task:

1. to explain and explicate the implication of what Freud wanted to say,

2. to make clear what happened to Freud's ideas in subsequent development,

3. present disagreements and modification of Freud's ideas.

To achieve all these aims well is not an easy task, particularly if these three aims are not clearly separated. Having criticized the monographs, I also want to say something in their praise. While they make too many demands on the beginner, they are nevertheless excellent for seminar discussion with a leader, particularly if students are encouraged to bring their own clinical material that can be understood in a new way when Freud's paper is discussed. Such clinical data often succeed in throwing unexpected light on Freud's original papers.

As in the other monographs, so here, too, Freud's paper forms the centre out of which the contributors radiate in different directions. What is striking is the variety of the contributions. The current monograph contains ten essays written by contributors from seven countries. The prerequisite for enjoying reading it is a positive attitude towards the current diversity of views within the IPA. For a psychoanalyst, this feeling of pleasure in diversity cannot be taken for granted. Freud's example in this respect is not encouraging: he tended to equate at least certain types of disagreement with resistance to the painful discoveries he made and a retreat from the difficult truth that it was his lot to discover (Bergmann, 2004). In my previous publications (Bergmann, 1993, 1997) I tried to cope with this diversity by dividing psychoanalysts who write into three groups: heretics (Adler, Jung, Rank), modifiers (Klein, Hartmann, Kohut, Winnicott), and extenders (Nunberg, Fenichel, Wälder). The heretic leaves or is expelled, the modifier asks for or implies that something crucial in Freud's work remained incomplete and something new has to be added, while the extender extends Freud's findings beyond what Freud explored. This division is not airtight but in my opinion important to make sense of the way we understand the history of psychoanalysis. In a monograph of this kind one would not expect to find either "heretics" or modifiers, but the idea of the "perennial mourner" developed by Volkan comes close to being a modification of Freud's views, since for the latter the fact that mourning is by definition terminable was central to his thinking.

There are two ways of looking at "Mourning and Melancholia": primarily as a further extension of Freud's paper "On Narcissism: An

Introduction" (1914c) or as the paper in which Freud transformed psychoanalysis into an object relations theory. The two viewpoints need not contradict each other, but the significance of the paper will be seen in a different light. It so happened that most contributors to this monograph are writing under the influence of Melanie Klein, and they tend to look upon "Mourning and Melancholia" as Freud's changing position from the so-called drive theory to an object relations theory. I quote from Ogden's chapter (chapter 6):

> I look at the way Freud made use of this seemingly focal exploration of these two psychological states [mourning and melancholia] as a vehicle for introducing—as much implicitly as explicitly—the foundation of his theory of internal object relations.

Quinodoz supports Ogden's point of view when he writes that Klein and her followers' views are "rooted" in Freud's "Mourning and Melancholia".

It is of historical interest that in her 1940 paper "Mourning and Its Relation to Manic Depressive States" Melanie Klein did not attribute her object relationship point of view to Freud's paper. But in subsequent developments, when Klein and her followers were threatened with expulsion from the IPA by Anna Freud and her followers (King & Steiner, 1991), it became important for the Kleinians to show that Klein was a loyal Freudian, if not an Anna Freudian. It was within this "political" context that it became important to emphasize that Freud himself, in "Mourning and Melancholia", took a major step towards the Kleinian point of view. In my opinion Melanie Klein was a most significant modifier of Freud's ideas as someone who developed Freud's dual instinct theory further than Freud did, but when the controversies broke out it was expedient to see her primarily as an extender of Freud's latest theories. A favourite way of maintaining the continuity between Freud and Klein is to claim that her views are implicit in Freud.

The concept of "implicit" implies that we can read backwards from a later point of view. It has a powerful emotional appeal and brings Klein closer to Freud, but it interferes with understanding the Freudian models—either his topographic model or his structural model. It is my belief that we will have a clearer picture of the history of psychoanalysis if we see Klein's model of inner object relations as distinct from either Freud's topographic or his structural model.

The most cogent argument against the view that "Mourning and Melancholia" is the beginning of Freud's conversion to object relations is that Freud's subsequent papers do not support this conversion. The object relations emphasis in "Mourning and Melancholia" was confined, in Freud's view, only to the successful and unsuccessful process of mourning.

In contrast to the contributors to this monograph, who typically only added Melanie Klein's work to Freud's, Kernberg (2004), in a chapter titled "Mourning and Melancholia Revisited", derived the whole extensive literature on depression from "Mourning and Melancholia", including such well-known works as those of Bibring (1953) and Jacobson (1971).

Between "On Narcissism" and "Mourning and Melancholia", Freud wrote a short and charming essay, "On Transience" (1916a), in which he takes a walk with the already famous poet Rainer Maria Rilke (for a theory that the unnamed poet of "On Transience" was Rilke, see Lehmann, 1966). Rilke could take no pleasure in the beauty of the landscape of the Dolomites because "all this beauty was fated to extinction". This led Freud to the important realization that transience is essential to the enjoyment of beauty and that therefore the capacity to mourn is a crucial capacity we all must acquire. He then reached the conclusion, so essential to "Mourning and Melancholia", that Rilke's mind was revolting against mourning. In that essay, Freud said something he would repeat in "Mourning and Melancholia": "We only see that libido clings to its objects and will not renounce those that are lost even when a substitute lies ready to hand. Such then is mourning" (pp. 306–307). Greek mythology as well as the Bible assume that mortal humanity is inferior to the gods because of our mortality; in this essay Freud reverses this tradition to assert that our very mortality makes it possible for us to value beauty.

There is an aspect of Freud's way of thinking that deserves our attention. In the world of thought, everything can be compared with everything else—or, as my teacher Robert Wälder used to say, "You can dig anywhere, but you will not always find oil." Similarly certain comparisons are highly productive, while others are not. The comparison between mourning and melancholia turned out to be extremely productive. Freud used other comparisons that proved productive, such as that between the play of children and stories invented by creative writers in "Creative Writers and Day-

Dreaming" (1908e [1907]), and the paper "On Narcissism" (1914c) was so productive because Freud found something in common among psychosis, homosexuality, sleep, love, and hypochondria and derived the concept of narcissism from a common abstraction among these diverse psychic events. Nobody before him would have thought of extracting a common denominator from such diverse phenomena.

An unusual capacity both to compare and to contrast is at the core of Freud's originality. Infantile sexuality is contrasted with adult sexuality as well as with latency; masculinity is contrasted with femininity, transference manifestations with transference neurosis, neurosis with perversion, neurosis with psychosis. Whether or not we are aware of it, Freud has taught us to think in contrasts.

The contrast between transference neurosis and narcissistic neurosis that Freud described in 1914 is paralleled by the distinction between mourning and melancholia. Mourning relates to a person lost, while melancholia takes place within the narcissistic realm. The two papers are powerfully linked: without the essay "On Narcissism", "Mourning and Melancholia" could not have been written, and if "Mourning and Melancholia" had not followed the paper "On Narcissism", one of the most important clinical implications of the concept of narcissism would not have become clinically available to psychoanalysis.

When Freud contrasted mourning and melancholia, he compared mourning—a normal if painful event from which hardly anyone can be spared—with a pathological although very common one: melancholia. The continuous comparison between the normal and the pathological was one of Freud's great gifts and is largely responsible for making a psychiatrist one of the immortal names in the twentieth century. The latent meanings of dreams, slips of the tongue, infantile sexuality, and the Oedipus complex are all normal phenomena with special significance for treating mental illness. Contrasting mourning with melancholia bridges the gap once again between the normal and the pathological realms.

We owe Carlos Mario Aslan (chapter 8) the important historical observation that Freud's interest in the impact of death on the living goes back further than "Mourning and Melancholia", for in *Totem and Taboo* (1912–13) Freud noted with some astonishment that a dearly beloved relative may, at the moment of death, change into a demon.

In Freud's hands the contrast between mourning and melancholia is stark and absolute. In the contributions to this volume it becomes more nuanced. In this monograph Volkan introduces subtle intermediary stages between mourning and melancholia with the concept of the "perennial mourner" whose mourning never comes to an end. I recall an adult patient who never overcame mourning the death, during childhood, of her mother. She was a perennial mourner because the object of her mourning remained conscious; but because she never stopped mourning, she was also melancholic.

The discerning reader will notice how very long the reference list is and how varied its contents. What the bibliography conveys is how very rich and variable the psychoanalytic literature has become, but also how very difficult it is for many of us to organize and synthesize this heritage into a coherent structure that makes sense and gives us a reliable background for our work. I was particularly struck by this strain in my attempt to understand Roosevelt Cassorla's contribution (chapter 3). We must be ready to accept the fact that the very volume and richness of the psychoanalytic heritage strains the integrative capacities of the presenter, resulting in the requirement of continuous attention while reading, so we do not get lost in the details.

One of the difficulties in producing the monographs of the IPA is that the participants do not have the chance to read the other essays before they sit down to write their own. The only one so privileged is the introducer, whose duty, as I see it, is to transform these contributions into something like a symposium, engaging the participants in more direct contact with one another. This I will now attempt to do for this monograph.

When the invitation to write this introduction reached me, I decided to read, line by line, the German original, together with the Strachey translation. I took out my German Freud and compared the original with Strachey's translation word for word. It proved an interesting endeavour: the line-by-line comparison greatly increased my understanding of "Mourning and Melancholia". Space allows me to mention the first two items of comparative interest. Freud writes on the second page: "*Die Melancholie ist seelisch ausgezeichnet durch innere tief schmerzliche Verstimmung*", which Strachey translates as: "The distinguishing mental features of melancholia are a profoundly painful dejection" (p. 244). This is very far from a literal translation. *Verstim-*

mung is not dejection, dejection being a much stronger word, but Strachey's rendering has a power of its own that evokes respect.

The second example is the suggestion in Priscilla Roth's essay (chapter 1) that Freud's statement that "People never willingly abandon a libidinal position even, indeed, when a substitute is already beckoning to them" should be regarded among Freud's richest formulations. When we compare Freud's original essay with Strachey's translation, we will note that Freud did not use the word "people" but the singular *der Mensch*—a reference to man as singular, a more powerful formulation, strictly speaking. Roth asks us to remember Strachey, not Freud. I recall the famous Italian proverb that translators are traitors, as well as the famous German translator of Greek tragedies who proclaimed: "Reader, learn Greek and throw away my translation." To me it seems that translation without a bias is a wish that cannot be realized and that by now the Strachey translation is so well known and so often quoted that a new translation will not undo Strachey's influence, for better or worse.

Roth's chapter is written within the Kleinian frame of reference—a frame that sees "Mourning and Melancholia" as introducing object relations into psychoanalysis. For Roth, the mind is not unitary: "Separate parts of the self and different internalized love objects, all relating to each other in complex ways—sometimes friendly and sometimes powerfully hostile" (opening paragraph). In melancholia a double identification takes place. The ego takes over the qualities of the "object of desire", and feelings of worthlessness are projected on the object that is identified with the unloved self, the comfort being, "I have not lost the object because I am it." Roth's concept of mourning is significantly wider than the way many of us use the term. The leading case she presents is neither a case of melancholia nor one of mourning: it is a case frequently encountered among women "who fail to establish a meaningful relationship to a man because they remain enslaved to an early libidinal love". These women are aggressive and deprecatory to their boyfriends and jealous of other women who have better love relationships. These women must, in Roth's view, learn to mourn the loss of their original love objects before they can be free to love. The work of mourning of these patients consists in relinquishing the tie to the original object. If we accept Roth's wider definition of mourning, then mourning is ever-present in our work.

It is well known that Holocaust survivors did not become psy-choanalytic patients as long as they were struggling against realistic difficulties in their lives after the war. However, once their social and economic conditions had improved, the unbearable memories of the Holocaust years returned from a kind of latency during which they had been repressed. The social dimension of that catastrophe forced psychoanalysts to rethink the question of how these victims were to be worked with. I have also participated in this work (Bergmann & Jucovy, 1988). One of our main conclusions was that the therapist must help the survivor to mourn, because the terrible conditions had allowed no time for mourning.

In chapter 2 María Lucila Pelento reviews some of the Holocaust literature but proceeds to apply the finding to the missing persons [*desaparecidos*] during the period of the terrorist State in Argentina. These people were abducted, tortured, and murdered. For the survi-vors, it was impossible to know why there were abducted or to learn whether they were still alive or already murdered. The very act of searching for information was dangerous. The analysis of one of the survivors is the subject of her chapter. It is not an easy chapter to read but a valuable contribution to the interface between psychoanalysis and social catastrophe. It makes us see "Mourning and Melancholia" in a new perspective. Freud's paper was written in the middle of one of these catastrophes, and yet Freud describes mourning and melan-cholia only as a personal, not as a social, phenomenon.

I found Roosevelt Cassorla's essay (chapter 3) difficult to mas-ter. His cast of characters is very large, consisting, as it does, of Bion, Caper, Ellman and Moskovitz, Greenberg, Grotstein, Paula Heimann, Betty Joseph, Meltzer, Ogden, Racker, Rosenfeld, Sandler, Segal, and Strachey, and the spirit of Melanie Klein presides over them all. The number of new concepts that the reader may have to assimilate is also very large. "The patient's shadow falls upon the analyst" is a variation on Freud's "The shadow of the object fell upon the ego"—a phrase employed to explain when the patient is successful in evoking in the analyst a powerful countertransference reaction. In this modern view patients are seen as being capable of penetrating the analyst and attacking her or his mental function-ing. The differences between patient and analyst tend to become obliterated in the analyst's projective counteridentification. The in-teraction between therapist and patient creates "a third analytical intersubjective product". A further important concept for Cassorla is the "non-dream"—the dream the patient dares not dream. In such situations not knowing can become an internal persecuting object. The non-dream of the patient can, in turn, fall upon the analyst's ego. A further danger visualized is the involvement of the analyst in a "chronic enactment" and a "non-dream for two". It seems to me that the evolving object relations theory resulted in an increase of the psychoanalytic vocabulary. It aimed to account for the increasingly complex interaction between patient and therapist, in which the vulnerability of the analyst to the attacks of the aggressive melancholic patient has kept on gaining significance.

Vamık Volkan (chapter 4) is a psychoanalyst with a reputation well beyond the confines of our discipline. The bibliography contains 14 references to his own work and that of his colleagues at the University of Virginia, with six of them being books. His contributions go back to 1972. Unlike Freud, who defined mourning as a process that comes to a termination point, Volkan speaks of "perennial mourners" who nevertheless do not develop a depression. The perennial mourners keep the object representation of the lost person as a foreign body, which in the psychoanalytic literature is known as an introject. Because of their ambivalence, they spend a great deal of energy to "kill" as well as to bring back the lost object. "Linking objects" such as photographs play a special role in perennial mourning. These linking objects tend to freeze the mourning process. Volkan differentiates the grief that follows loss from the mourning process. Since adults are capable of keeping the mental representation of a lost love object "alive", the adult mourning process never comes to an end. Melancholia occurs when the relationship was ambivalent and the mental representations of the lost object are taken into the self-representations. When death is associated with a trauma such as a failure to rescue from drowning or from a fire, persistent guilt feelings make mourning difficult or impossible.

The last section of Volkan's chapter is devoted to societal mourning. At this point Volkan's chapter forms a link to Pelento's contribution. Social catastrophes and natural calamities can affect large groups, consisting of thousands and even millions of people. Such societies behave like "perennial mourners". Monuments are a common expression of societal mourning: they may help to "contain" societal mourning. Group trauma, if not mastered, is transmitted to the second generation. (Volkan does not mention our book, *Generations of the Holocaust*—Bergmann & Jucovy, 1988—but it illustrates his thesis.) Political leaders can choose to inflame such traumatic events for their own political purposes. Societies that undergo perennial mourning develop "entitlement ideologies" based on what they had suffered in the past. Volkan's analysis made it possible for me to understand aspects of Jewish history in a new way. The day of fasting on the ninth day of the Hebrew month Av is dedicated to mourning the destruction of the Temple in AD 70; it can be seen as an example of societal mourning. And Zionism, which declared the right of the Jews to return to their ancestral home, can be seen as an example of "entitlement ideology". Volkan greatly expanded the boundaries of "Mourning and Melancholia" into the social and political domain.

Volkan's fascinating essay left me with some questions. Is the "perennial mourner" really a special variant on the mourning theme, or should we look upon him as a melancholic hiding behind a mourning mask? And by what mechanisms do the "societal mourners" transform their humiliation into an entitlement? It seems to me that if they succeed to do this, it is because their mourning increased their narcissism, and if so, they, too, are disguised melancholics.

María Cristina Melgar's essay on the relationship between mourning and creativity (chapter 5) can be described as poetic. It is rich in creative observation but not easy to follow and may be particularly difficult for non-Kleinians. The chapter opens with an observation by Borges that Plato wrote his dialogues out of mourning for Socrates. In them, Socrates comes to life, undoing the fatal drinking of the hemlock. Melgar's example of the creative transformation of mourning is Carpaccio's painting "Saint Augustine in His Study (The Vision of Saint Augustine)". In the legend, Saint Jerome visits Saint Augustine to announce his coming death. Carpaccio does not portray the presence of Saint Jerome but illuminates the empty space. Saint Augustine's expression is one of astonishment, depicting the void that death leaves behind. Melgar also cites George Pollock's observation (1975) that funeral music may express composers mourning for their own anticipated deaths. Mourning can lead to new paths of creativity without being an example of the more mundane "working through".

Thomas Ogden's essay (chapter 6) is a strong plea to read "Mourning and Melancholia" as the paper that initiated object relations theory, with its emphasis on unconscious internal objects as the most important reason for intrapsychic conflict. Freud's statement on p. 245 that the melancholic "knows *whom* he has lost but not *what* he has lost" has two meanings for Ogden: the first refers to the significance of the tie to the object, the second to the loss within the individual as a result of losing the object. The melancholic abandons the object, while the mourner loses the object. Because the melancholic disconnects himself from large portions of external reality, he forfeits a substantial part of his own life. Ogden agrees with Freud that in melancholia the ego has identified with the lost object. He adds that as a result of this identification, the two—ego and object—remain imprisoned by each other.

Ogden then presents a most interesting dream. It is the interpretation of this dream that showed me how far Ogden has moved away from what seems to me traditional psychoanalysis. In the dream a guest of honour is to be celebrated but a series of men get up and pay homage to the dreamer. Every time the dreamer thanks them but reminds the speaker that he is not the guest of honour, the scene is repeated, time and again, without resolution. A traditional analyst would interpret this dream as a conflict between the narcissism of the patient and his relationship to the analyst. The men in the audience who speak glowingly of the patient represent the patient's narcissism, while the patient himself—that is, his non-narcissistic part—wishes to pay homage to the analyst, who is seen as the guest of honour at the party. The terrifying realization of the dreamer is that this sequence could go on forever and indicates the patient's unconscious belief that the battle between self-love and transference love will never be resolved. I will not reproduce Ogden's own interpretation, leaving it to the reader to decide which interpretation he finds convincing. That different analysts can interpret dreams very differently is a fact of life we must learn to live with. Freud believed that any dream has only one latent meaning: we have since learned that the "model" from which analysts draw their interpretations consciously or unconsciously plays a significant role in determining what the latent content of a dream turns out to be.

To my knowledge Ogden's essay is the only one that is reproduced from the literature (having appeared in the *International Journal of Psychoanalysis*, Vol. 83, 2002). I take it to mean that those who selected the participants considered it to be particularly noteworthy. That fact should make the difference between my interpretation and Ogden's interpretation of the dream more interesting.

Florence Guignard's point of departure (chapter 7) is the view that the Western world has changed more radically since Freud than most psychoanalysts admit. The latency period, so significant to Freud's thinking in *Three Essays* (1905d), which separates infantile sexuality from adult sexuality, is rapidly disappearing. This threatening disappearance takes with it one of the cornerstones of Western civilization. Globalization has given us global anxiety. For Freud, individual fantasy was the great counterforce to the reality principle, whereas today's culture enables most people to live in "virtual reality". Virtual reality does not require the capacity for symbolization stressed by Melanie Klein and Hannah Segal. To confuse fantasy with reality requires an intense and pathological projective organization, while virtual reality offers an illusion of what is real.

The mourning process takes place when the pleasure–unpleasure principle clashes with the reality principle, when the major drives interact, when external objects are at variance with the internal object, and when ego, object, and symbol interact. Apart from Freud, the lion's share of the chapter is devoted to Melanie Klein's ideas. Together with Pelento and Volkan, Guignard is one of the three contributors in this monograph to have stressed the impact of a changed social reality on analytic work.

Carlos Mario Aslan's chapter (chapter 8) is, as the title indicates, an attempt to update the metapsychology of the mourning process. Aslan sees mourning as a detachment from a love object with whichever acts of love can no longer be exchanged. Further on he notes: "Mourning processes have two main purposes: to work through the loss of a love object, and to get rid of an internal persecutory thanatic object that is against pleasure and life." The first half of the definition agrees with Freud's "Mourning and Melancholia"; the second, with the use of the term "thanatic"—derived from Thanatos, Freud's term for the death instinct—is in keeping with Freud's death instinct theory and is written under Melanie Klein's influence. Freud, in Aslan's view, failed to differentiate between the internal object and identification with it.

The mourning process becomes pathological when it is interrupted in its normal evolution; it then becomes a depressive experience. Normal mourning consists of a group of functions. Different types of internalizations do not, as it is so often stated, go into the ego, superego, or ego ideal but function as ego, superego, or ego ideal. The process of mourning begins with denial ("I can't believe it!"). When reality-testing teaches the ego to accept the loss, the ego withdraws its libidinal attachment from the internalized object representation of the dead person. This withdrawal of the libido creates an "unmixing" of the two drives, leaving the internal object prey to the death drive. Thanatos, or the death drive, is released due to the unmixing of the two drives, creating a dangerous situation and evoking wishes to die. An example cited is that of a widower who wishes to have a sexual relationship. If the internal object functions as the superego, the widower will feel guilty; if the identification is an ego identification, he will lose the desire. The chapter requires close reading. I did not find it easy to follow, but the effort invested was worth while.

Jean-Michel Quinodoz's essay "Teaching Mourning and Melancholia" (chapter 9) is, as the title indicates, a primer on how to teach Freud's paper. It is part of his book *Reading Freud: A Chronological Exploration of Freud's Writings* (2004). It is noteworthy for the clarity of its exposition, and a reader not yet familiar with Freud's "Mourning and Melancholia" should read this chapter first. Quinodoz divides his chapter into four sections. In the first he deals with Abraham's writings on depression in 1911, a few years before "Mourning and Melancholia" was written. The second is his analysis of Freud's paper, concise and well formulated. The third deals with Melanie Klein's contribution, while the fourth goes beyond the confines of this monograph to suggest how Freud's writings in general should be taught. Quinodoz treats the Kleinian observation that the conflict between aggression and libido takes place during infancy as a discovery, whereas I see it as a leading hypothesis that largely determined her new model, but otherwise he presents the Kleinian model succinctly.

I would like to add something to Quinodoz's discussion of Abraham's work. He mentions Abraham's 1911 paper "Notes on the Psychoanalytic Investigation and Treatment of Manic-Depressive Insanity and Allied Conditions". He emphasizes Abraham's insight that these patients cannot love because of the over-strong sadistic component of their libido. The statement is of interest because prior to the dual instinct theory, sadism had been considered part of the libido. In Abraham's 1911 view, "Depression sets in when he has to give up his sexual aim without having obtained gratification" (p. 137). Among the participants in this monograph, Quinodoz is the only one to trace the history of the subject back to Abraham, and for that

we are grateful. I would like, however, to highlight a basic difference
between Abraham and Freud's "Mourning and Melancholia". In a
paper published in 1916—that is, a year before Freud's paper—
Abraham wrote of the fixation of the melancholic on the oral
stage:

> In his unconscious the melancholic depressed person directs
> upon his sexual object the wish to incorporate it. In the depth
> of his unconscious there is a tendency to devour and demolish
> his object. [p. 216]

> In contrast to the sadistic desires of the obsessional neurotic, the
> unconscious wish of the melancholic is to destroy his love object
> by eating it up. [p. 227]

Abraham is writing entirely within the then-correct view that neither
illness was the result of fixation, while Freud, in his paper, introduced
the new dimension of a relationship to an object. It is of historical
interest that this simple view may have been the psychoanalytic view
on depression had Freud not revolutionized our understanding of
depression in "Mourning and Melancholia". Even the very gifted
Abraham had no premonition of what Freud would discover about
mourning and melancholia.

I would like to end this Introduction on a personal note. The
privilege of introducing this panel to the readers was not an easy job
for me in my 93rd year of life, but it was a very rewarding task, as
I hope it will be for the reader of this monograph. I was not aware
of the very large shadow that Melanie Klein's work has thrown on
Freud's "Mourning and Melancholia" and how very complex the
work of mourning has become in current psychoanalysis. But even
more impressive was the realization that the work of mourning goes
far beyond the death of a loved one, important as this is in so many
lives. In our lives we always make choices: every choice we make implies that we do not select some other choices and every significant
choice not made evokes some sense of mourning. This was brought
home to me by a patient of mine who regrets nearly all the deci-
sions she has made in her life. Her regrets had more the quality of
a persecuting melancholia than of mourning. Cure came when the
ego was strong enough to mourn the choices not taken rather than
submit to a persecuting superego that tortured her. The importance
of the work of mourning also became clearer to me in another case

where a man had to choose between the woman he loved and the woman he could not live without. It became clear to us that either choice meant mourning for what he would have to give up. This patient taught me that there are situations in life where we must choose between two types of mourning. The capacity to mourn is an indispensable capacity we all must acquire.

PART I

"Mourning and Melancholia"
(1917e [1915])

Sigmund Freud

MOURNING AND MELANCHOLIA

DREAMS having served us as the prototype in normal life of narcissistic mental disorders, we will now try to throw some light
on the nature of melancholia by comparing it with the normal
affect of mourning.[1] This time, however, we must begin by
making an admission, as a warning against any over-estimation
of the value of our conclusions. Melancholia, whose definition
fluctuates even in descriptive psychiatry, takes on various clinical forms the grouping together of which into a single unity
does not seem to be established with certainty; and some of these
forms suggest somatic rather than psychogenic affections. Our
material, apart from such impressions as are open to every
observer, is limited to a small number of cases whose psychogenic nature was indisputable. We shall, therefore, from the
outset drop all claim to general validity for our conclusions,
and we shall console ourselves by reflecting that, with the
means of investigation at our disposal to-day, we could hardly
discover anything that was not typical, if not of a whole class of
disorders, at least of a small group of them.

The correlation of melancholia and mourning seems justified
by the general picture of the two conditions.[2] Moreover, the
exciting causes due to environmental influences are, so far as
we can discern them at all, the same for both conditions. Mourning is regularly the reaction to the loss of a loved person, or to
the loss of some abstraction which has taken the place of one,
such as one's country, liberty, an ideal, and so on. In some
people the same influences produce melancholia instead of
mourning and we consequently suspect them of a pathological
disposition. It is also well worth notice that, although mourning
involves grave departures from the normal attitude to life, it
never occurs to us to regard it as a pathological condition and to

---

[1] [The German '*Trauer*', like the English 'mourning', can mean both
the affect of grief and its outward manifestation. Throughout the present
paper, the word has been rendered 'mourning'.]

[2] Abraham (1912), to whom we owe the most important of the few
analytic studies on this subject, also took this comparison as his starting
point. [Freud himself had already made the comparison in 1910 and
even earlier. (See Editor's Note, p. 240 above.)]

243

refer it to medical treatment. We rely on its being overcome after a certain lapse of time, and we look upon any interference with it as useless or even harmful.

The distinguishing mental features of melancholia are a profoundly painful dejection, cessation of interest in the outside world, loss of the capacity to love, inhibition of all activity, and a lowering of the self-regarding feelings to a degree that finds utterance in self-reproaches and self-revilings, and culminates in a delusional expectation of punishment. This picture becomes a little more intelligible when we consider that, with one exception, the same traits are met with in mourning. The disturbance of self-regard is absent in mourning; but otherwise the features are the same. Profound mourning, the reaction to the loss of someone who is loved, contains the same painful frame of mind, the same loss of interest in the outside world—in so far as it does not recall him—the same loss of capacity to adopt any new object of love (which would mean replacing him) and the same turning away from any activity that is not connected with thoughts of him. It is easy to see that this inhibition and circumscription of the ego is the expression of an exclusive devotion to mourning which leaves nothing over for other purposes or other interests. It is really only because we know so well how to explain it that this attitude does not seem to us pathological.

We should regard it as an appropriate comparison, too, to call the mood of mourning a 'painful' one. We shall probably see the justification for this when we are in a position to give a characterization of the economics of pain.[1]

In what, now, does the work which mourning performs consist? I do not think there is anything far-fetched in presenting it in the following way. Reality-testing has shown that the loved object no longer exists, and it proceeds to demand that all libido shall be withdrawn from its attachments to that object. This demand arouses understandable opposition—it is a matter of general observation that people never willingly abandon a libidinal position, not even, indeed, when a substitute is already beckoning to them. This opposition can be so intense that a turning away from reality takes place and a clinging to the object through the medium of a hallucinatory wishful psychosis.[2] Normally, respect for reality gains the day. Nevertheless its

[1] [See footnote 1, p. 147 above.]
[2] Cf. the preceding paper [p. 230].

orders cannot be obeyed at once. They are carried out bit by bit, at great expense of time and cathectic energy, and in the meantime the existence of the lost object is psychically prolonged. Each single one of the memories and expectations in which the libido is bound to the object is brought up and hyper-cathected, and detachment of the libido is accomplished in respect of it.[1] Why this compromise by which the command of reality is carried out piecemeal should be so extraordinarily painful is not at all easy to explain in terms of economics. It is remarkable that this painful unpleasure is taken as a matter of course by us. The fact is, however, that when the work of mourning is completed the ego becomes free and uninhibited again.[2]

Let us now apply to melancholia what we have learnt about mourning. In one set of cases it is evident that melancholia too may be the reaction to the loss of a loved object. Where the exciting causes are different one can recognize that there is a loss of a more ideal kind. The object has not perhaps actually died, but has been lost as an object of love (e.g. in the case of a betrothed girl who has been jilted). In yet other cases one feels justified in maintaining the belief that a loss of this kind has occurred, but one cannot see clearly what it is that has been lost, and it is all the more reasonable to suppose that the patient cannot consciously perceive what he has lost either. This, indeed, might be so even if the patient is aware of the loss which has given rise to his melancholia, but only in the sense that he knows *whom* he has lost but not *what* he has lost in him. This would suggest that melancholia is in some way related to an object-loss which is withdrawn from consciousness, in contradistinction to mourning, in which there is nothing about the loss that is unconscious.

In mourning we found that the inhibition and loss of interest are fully accounted for by the work of mourning in which the ego is absorbed. In melancholia, the unknown loss will result in a similar internal work and will therefore be responsible for the melancholic inhibition. The difference is that the inhibition

[1] [This idea seems to be expressed already in *Studies on Hysteria* (1895*d*): a process similar to this one will be found described near the beginning of Freud's 'Discussion' of the case history of Fräulein Elisabeth von R. (*Standard Ed.*, **2**, 162).]

[2] [A discussion of the economics of this process will be found below on p. 255.]

of the melancholic seems puzzling to us because we cannot see what it is that is absorbing him so entirely. The melancholic displays something else besides which is lacking in mourning— an extraordinary diminution in his self-regard, an impoverishment of his ego on a grand scale. In mourning it is the world which has become poor and empty; in melancholia it is the ego itself. The patient represents his ego to us as worthless, incapable of any achievement and morally despicable; he reproaches himself, vilifies himself and expects to be cast out and punished. He abases himself before everyone and commiserates with his own relatives for being connected with anyone so unworthy. He is not of the opinion that a change has taken place in him, but extends his self-criticism back over the past; he declares that he was never any better. This picture of a delusion of (mainly moral) inferiority is completed by sleeplessness and refusal to take nourishment, and—what is psychologically very remarkable—by an overcoming of the instinct which compels every living thing to cling to life.

It would be equally fruitless from a scientific and a therapeutic point of view to contradict a patient who brings these accusations against his ego. He must surely be right in some way and be describing something that is as it seems to him to be. Indeed, we must at once confirm some of his statements without reservation. He really is as lacking in interest and as incapable of love and achievement as he says. But that, as we know, is secondary; it is the effect of the internal work which is consuming his ego— work which is unknown to us but which is comparable to the work of mourning. He also seems to us justified in certain other self-accusations; it is merely that he has a keener eye for the truth than other people who are not melancholic. When in his heightened self-criticism he describes himself as petty, egoistic, dishonest, lacking in independence, one whose sole aim has been to hide the weaknesses of his own nature, it may be, so far as we know, that he has come pretty near to understanding himself; we only wonder why a man has to be ill before he can be accessible to a truth of this kind. For there can be no doubt that if anyone holds and expresses to others an opinion of himself such as this (an opinion which Hamlet held both of himself and of everyone else[1]), he is ill, whether he is speaking the

[1] 'Use every man after his desert, and who shall scape whipping?' (Act II, Scene 2).

truth or whether he is being more or less unfair to himself. Nor is it difficult to see that there is no correspondence, so far as we can judge, between the degree of self-abasement and its real justification. A good, capable, conscientious woman will speak no better of herself after she develops melancholia than one who is in fact worthless; indeed, the former is perhaps more likely to fall ill of the disease than the latter, of whom we too should have nothing good to say. Finally, it must strike us that after all the melancholic does not behave in quite the same way as a person who is crushed by remorse and self-reproach in a normal fashion. Feelings of shame in front of other people, which would more than anything characterize this latter condition, are lacking in the melancholic, or at least they are not prominent in him. One might emphasize the presence in him of an almost opposite trait of insistent communicativeness which finds satisfaction in self-exposure.

The essential thing, therefore, is not whether the melancholic's distressing self-denigration is correct, in the sense that his self-criticism agrees with the opinion of other people. The point must rather be that he is giving a correct description of his psychological situation. He has lost his self-respect and he must have good reason for this. It is true that we are then faced with a contradiction that presents a problem which is hard to solve. The analogy with mourning led us to conclude that he had suffered a loss in regard to an object; what he tells us points to a loss in regard to his ego.

Before going into this contradiction, let us dwell for a moment on the view which the melancholic's disorder affords of the constitution of the human ego. We see how in him one part of the ego sets itself over against the other, judges it critically, and, as it were, takes it as its object. Our suspicion that the critical agency which is here split off from the ego might also show its independence in other circumstances will be confirmed by every further observation. We shall really find grounds for distinguishing this agency from the rest of the ego. What we are here becoming acquainted with is the agency commonly called 'conscience'; we shall count it, along with the censorship of consciousness and reality-testing, among the major institutions of the ego,[1] and we shall come upon evidence to show that it can become diseased on its own account. In the clinical picture of

[1] [See above, p. 233.]

melancholia, dissatisfaction with the ego on moral grounds is the most outstanding feature. The patient's self-evaluation concerns itself much less frequently with bodily infirmity, ugliness or weakness, or with social inferiority; of this category, it is only his fears and asseverations of becoming poor that occupy a prominent position.

There is one observation, not at all difficult to make, which leads to the explanation of the contradiction mentioned above [at the end of the last paragraph but one]. If one listens patiently to a melancholic's many and various self-accusations, one cannot in the end avoid the impression that often the most violent of them are hardly at all applicable to the patient himself, but that with insignificant modifications they do fit someone else, someone whom the patient loves or has loved or should love. Every time one examines the facts this conjecture is confirmed. So we find the key to the clinical picture: we perceive that the self-reproaches are reproaches against a loved object which have been shifted away from it on to the patient's own ego.

The woman who loudly pities her husband for being tied to such an incapable wife as herself is really accusing her *husband* of being incapable, in whatever sense she may mean this. There is no need to be greatly surprised that a few genuine self-reproaches are scattered among those that have been transposed back. These are allowed to obtrude themselves, since they help to mask the others and make recognition of the true state of affairs impossible. Moreover, they derive from the *pros* and *cons* of the conflict of love that has led to the loss of love. The behaviour of the patients, too, now becomes much more intelligible. Their complaints are really 'plaints' in the old sense of the word. They are not ashamed and do not hide themselves, since everything derogatory that they say about themselves is at bottom said about someone else. Moreover, they are far from evincing towards those around them the attitude of humility and submissiveness that would alone befit such worthless people. On the contrary, they make the greatest nuisance of themselves, and always seem as though they felt slighted and had been treated with great injustice. All this is possible only because the reactions expressed in their behaviour still proceed from a mental constellation of revolt, which has then, by a certain process, passed over into the crushed state of melancholia.

There is no difficulty in reconstructing this process. An object-choice, an attachment of the libido to a particular person, had at one time existed; then, owing to a real slight or disappointment coming from this loved person, the object-relationship was shattered. The result was not the normal one of a withdrawal of the libido from this object and a displacement of it on to a new one, but something different, for whose coming-about various conditions seem to be necessary. The object-cathexis proved to have little power of resistance and was brought to an end. But the free libido was not displaced on to another object; it was withdrawn into the ego. There, however, it was not employed in any unspecified way, but served to establish an *identification* of the ego with the abandoned object. Thus the shadow of the object fell upon the ego, and the latter could henceforth be judged by a special[1] agency, as though it were an object, the forsaken object. In this way an object-loss was transformed into an ego-loss and the conflict between the ego and the loved person into a cleavage between the critical activity of the ego and the ego as altered by identification.

One or two things may be directly inferred with regard to the preconditions and effects of a process such as this. On the one hand, a strong fixation to the loved object must have been present; on the other hand, in contradiction to this, the object-cathexis must have had little power of resistance. As Otto Rank has aptly remarked, this contradiction seems to imply that the object-choice has been effected on a narcissistic basis, so that the object-cathexis, when obstacles come in its way, can regress to narcissism. The narcissistic identification with the object then becomes a substitute for the erotic cathexis, the result of which is that in spite of the conflict with the loved person the love-relation need not be given up. This substitution of identification for object-love is an important mechanism in the narcissistic affections; Karl Landauer (1914) has lately been able to point to it in the process of recovery in a case of schizophrenia. It represents, of course, a *regression* from one type of object-choice to original narcissism. We have elsewhere shown that identification is a preliminary stage of object-choice, that it is the first way—and one that is expressed in an ambivalent fashion —in which the ego picks out an object. The ego wants to incorporate this object into itself, and, in accordance with the oral or cannibalistic phase of libidinal development in which it is,

[1] [In the first (1917) edition only, this word does not occur.]
P.A.M.—R

it wants to do so by devouring it.[1] Abraham is undoubtedly right in attributing to this connection the refusal of nourishment met with in severe forms of melancholia.[2]

The conclusion which our theory would require—namely, that the disposition to fall ill of melancholia (or some part of that disposition) lies in the predominance of the narcissistic type of object-choice—has unfortunately not yet been confirmed by observation. In the opening remarks of this paper, I admitted that the empirical material upon which this study is founded is insufficient for our needs. If we could assume an agreement between the results of observation and what we have inferred, we should not hesitate to include this regression from object-cathexis to the still narcissistic oral phase of the libido in our characterization of melancholia. Identifications with the object are by no means rare in the transference neuroses either; indeed, they arc a well-known mechanism of symptom-formation, especially in hysteria. The difference, however, between narcissistic and hysterical identification may be seen in this: that, whereas in the former the object-cathexis is abandoned, in the latter it persists and manifests its influence, though this is usually confined to certain isolated actions and innervations. In any case, in the transference neuroses, too, identification is the expression of there being something in common, which may signify love. Narcissistic identification is the older of the two and it paves the way to an understanding of hysterical identification, which has been less thoroughly studied.[3]

Melancholia, therefore, borrows some of its features from mourning, and the others from the process of regression from narcissistic object-choice to narcissism. It is on the one hand, like mourning, a reaction to the real loss of a loved object; but over and above this, it is marked by a determinant which is absent in normal mourning or which, if it is present, transforms the latter into pathological mourning. The loss of a love-object is an excellent opportunity for the ambivalence in love-rela-

---

[1] [See above, p. 138. Cf. also Editor's Note, pp. 241–2.]

[2] [Abraham apparently first drew Freud's attention to this in a private letter written between February and April, 1915. See Jones's biography (1955, 368).]

[3] [The whole subject of identification was discussed later by Freud in Chapter VII of his *Group Psychology* (1921c), *Standard Ed.*, **18**, 105 ff. There is an early account of hysterical identification in *The Interpretation of Dreams* (1900a), *Standard Ed.*, **4**, 149–51.]

tionships to make itself effective and come into the open.[1] Where there is a disposition to obsessional neurosis the conflict due to ambivalence gives a pathological cast to mourning and forces it to express itself in the form of self-reproaches to the effect that the mourner himself is to blame for the loss of the loved object, i.e. that he has willed it. These obsessional states of depression following upon the death of a loved person show us what the conflict due to ambivalence can achieve by itself when there is no regressive drawing-in of libido as well. In melancholia, the occasions which give rise to the illness extend for the most part beyond the clear case of a loss by death, and include all those situations of being slighted, neglected or disappointed, which can import opposed feelings of love and hate into the relationship or reinforce an already existing ambivalence. This conflict due to ambivalence, which sometimes arises more from real experiences, sometimes more from constitutional factors, must not be overlooked among the preconditions of melancholia. If the love for the object—a love which cannot be given up though the object itself is given up—takes refuge in narcissistic identification, then the hate comes into operation on this substitutive object, abusing it, debasing it, making it suffer and deriving sadistic satisfaction from its suffering. The self-tormenting in melancholia, which is without doubt enjoyable, signifies, just like the corresponding phenomenon in obsessional neurosis, a satisfaction of trends of sadism and hate[2] which relate to an object, and which have been turned round upon the subject's own self in the ways we have been discussing. In both disorders the patients usually still succeed, by the circuitous path of self-punishment, in taking revenge on the original object and in tormenting their loved one through their illness, having resorted to it in order to avoid the need to express their hostility to him openly. After all, the person who has occasioned the patient's emotional disorder, and on whom his illness is centred, is usually to be found in his immediate environment. The melancholic's erotic cathexis in regard to his object has thus undergone a double vicissitude: part of it has regressed to identification, but the other part, under the influence of the conflict due to

---

[1] [Much of what follows is elaborated in Chapter V of *The Ego and the Id* (1923*b*).]
[2] For the distinction between the two, see my paper on 'Instincts and their Vicissitudes' [pp. 138–9 above].

ambivalence, has been carried back to the stage of sadism, which is nearer to that conflict.

It is this sadism alone that solves the riddle of the tendency to suicide which makes melancholia so interesting—and so dangerous. So immense is the ego's self-love, which we have come to recognize as the primal state from which instinctual life proceeds, and so vast is the amount of narcissistic libido which we see liberated in the fear that emerges at a threat to life, that we cannot conceive how that ego can consent to its own destruction. We have long known, it is true, that no neurotic harbours thoughts of suicide which he has not turned back upon himself from murderous impulses against others, but we have never been able to explain what interplay of forces can carry such a purpose through to execution. The analysis of melancholia now shows that the ego can kill itself only if, owing to the return of the object-cathexis, it can treat itself as an object—if it is able to direct against itself the hostility which relates to an object and which represents the ego's original reaction to objects in the external world.[1] Thus in regression from narcissistic object-choice the object has, it is true, been got rid of, but it has nevertheless proved more powerful than the ego itself. In the two opposed situations of being most intensely in love and of suicide the ego is overwhelmed by the object, though in totally different ways.[2]

As regards one particular striking feature of melancholia that we have mentioned [p. 248], the prominence of the fear of becoming poor, it seems plausible to suppose that it is derived from anal erotism which has been torn out of its context and altered in a regressive sense.

Melancholia confronts us with yet other problems, the answer to which in part eludes us. The fact that it passes off after a certain time has elapsed without leaving traces of any gross changes is a feature it shares with mourning. We found by way of explanation [pp. 244–5] that in mourning time is needed for the command of reality-testing to be carried out in detail, and that when this work has been accomplished the ego will have succeeded in freeing its libido from the lost object. We may imagine

---

[1] Cf. 'Instincts and their Vicissitudes' [p. 136 above].
[2] [Later discussions of suicide will be found in Chapter V of *The Ego and the Id* (1923b) and in the last pages of 'The Economic Problem of Masochism' (1924c).]

that the ego is occupied with analogous work during the course of a melancholia; in neither case have we any insight into the economics of the course of events. The sleeplessness in melancholia testifies to the rigidity of the condition, the impossibility of effecting the general drawing-in of cathexes necessary for sleep. The complex of melancholia behaves like an open wound, drawing to itself cathectic energies—which in the transference neuroses we have called 'anticathexes'—from all directions, and emptying the ego until it is totally impoverished.[1] It can easily prove resistant to the ego's wish to sleep.

What is probably a somatic factor, and one which cannot be explained psychogenically, makes itself visible in the regular amelioration in the condition that takes place towards evening. These considerations bring up the question whether a loss in the ego irrespectively of the object—a purely narcissistic blow to the ego—may not suffice to produce the picture of melancholia and whether an impoverishment of ego-libido directly due to toxins may not be able to produce certain forms of the disease.

The most remarkable characteristic of melancholia, and the one in most need of explanation, is its tendency to change round into mania—a state which is the opposite of it in its symptoms. As we know, this does not happen to every melancholia. Some cases run their course in periodic relapses, during the intervals between which signs of mania may be entirely absent or only very slight. Others show the regular alternation of melancholic and manic phases which has led to the hypothesis of a circular insanity. One would be tempted to regard these cases as non-psychogenic, if it were not for the fact that the psycho-analytic method has succeeded in arriving at a solution and effecting a therapeutic improvement in several cases precisely of this kind. It is not merely permissible, therefore, but incumbent upon us to extend an analytic explanation of melancholia to mania as well.

I cannot promise that this attempt will prove entirely satisfactory. It hardly carries us much beyond the possibility of taking one's initial bearings. We have two things to go upon:

---

[1] [This analogy of the open wound appears already (illustrated by two diagrams) in the rather abstruse Section VI of Freud's early note on melancholia (Freud, 1950a, Draft G, probably written in January, 1895). See Editor's Note, p. 229.]

the first is a psycho-analytic impression, and the second what we may perhaps call a matter of general economic experience. The impression which several psycho-analytic investigators have already put into words is that the content of mania is no different from that of melancholia, that both disorders are wrestling with the same 'complex', but that probably in melancholia the ego has succumbed to the complex whereas in mania it has mastered it or pushed it aside. Our second pointer is afforded by the observation that all states such as joy, exultation or triumph, which give us the normal model for mania, depend on the same economic conditions. What has happened here is that, as a result of some influence, a large expenditure of psychical energy, long maintained or habitually occurring, has at last become unnecessary, so that it is available for numerous applications and possibilities of discharge—when, for instance, some poor wretch, by winning a large sum of money, is suddenly relieved from chronic worry about his daily bread, or when a long and arduous struggle is finally crowned with success, or when a man finds himself in a position to throw off at a single blow some oppressive compulsion, some false position which he has long had to keep up, and so on. All such situations are characterized by high spirits, by the signs of discharge of joyful emotion and by increased readiness for all kinds of action —in just the same way as in mania, and in complete contrast to the depression and inhibition of melancholia. We may venture to assert that mania is nothing other than a triumph of this sort, only that here again what the ego has surmounted and what it is triumphing over remain hidden from it. Alcoholic intoxication, which belongs to the same class of states, may (in so far as it is an elated one) be explained in the same way; here there is probably a suspension, produced by toxins, of expenditures of energy in repression. The popular view likes to assume that a person in a manic state of this kind finds such delight in movement and action because he is so 'cheerful'. This false connection must of course be put right. The fact is that the economic condition in the subject's mind referred to above has been fulfilled, and this is the reason why he is in such high spirits on the one hand and so uninhibited in action on the other.

If we put these two indications together,[1] what we find is this.

---

[1] [The 'psycho-analytic impression' and the 'general economic experience'.]

In mania, the ego must have got over the loss of the object (or its mourning over the loss, or perhaps the object itself), and thereupon the whole quota of anticathexis which the painful suffering of melancholia had drawn to itself from the ego and 'bound' will have become available [p. 253]. Moreover, the manic subject plainly demonstrates his liberation from the object which was the cause of his suffering, by seeking like a ravenously hungry man for new object-cathexes.

This explanation certainly sounds plausible, but in the first place it is too indefinite, and, secondly, it gives rise to more new problems and doubts than we can answer. We will not evade a discussion of them, even though we cannot expect it to lead us to a clear understanding.

In the first place, normal mourning, too, overcomes the loss of the object, and it, too, while it lasts, absorbs all the energies of the ego. Why, then, after it has run its course, is there no hint in its case of the economic condition for a phase of triumph? I find it impossible to answer this objection straight away. It also draws our attention to the fact that we do not even know the economic means by which mourning carries out its task [p. 245]. Possibly, however, a conjecture will help us here. Each single one of the memories and situations of expectancy which demonstrate the libido's attachment to the lost object is met by the verdict of reality that the object no longer exists; and the ego, confronted as it were with the question whether it shall share this fate, is persuaded by the sum of the narcissistic satisfactions it derives from being alive to sever its attachment to the object that has been abolished. We may perhaps suppose that this work of severance is so slow and gradual that by the time it has been finished the expenditure of energy necessary for it is also dissipated.[1]

It is tempting to go on from this conjecture about the work of mourning and try to give an account of the work of melancholia. Here we are met at the outset by an uncertainty. So far we have hardly considered melancholia from the topographical point of view, nor asked ourselves in and between what psychical systems the work of melancholia goes on. What

---

[1] The economic standpoint has hitherto received little attention in psycho-analytic writings. I would mention as an exception a paper by Victor Tausk (1913) on motives for repression devalued by recompenses.

part of the mental processes of the disease still takes place in connection with the unconscious object-cathexes that have been given up, and what part in connection with their substitute, by identification, in the ego?

The quick and easy answer is that 'the unconscious (thing-) presentation[1] of the object has been abandoned by the libido'. In reality, however, this presentation is made up of innumerable single impressions (or unconscious traces of them), and this withdrawal of libido is not a process that can be accomplished in a moment, but must certainly, as in mourning, be one in which progress is long-drawn-out and gradual. Whether it begins simultaneously at several points or follows some sort of fixed sequence is not easy to decide; in analyses it often becomes evident that first one and then another memory is activated, and that the laments which always sound the same and are wearisome in their monotony nevertheless take their rise each time in some different unconscious source. If the object does not possess this great significance for the ego—a significance reinforced by a thousand links—then, too, its loss will not be of a kind to cause either mourning or melancholia. This characteristic of detaching the libido bit by bit is therefore to be ascribed alike to mourning and to melancholia; it is probably supported by the same economic situation and serves the same purposes in both.

As we have seen, however [p. 250 f.], melancholia contains something more than normal mourning. In melancholia the relation to the object is no simple one; it is complicated by the conflict due to ambivalence. The ambivalence is either constitutional, i.e. is an element of every love-relation formed by this particular ego, or else it proceeds precisely from those experiences that involved the threat of losing the object. For this reason the exciting causes of melancholia have a much wider range than those of mourning, which is for the most part occasioned only by a real loss of the object, by its death. In melancholia, accordingly, countless separate struggles are carried on over the object, in which hate and love contend with each other; the one seeks to detach the libido from the object, the other to maintain this position of the libido against the assault. The location of these separate struggles cannot be assigned to any system but the *Ucs.*, the region of the memory-traces of *things*

[1] ['*Dingvorstellung.*' See above p. 201*n*.]

(as contrasted with *word*-cathexes). In mourning, too, the efforts to detach the libido are made in this same system; but in it nothing hinders these processes from proceeding along the normal path through the *Pcs.* to consciousness. This path is blocked for the work of melancholia, owing perhaps to a number of causes or a combination of them. Constitutional ambivalence belongs by its nature to the repressed; traumatic experiences in connection with the object may have activated other repressed material. Thus everything to do with these struggles due to ambivalence remains withdrawn from consciousness, until the outcome characteristic of melancholia has set in. This, as we know, consists in the threatened libidinal cathexis at length abandoning the object, only, however, to draw back to the place in the ego from which it had proceeded. So by taking flight into the ego love escapes extinction. After this regression of the libido the process can become conscious, and it is represented to consciousness as a conflict between one part of the ego and the critical agency.

What consciousness is aware of in the work of melancholia is thus not the essential part of it, nor is it even the part which we may credit with an influence in bringing the ailment to an end. We see that the ego debases itself and rages against itself, and we understand as little as the patient what this can lead to and how it can change. We can more readily attribute such a function to the *unconscious* part of the work, because it is not difficult to perceive an essential analogy between the work of melancholia and of mourning. Just as mourning impels the ego to give up the object by declaring the object to be dead and offering the ego the inducement of continuing to live [p. 255], so does each single struggle of ambivalence loosen the fixation of the libido to the object by disparaging it, denigrating it and even as it were killing it. It is possible for the process in the *Ucs.* to come to an end, either after the fury has spent itself or after the object has been abandoned as valueless. We cannot tell which of these two possibilities is the regular or more usual one in bringing melancholia to an end, nor what influence this termination has on the future course of the case. The ego may enjoy in this the satisfaction of knowing itself as the better of the two, as superior to the object.

Even if we accept this view of the work of melancholia, it still does not supply an explanation of the one point on which we were seeking light. It was our expectation that the economic condition for the emergence of mania after the melancholia has run its course is to be found in the ambivalence which dominates the latter affection; and in this we found support from analogies in various other fields. But there is one fact before which that expectation must bow. Of the three preconditions of melancholia—loss of the object, ambivalence, and regression of libido into the ego—the first two are also found in the obsessional self-reproaches arising after a death has occurred. In those cases it is unquestionably the ambivalence which is the motive force of the conflict, and observation shows that after the conflict has come to an end there is nothing left over in the nature of the triumph of a manic state of mind. We are thus led to the third factor as the only one responsible for the result. The accumulation of cathexis which is at first bound and then, after the work of melancholia is finished, becomes free and makes mania possible must be linked with regression of the libido to narcissism. The conflict within the ego, which melancholia substitutes for the struggle over the object, must act like a painful wound which calls for an extraordinarily high anti-cathexis.—But here once again, it will be well to call a halt and to postpone any further explanation of mania until we have gained some insight into the economic nature, first, of physical pain, and then of the mental pain which is analogous to it.[1] As we already know, the interdependence of the complicated problems of the mind forces us to break off every enquiry before it is completed—till the outcome of some other enquiry can come to its assistance.[2]

[1] [See footnote 1, p. 147 above.]
[2] [*Footnote added* 1925:] Cf. a continuation of this discussion of mania in *Group Psychology and the Analysis of the Ego* (1921c) [*Standard Ed.*, **18**, 130-3].

PART II

Discussion of
"Mourning and Melancholia"

11

Discussion of
"Mourning and Melancholia"

1

Melancholia, mourning, and the countertransference

Priscilla Roth

"Mourning and Melancholia" is a psychoanalytic treasure that changed the way psychoanalysts think. Though written as one of the metapsychological papers, it is profoundly concerned with emotions. In its insistence that the mind is not unitary, it led to the conceptualization of an internal world in which there are different and separate parts of the self and different internalized love objects all relating to each other in complex ways—sometimes friendly and sometimes powerfully hostile. And it introduced the idea that the quality of these relations between parts of our self and our internalized love objects is what defines our moods, our sense of well-being, and, indeed, our character.

Like Shakespeare's Hamlet, Freud's "Mourning and Melancholia" is full of famous quotes; I want especially to focus on one of them. The statement "People never willingly abandon a libidinal position, not even, indeed, when a substitute is already beckoning to them" is among Freud's richest formulations. For many years I have suggested to students, only half jokingly, that it ought to be emblazoned in large letters on the wall of every consulting-room, where the analyst can be reminded of its message during every session with every patient. "People never willingly abandon a libidinal position". A fulcrum, embracing discoveries first adumbrated in *On Narcissism* and the Leonardo Da Vinci paper and pointing ahead to *Beyond the Pleasure Principle* and *The Ego and The Id*, the sentence succinctly describes that which is most puzzlingly intransigent in human nature. The repetition compulsion, manic defences, obsessional disorders all have their roots in the behavioural pattern described in these eighteen words.

Freud famously tells us in "Mourning and Melancholia" that the lost loved object is incorporated and established, by identification, within the ego, in order to obviate the unbearable experience of object loss. The meaning of "object loss" is important. It does not mean that the loved object has died or gone away or been unfaithful, though any of these may have been the precipitating event that created the danger of the loss of the object, and though psychologically any and all of these things may have happened. Object loss means that something catastrophic has happened to the subject's internal connection with his object. To understand this is to recognize how essential is the internalized object to an individual's sense of well-being, the sense of cohesion within his ego. Freud's *On Narcissism* allows us to understand that the danger that arises to someone when a love object is "lost"—through death, or betrayal, or disappointment—is not primarily the loss of that particular person or institution or ideal; the danger is to the person's sense of himself, which depends on his sense of an ongoing internal attachment to his loved object.

Freud makes clear, in this and later papers (1917e [1915], 1923b), the connection between loving one's objects and the psychological experience of being internally loved and protected by these objects; Melanie Klein (1935, 1940) continued the exploration of this connection. The moment one is threatened with loss of this fundamental attachment, the primary psychological task becomes that of preserving feelings of love, since the loss of these feelings leaves desolation and terror. The melancholic solution to this threat rearranges the perception of reality, so that when the external love object is lost—by whatever circumstances—the attachment to the *internal* object relation is maintained, even though this requires that the object change its external identity. That is, it is only the *external* object that changes; the libidinal position, the patterning of a relationship with the internal object, remains the same.

In analysis, the patient is at the mercy of intense feelings—love and hate—directed towards his analyst: this attachment is the transference. It may become something else one day: gratitude, admiration, appreciation of real qualities and real help. But for a long time these feelings, no matter how powerful, are a way of not giving up the familiar libidinal object—that is, loving the analyst is the patient's way of re-organizing reality so that the familiar love remains while the object has changed its external identity. And the same is true for hatred—the patient's hatred of his analyst is always profoundly rooted in his hatred for his original disappointing object. Subjectively the experience of the patient may be "I can't feel anything for my mother; I love *you*." But we know that not only are certain feelings for the mother—meaning original object—displaced onto the analyst, but that their attachment onto the person of the analyst is both tenacious and shallow. Helene Deutsch's (1930) patient who, having apparently weathered the death of her mother and the later abandonment by her beloved sister, loses her mind when her little dog is killed, is a telling example. The internal object relationship is constant—its external manifestations change.

When this happens, love for this substitute object—indeed, for each of the substitutes—is not for the unique qualities of the new object, but for how well the object relationship stands in for the original object relationship, lost since the earliest disappointments and re-established to avoid experiencing loss. The more this is so, the more tenacious the tie to the replacement object. And it is also clear that insofar as the objects lose their unique qualities for the subject, they become variations on the same theme—repeated examples of an unchanging original. Thus the shallowness of the tie to any one of them and the relative ease with which any particular one can be psychologically replaced.

For the analyst, the relationship with the patient also represents lost object relationships: a relationship with his child self, but also a relationship with parents needing to be cared for and cured of their unhappiness or, alternatively, punished for their failures. Or both. There is a clash between the analyst's wish to be loved by his patients and the fact that he is largely a transference object to them, which means that the patient's view of him is only partly related to anything he actually is. The analyst is often required to allow himself to be what the patient sees him as—which frequently means temporarily accepting a role that is inimical to his sense of himself. If we can allow ourselves this "role actualization", in Sandler's phrase, we may become able meaningfully to understand our patients' internal relationships. This often, and sometimes repeatedly and for long periods, requires us to do the mourning that our patients, locked in the melancholic experience, are unable to do.

Inherent and implied in the idea that no one gives up a *libidinal position* willingly (note that Freud does not write "a libidinal *object*") is the understanding that what is transferred in analysis is not a single object, or a single discrete object relationship, but what has come to be called the "total situation" (Klein, Joseph). It is also important to keep in mind that maintaining the same libidinal position does not at all imply maintaining the same location within that position: processes of projection, introjection, identification, and projective identification enable the subject to locate and dislocate himself from one point in a configuration to another.

There is always something of the earliest libidinal relationships—both love and hatred—going on in the transference and therefore also in the countertransference. This is not in doubt. What is in question is our ability to understand the way these most primitive relationships manifest themselves in any particular analysis. To help us, we have our countertransference experiences and the tools that enable us to make sense of these experiences: the structure afforded us by the analytic situation, our role as analyst, and those fertile theories that illuminate and make sense of the experiences in which we are participating.

In a beautiful discussion of "Mourning and Melancholia", Ignês Sodré (2005, pp 124–141) has described the way the melancholic "wound" embodies a paradoxical situation: on the one hand a powerful melancholic longing for a lost love relationship and, on the other, a tormenting, imprisoning tie to the object—a "wound", remorselessly gnawed and picked at. The analysis I want to discuss was marked by these features. In this often confusing analysis, the peculiar countertransference reactions and enactments that developed became my most important guide to understanding this paradoxical and painful situation.

Clinical material

Over the years I have treated in analysis a number of young women, each of whom was attractive and intelligent, somewhere over 30 years old, and frightened at finding that something about herself prevented her from establishing a meaningful relationship with a man. Each, I came to feel, was hampered by an enslavement to an early libidinal tie that which she was unable to relinquish.

In her early 30s when her analysis began, K had had several boy-friends, but none of the relationships had lasted. She was afraid she would never get married and have children, never be "normal".

She is a lawyer in an established firm; beautiful, from a wealthy family. She remembers constant battles between her parents, who divorced when she was at University. She reports that she was a dif-ficult child: she had temper tantrums and was impossible to control. Her parents are puzzled by her and don't understand why she isn't married. Her father pays for her analysis while being contemptuous of it. She has one sister who is three years younger.

For the first year K expressed only positive feelings about the analysis, often remarking on how much "progress" she was making. She had had a previous unsuccessful analysis, and she saw this new analysis as full of promise. From the beginning her material was strikingly narcissistic—a running commentary on her feelings, in a vacuum, with almost no content: "first I felt this, then I felt that, when I feel this it makes me feel thus and so". She could never, for example, describe a film she had seen, nor even mention its name, lest I become interested in the film. After the first year there was some change in this as she became angry about breaks or occasional changes to the structure of the analysis: the rare changed session time infuriated her, as did any alteration to what she saw as usual ana-lytic practice: "No one else's analyst takes off the week *before* Easter; everyone else's analyst takes the week *after* Easter."

During the first two years she went on occasional dates and had some sexual relationships; none of these had any particular impor-tance to her. Early in the third year of analysis she had a date with a young man, B, which became a weekend spent together. She was delighted and reported that she thought she was in love. Within weeks, however, these feelings of attraction became transformed into complaints, demands, and assertions of entitlement, which periodi-cally gave way to terror that he would leave her. By the third week after the exciting weekend, the patient was irritated by B's wanting to spend time with his friends, which she saw as not being "com-mitted": she nagged him with increasing bitterness about smoking, untidiness, not having a driving licence, not answering her text mes-sages quickly enough, not "going around the car and opening the car door" for her like her friend's boyfriend did, having to work so much, and not taking her on romantic holidays. He was now her possession, expected to provide her with all the accoutrements of a "relationship". From this point on, I rarely heard about the pleasures of getting to know B, delight in his company, or anything specific to him that might interest or please her. He was consistently described in terms of what "a boyfriend" or "a relationship" should be; his only function was that of a servant, whose job was to bring her, as if on a tray, the "boyfriend experiences" to which she was entitled. When he occasionally rebelled and became angry, she would arrive at her session in despair about having "gone too far", wanting help to control her behaviour. This never lasted long; within minutes she would find reasons to justify her attack on him and to find further fault with him.

My role became defined purely in terms of my usefulness to "the relationship". She often mixed me up with one or another of her girlfriends with whom she discussed the relationship in identical terms and would demand that I give her advice or reassurance, as her friends did. "Zoe thinks I should phone B even though he hasn't phoned me; what do you think?" Attempts to explore what was going on between us were met with dismissal and, if I persisted, contempt: "I am not interested in you; I am only interested in my relationship." This was persistent and unwavering. The effect was to deprive both herself and me of any depth: she would make herself shallow and as-if stupid in the service of the tie to this "relationship", which obliterated everything else, and she wanted nothing from me except advice on how she should conduct the relationship. She was similarly subtractive of B, whose qualities were limited to how he did or did not play into her picture of what "a relationship" should be and, by not providing her with her ideal relationship, enacted with her the other side of such relationships—marked by criticism, disappointment, and failure.

The dual quality of the melancholic experience as Freud describes it in "Mourning and Melancholia" includes an overwhelming longing for the lost object relationship, felt to have been ideal and irreplaceable, and, at the same time, a hatred of the object for denying one this longed-for relationship. The loss of the idealized object brings unbearable anguish, which seems as if it can only be assuaged by a restoration of the lost relationship. It was Freud's genius to understand that for the melancholic this restoration is

psychically accomplished by the process of identification—we become what we would otherwise lose. The identifications that take
place—in order to deny the loss—are with both aspects of this object:
the ideal and the hateful. In K's case the identification was with an
object experienced as, at the same time, demanding, impenetrable,
withholding, irritating, and frustrating. Everything in her mind centred around this—the enactment, in her life and in her analysis, of
a relationship both all-consuming and fraught with disappointment
and violent feelings. .
Some material will show how this was manifested in the analysis:

One day I spoke to her about a fee rise. The following day she
responded.

"I really don't want to come to analysis any more. Don't want
four times week. I just find I don't want to get up and come here.
Most days I'd rather sleep. I want to come once a week. I want
to be able to come if I feel bad . . . but not all the time. I used to
feel bad, needed to come more. Now I don't. I came to analysis
because I wanted to have a relationship—well, now I've got one,
I just want to live my life, not have to analyse myself all the time,
just have an ordinary life. Like normal people."

It was clear that the proposed fee-rise had hurt her feelings. The
fee—and the raising of it—stood for everything that keeps her out
and differentiates her role from mine, her position from mine. She
experiences this as an expulsion—a brutal loss of her hold on the
object. Threatened in this way with having to know that we are separate, each from the other, and the loss to her sense of herself that
knowing this would entail, she instead incorporated a particular picture of me into herself and, as it were, became this view of me: she
identified with a cold and unavailable object and became someone
who has no needs and has everything desirable. At the same time
she projected all her sense of inadequacy, of worthlessness, into me.
Once that has happened, why would she want to come to useless me
for analysis? This is object loss followed by an identification with the
loved and hated object—the process Freud described. The patient
pulls her analyst into an enactment of her primary libidinal relationship. In this situation—I raise her fee / she is hurt = she is cold
and smug / I am hurt—the relationship: subject to object—child

to parent—remains the same; one party is a useless supplicant, the other a cold and impenetrable object. Relations between the two are exploitative and ruthless one way or the other, but the basic relationship stays the same.

This is the double identification of melancholia—on the one hand taking over the qualities of the object of desire and, on the other, projecting the unwanted feelings of worthlessness into the object who is identified with the unloved self.

Melancholia is a narcissistic condition; the hatred of the object in melancholia is because of its separateness from the self. So when K incorporates and identifies with me, it is with a picture of me whose most desirable and enviable quality is the ease with which I can reject and abandon.

But this is only one side of melancholia.

That night the patient had a dream that she brought to the next day's session:

I was coming here, to my session. Maybe it was summer, because it was warm and sunny. All around the building was water, there was a big lake and a beautiful garden—a beautiful landscape, a much bigger space than there actually is. To get to the door I had to climb onto a ladder, and there was a pulley system which pulled me in, over the lake, as if over a moat. At the door, three girls came out—they'd been in the consulting-room with you. They said, "She's marking one of your essays—she's got some of your work on her table." I realized that they were just supervisees, and they thought I was just a supervisee; they didn't realize I'm in analysis. When I went in you said "K", very warmly and friendly and nice, and you showed me pictures of plans for the gardens. As if we were friends."

This is the other side of the melancholia—a dream-memory of an idealized place from which she is not excluded; instead, in this place my arms reach out and lift her, like a small infant, up and over all the obstacles and bring her to me. And I have her on my table, in my mind, all the time. In this place she will have not four ordinary sessions, coming and going, but one forever-in-my-mind never-ending session in which I show her beautiful gardens, as if we were friends, forever. This is an idealized picture, an idealized relationship; but it is what she feels she has lost and desperately longs for and is condemned to spend her life fighting to get back.

This longing for what is lost and felt to be entirely necessary for happiness and well-being is the other side of the coldness and ruthlessness of the previous day's takeover: the patient could only maintain a balance inside herself by incorporating and identifying with the experienced-as-impenetrable and unavailable object. Thus identification makes an impossible state seem possible—I *am* the object, I have not lost the object, I am not separate from the object. I *am* the object.

Since the only bearable state is one of complete non-differentiation from the object, the fee-rise feels disastrous. She feels that a cruel and punitive object has pushed her away because she is a failure. It is as if she hears me saying, "You pay, I receive, because I have everything desirable and valuable, and you have nothing." This version of the object—cruel, smug, and punitive—is what Freud (1914c) called the "special psychic agency" and what became the superego. K deals with the blow to her wish that she and I are undifferentiated by identifying with her cruel superego and turning its disdain and contempt on me as the felt-to-be-disposable her.

This pattern, in which someone is always trying to get in and is always being cruelly kept out—which has its roots in her history— played out again and again in the analysis: I would try to make contact with my patient, she would be impenetrable, and seemed to strip her own mind and mine of singularity and meaning. Everything I did was judged only in relation to—as either helpful to or interfering with—her "relationship". (An example: "I'm getting very irritated thinking about how your going away yesterday with such short notice impacted on my relationship all weekend. I was in a bad mood, irritated with B, I knew it was your fault. If I left analysis, I wouldn't have this problem, would I?"). The countertransference experience during this period was of being emptied of any desirable qualities. The patient maintained that I had no unique value to her and that she had no interest in thought or insight, and often in her presence I felt gutted of any ability to think or reflect and left with a primitive impulse to bat back at her in the way she batted my interpretations back at me. Most of the time I did not actually enact this, but the impulse was frequently there, and what was missing for periods was my confidence in my psychoanalytic identity—my capacity to feel and think as a psychoanalyst.

The following material demonstrates the interaction I am describing. [I note my countertransference experience in brackets.]

After a summer break K announced that things had been terrible the whole time "we were away". She was horrible to B, critical and nasty, constantly comparing him to other people's boyfriends, feeling that he wasn't good enough.

Yesterday, she said, they nearly got to the end. Saturday her sister gave birth. "We went to see them in the hospital yesterday. B and I were both born in that same hospital. I said to B, "Isn't it amazing that we were born here too?" He said, "Yeah", but didn't seem very interested. Well, I just went nuts. We went in to see my sister and brother-in-law and the baby—there they were, with their baby: my younger sister now has two children!! and I was just furious! I hated B. Later I told him he isn't what I want, he isn't good enough."

I said to K that I thought the experience of being in the hospital visiting the new baby was both upsetting to her in itself, but also powerfully representative of a frequent experience she has: that there is always a picture in the back of her mind of where she'd really like to be and can't be, and it is defined exactly as *where she is not.* I said the picture of the mother and father and baby—with her having to look on, feeling completely left out—is the awful and painful apotheosis of it. In the background is the picture she has of me on holiday, not remembering that she was born here too—that *she* is an adored baby. When she feels so forgotten, so jealous, then B seems to her not good enough, however he behaves. [Making this interpretation, I felt sympathetic and tender towards her.]

K immediately said that she didn't understand. The baby visit only happened yesterday, and she was horrible all through the holiday.

I explained again that this was only the culmination . . . that the whole holiday "when we were away" felt like having to watch a happy family in her mind. I mentioned also her parents and baby sister—that watching this new baby brought back these ever-threatening feelings.

[I felt uncomfortable explaining this again; I feared that her question was disingenuous and that she had become inaccessible, and I thought I had probably lost her participation in a conversation in which we could understand each other.]

She responded, "But how can I have felt that about two parents who were always fighting with each other?"

[This was heart-sinkingly familiar: K would ask questions that were a kind of nit-picking, a process in which the questions themselves had nothing to do with interest or curiosity but felt, instead, like arguments designed only to keep me out. I found myself trying clumsily to answer her questions, to explain. This felt false, and I sensed the loss of what had felt like a meaningful communication between us.]

This is the countertransference experience I want to illustrate. In this state, I am stuck in a narrow space, finding myself having to explain "the internal world" to her—the way this scene with baby and mother and father are emblematic of a long-standing misery—and as I do this, it is as if there is no other mind in the room to understand what I'm talking about. As I go on trying somehow to "explain" why she might have found the hospital visit so disturbing, I, too, begin to behave as though something enormous hasn't just happened: a loss of meaning, a loss of a connection between us. When that happens, we are both unable to relate to each other within a world of richness of contact and thought, we are both left in the narrow confines of concrete meaning. What has been lost to the patient is the actual experience of an object (here an analyst) who could hear what she was saying, hear "I was born here too!", understand her terrible jealousy and envy—that is, actually be a "we" with her. Instead, we are batting at each other, neither making contact.

After a few minutes she said, "I *was* jealous of L (her friend) this weekend . . . in fact, mad with jealousy." L's new boyfriend had "whisked L away to Prague on a holiday to a glamorous hotel. He planned it all!" She said to B, "You never do this!" She was overcome with jealousy—thought she wouldn't be able to bear it, wouldn't be able to live. There was a long pause. During the holiday she didn't love B at all. Didn't even respect him. She had to go through the motions. Pause. "So what does what you've been saying have to do with *that*??? I mean, why didn't I feel any respect for him?"

Once again there is a moment of some understanding—she tells me that she *is* able to be aware of jealousy and of how powerful it is—so powerful that, embedded in her jealous feelings, she was unable to love B during the holiday. ("People never willingly abandon a libidinal object, not even when a substitute is already beckoning.") But when she experiences a wish that I help her to understand this, she immediately feels jealous and envious of the privileged position this gives me: as if I am now the lucky one, like L, who is being "whisked off" by her boyfriend to some glamorous, enviable place. So she reverts to the familiar position in which I am locked out of her thoughtful mind: "So what does what you've been saying have to do with *that*?"—and I am suddenly being accused and held to account.

This was a recurring pattern in the analysis: my feeling of being repeatedly shifted to a thin spot from which I have no access to her, and then she has none to me, and we can only each be disappointed in the other. My job, at these moments, was to do her work of mourning, over and over again. My frequent experience was of feeling I had found an object to talk to, to understand and be understood by, and then to lose it. Having lost it, I was often pulled into an identification with my patient's projection into me: I repeatedly experienced a sense of failure, of uselessness, of being disposable. Each time, the work of mourning involved bearing these projections and then separating myself from them and finding my own identity once again.

The patient's description of visiting the couple and baby in the hospital, and the following material about L and not being able to love B on holiday, *does* have content and meaning within it: jealousy, which she is aware of feeling and of finding extremely painful, and also a sense that other people have experiences that she can only mimic. This material came from feelings that are real and powerful and are very different from "What does that have to do with what you say?"

What causes such a dramatic change? The patient yearns for contact with a love object experienced as lost—lost because finite, because not-her, because in every way imperfect. But any present experience of contact is immediately interrupted by hatred of the actual object because at the moment it is desirable it is also recognized as finite, not-her, imperfect. The act of double identification—she is the desirable object, I am disposable—makes this impossible situation possible for her; it is a manic defence that "whisks" her away from loss to triumph.

It is not possible to have a perfect relationship with a perfectly possessed object. We all know this in theory, but we all struggle with its inexorable truth. This is what Freud so brilliantly insisted on: we don't easily give up our very first loves, our original libidinal ties. And so long as we don't give them up, we are unable to benefit from, to enjoy, to learn from, new contacts and new relationships. Giving up our first, idealized, love is a long and painful struggle and involves bearing feelings that are difficult to bear: weakness, dependency, humiliation, and the terror of being alone.

Some time later, two weeks before a three-week break

The patient has four sessions a week—Monday to Thursday. She had, unusually, cancelled two Monday mornings in a row.

> When she returned on Tuesday, she reported that she'd had a miserable weekend, and that she now felt depressed, mean, and ungenerous. She reported a dream. In this dream, *she and B take her sister's two small children into their bed. They were all in bed together; it was very very nice.*
>
> She added that on her way to analysis she always sees women in big cars, with children. Why can't she be happy like them? They always look so happy. She is fed up with her life, fed up with B. Sometimes she thinks she'd be happier on her own.

The dream was like her dream about coming to the consulting-room in the idyllic landscape. Here it is about grownups and children all in her bed, all very happy. Like the idyllic landscape dream, this is a dream about something she feels is lost forever and, compared with which everything else, is tormentingly disappointing. This dream— in bed with children—is also a dream-solution to the hospital experience where she had visited her sister and brother-in-law after the birth of their second child. At that time she had said to B: "Isn't it amazing? We were born here too!" I think this meant that "we" are the babies, and "we" are the couple, and "WE" were born here! Not just sister's babies. This didn't work because in not responding, B seemed to be saying "I'm not going to join you in this, there isn't going to be a 'we'—I am not thinking as you are—I am me, and you are you." In this new dream, not only does she, together with B, replace the sister and brother-in-law, standing for the parents with their new baby, her sister, but she and B are also the children she has taken into her bed . All jealousy, all envy, all sense of being left and alone is obviated by this dream.

When she came back the following week, she was very angry:

"What you said Thursday really irritated me. I slept badly again. You said I was feeling fragmented because I missed the sessions last Monday and this. It's just stupid. A stupid thing to say."

[This was not what I had said, and I thought she knew this. I felt in a familiar uncomfortable spot.]

I said, "It sounds like this has become something I have said in your mind, though it's not what I said." [This felt a pathetic response—a feeble attempt to get back on my feet.]

She said, "I know . . . you said it's because you are taking the holiday as well. That makes me even more irritated. You're saying that I sleep badly, I feel bad, because of something you do. You always take things up in terms of here, as if I have no external life at all. Maybe you think it's your job. Its just stupid. And the answer is obviously to stop coming; if analysis is my problem, why bother coming? I can solve my problems by not coming."

[I felt irritated and constricted, wanting to argue with her; to say "I didn't say that." . . . I thought she knew more than this and it felt like an impenetrable game she was playing. I felt played with, swatted at, not allowed to make any contact with her.]

"You should think about the impact on me when you say these things. I leave on Thursday, you tell me it's my fault for missing last Monday and this Monday. Your job is to make me feel better. And if what you say is true, how come I slept fine on Thursday and Friday, then terribly on Saturday, Sunday, and Monday? How does that make sense? I don't find what you say interesting . . . I'm not interested in analysis."

[I had to consider that perhaps I had been interpreting to her without thinking about the impact on her of what I was saying. But in my memory of Thursday I had been feeling sympathetic to her, trying very hard to make contact with her. Not feeling irritated. "And anyway", I began to think, "she is now saying she slept FINE on Thursday and Friday . . . so how does THAT make sense?" I realized that now I was thinking as she does, wanting to defend myself and to pick holes in what she was saying, and that I'd lost my own sense of who I am and how to think about this.]

I reminded her of previous weeks, when she *was* interested, and said something had happened to her interest. [Here I was trying to make contact with the part of my patient who knows more about herself, and of course trying to locate another part of myself as her analyst.]

She said, "I haven't felt that in a long time." She paused. "I used to think you were wonderful. You understood me perfectly . . . all I ever wanted." And then: "How do you explain *that*!?"

[This last statement—"How do you explain *that*?" was taunting and triumphant, as though to contradict both my attempt to contact her and anything she might have been remembering a second before. When she'd remembered that "I used to think you were wonderful", she was somewhat softer, in touch for a moment with different feelings. But she immediately reverted to the flicking-back "How do you explain *that*"].

I want to try to describe what I think was going on. I think the dream of the previous week had disturbed her, and the work on the dream had touched her. But then, inevitably, the weekend arrived, this time longer because of her cancellation of Monday. I think her experience of the weekend was as if I had pulled something that belonged to her away from her—like a mother suddenly and unexpectedly pulling the nipple from her baby's mouth. In this session she is again identified with just such a sadistic object—each time I think I have a place on which to stand and speak to her, she pulls it away from me, doesn't allow me to have contact with her. And I am left on the outside, trying to get in. I am like the baby, falling apart because I've lost what I was holding on to.

This is a painful position to be in, and my feelings are once again a mixture of prickly irritation and sadness at the absence of contact. My ability to respond in a way that is helpful depends entirely on my capacity once again to mourn the loss of the contact. This involves a taking in of the patient's projection—I am an abandoned baby—and then separating myself from it and finding my identity as her analyst.

Pushed by my patient's projections to feel the rage and humilia-tion she must get rid of, I am helped not to enact the to-and-fro of the hating/hateful relationship by the structure of my role as her analyst and by a body of theory, most especially Freud's profound understanding of such events.

> After a few minutes I tried to talk to her about some of this. I said that my impression is as if I'm kept on a very thin ledge, that I can't make any contact with her at all—can't get in, can't feel any real understanding between us . . . that she swats me away so that I can't touch her. We're allowed only the thinnest of contact, no depth to it, her mind closed as if it doesn't want understanding either way between us—for me to understand her, or for her to understand me.

> She was silent and then said, "That's like my father. That's what he does. There is no contact, he doesn't allow it. This is just what it feels like to be with him. He talks only in clichés. And my mother . . . only neediness." She paused. "My father is moving house—after 30 years—the house I grew up in has been torn to the ground—they're building a new house on the property. The house is gone. It's very odd. He says it is a difficult time for him, but he only talks in clichés. 'It's a very emotional time for me.' Meaningless." She was silent for a minute. In fact, she said, she's in quite a good mood today. Not here—she's been in a bad mood since she got here—but she woke up in a good mood even though she didn't get much sleep. On the weekend they moved B's stuff into her flat—the vans came and delivered everything. On Saturday they put his stuff away. It was fun. There is still lots of crap around . . . boxes and things. But they did a lot. On Sunday they went to the wedding—then came back last night. . . . She's excited about the holiday, but not about the flights: there will be a long flight, then two internal short flights . . . she is afraid of the short flights.

> I said I thought that what I had said had made sense to her, and that as well as talking about her trip, she was describing a change that seems to have taken place, in which her mind can actually move and travel. I thought this was very different from where she

had been earlier in the session: that her thoughts seemed now to be able to move out of the flatness and thin-ness, the batting back. That she now had thoughts about her father and mother, about moving house, and putting stuff away, about travelling, and how it will all be. . . . Her mind and thoughts seemed freer, with more possibilities. I thought she had been able to make room for me in her mind, as she is able to make room for B in her flat.

She paused and then said, "I am meeting the woman from Human Resources today at work. She is a psychotherapist. She is apparently very odd. E says this woman will offer me supervision. That'll be weird." Then spoke again about the trips and that she wished she could stay in one place.

I said I thought that she was finding it "very odd" that something had happened inside her, that she felt freer and less constricted, without her being in charge of it, being able to predict it or explain it. I thought she didn't know how to think about that and found it "weird".

The following day she announced that she was furious at B. She had come home from work and found that he hadn't moved any of the boxes she'd asked him to get rid of.

"He doesn't do anything for US", she shouted. "He will do all sorts of things for himself, he tidies up HIS room, but he left boxes all around the house . . . he never thinks about US. Either he should earn the money, and drive me around in his car, or else he has to help me clean up the flat. He has to do one or other. He has to be a partner."

What has happened? Once again, something had momentarily changed for the patient in the previous day's session. There had been, though only briefly, a transformation: she had been more available, more open, her mind moving and connecting and flexible. She had been much freer to follow her thoughts and wanted to communicate them. But she found it "weird" to find that this alteration had occurred outside her bidding it to, "odd" that she felt that I had something to teach her.

This "Why can't he think about *us*" material that comes on Wednesday is back to the old intransigent libidinal position after the movement on Tuesday. On Tuesday, even if just for a few moments, she had a wish to be understood and in contact. This gets lost both because it is strange and uncontrollable, but also because there is an interruption to it—the end of the session—and she reverts to her default position: "You never take care of *US*."

What I am suggesting is that at the moment she experiences contact, she also experiences it as weird and odd—it is a momentary emerging from a narcissistic state in which she is resolutely playing out a primary libidinal relationship, into a real relationship with a real object. Then the session ends, and because at this stage the patient cannot yet feel she can keep alive an internal connection with me, the end of the session means she has no place to go and no way of sustaining the freer state of mind.

For many of our patients, the melancholic solution, which includes incorporation and identification, projection and manic states, is the only way they have of making an impossible situation feel possible: I have not lost the object because I am it. Mourning—a lengthy process, in which progress comes bit by bit and in fits and starts—can eventually allow the acceptance of the painful reality of separation: I am not the object. In order to accept this reality, we need gradually to learn that we can survive as separate beings from our objects.

We all need help to do this, particularly when we are in a situation that threatens our self-esteem and our sense of our own identity. When our patients push us into enacting their early object relationships with them, we analysts need help to extract ourselves from the enactment and think. The process of mourning takes place constantly in K's analysis: each time I give her an interpretation and she makes contact for a second and then takes the contact away, I feel irritation, depression, and loss. I have then to free myself from this state by a process of mourning: I have to give up the position I have been in and re-position myself so that I can begin to think as her analyst once again.

At these moments in the analyses we conduct, we analysts have the structure of our role and the analytic setting to help us return to our analytic selves; we also can call upon what we have learned from our own experiences. And we have what can eventually become an internalized body of theory, particularly about these processes from "Mourning and Melancholia" and the work that has grown out of it.

The patient has none of this. So she needs help from me, not to lift her up and over the obstacles, but to help her face them and accompany her while she does so from a point of view that understands her point of view and then helps her to see something more about it. This involves both an identification with my patient in distress and then a separation, a moving away from being what the patient has projected into me, back into the separateness of being her analyst, speaking to her about an experience we both know about.

It is this experience of her analyst working with her that may enable her gradually, piece by piece, to let go of the melancholic solution—the insistence on the ideal, the identification with the object—and begin to experience and internalize something more helpful to her development.

2

Mourning for "missing" people

María Lucila Pelento

After the death of a loved-one, forgetting—that "latent gift", as Blanchot (1962, p. 87) called it—requires a certain process to take place, which is part of the work of the psyche that Freud termed "mourning work" [*Trauerarbeit*] (Freud, 1917e [1915]). It begins with acknowledging the reality of death, which is an unavoidable condition for triggering a mourning process. This acknowledgement entails gathering "what was seen"—if the person witnessed the loved-one's illness and/or death—"what was heard"—if the death was also communicated, or only communicated—and "what was ratified"—through the various practices that are usual in society at certain points in time.

The "revolt of the minds against mourning"—as Freud described it in "On Transience" (1916a)—is immediately felt as an intense wish for the death not to have really happened.

Words pronounced in a state of shock, particularly in the case of unexpected death—such as "I can't believe it", "it can't be true"—express the need to deny the fact of death and reveal the refusal to abandon the former object of pleasure. This is a fluctuating process: the subject believes and does not believe the actual reality of this death by turns. Nevertheless, once the fact has become compellingly undeniable, convergence of all the above-mentioned components constrains the subject to accept the evidence of reality by withdrawing his investment in the object. But this is an extremely difficult and painful operation. The subject turns away from reality, withdraws all interest from it, while strongly cathecting each and every one of the memories that form a link with the object. This retreating to the most intimate relationship with the internal object, this hyper-cathecting movement, is absolutely indispensable, because through it the ego tries, unsuccessfully, to fill the libidinal loss it has suffered. During the first stages of mourning this entails a functional splitting of the ego, since, although one part of the ego, withdrawn from other interests, keeps a strong relationship with the internal object, another part must, once the initial shock is over, continue to fulfil some of its usual activities. This splitting will result in different outcomes if it persists while the work of mourning takes place and gradually dissolves, or if it becomes more intense, with mourning encysted in a part of the ego, thus causing an impact on the bereaved or their offspring. At other times, the absence of this splitting may be a sign of a possible evolution into melancholy.

The slow detachment from each of the memories that were links to the object floods the ego with pain—a feeling that Freud designated as "enigmatic". References and models for this feeling—physical pain and the pain of war—can be found in all Freud's writings (Freud, 1905e [1901], 1914c, 1920g, 1924c, 1950 [1895]).

The mourning process also implies a difficult task: "the attempt to work-through the messages of the other" (Laplanche, 1990). Trying to find clues to what the deceased would have wanted from the bereaved means understanding not only the former's wishes, but also his/her mandates. These mandates involve representations of ideal models to be followed and/or desires, prohibitions, and rules.

Under usual circumstances, the work of mourning ends—though never entirely: the grief is appeased, as are the dead person's idealization, guilt, and its mandates, so that some valences remain free to invest in a new love object. A particular mode of forgetting then emerges: one remembers, but without the lacerating grief that memories caused at first. As mentioned above, this de-cathecting of the object is never absolute: part of the object remains in the ego, leading to multiple identifications. This led to the idea that there was a second stage of the work of mourning, characterized by work of

de-identification (Baranger, Goldstein, & Zak de Goldstein, 1989).
In their paper, entitled "On de-identification", Baranger, Goldstein,
and Zak de Goldstein propose the hypothesis of a form of de-identification taking place during a second phase of the work of mourning. This "un-mourning", in the authors' words, would enable the
subject to disengage himself, after a differentiation process, from
identifications that are felt as disharmonious and that were received
by the ego and the ego ideal during the first phase of the work of
mourning. This would be a second opportunity to disengage from
the love object at a later point in life.

The mourning-work model that Freud bequeathed to us almost
a century ago was subsequently the origin of multiple broader and
more profound variations: (a) to discover the impact that the other's
mode of death—a long or unexpected illness; an accident; a suicide;
a murder, and so forth—can have; (b) to discern the different pathological effects that may be caused by trying to avoid any one of the
phases of the mourning work, either by not accepting the other's
death, through disavowal, or because the reality test is, for some
reason, interfered with; or because through various defence mechanisms, death is accepted but the feelings it elicits—grief, nostalgia,
guilt, anger, relief, and so on—are not; or because de-cathecting is
evaded, and mourning becomes interminable. As for the feeling of
guilt and the object to which it relates—the other, a third party, the
dead person, or oneself—why didn't they take better care of him/
her?; why wasn't he/she careful?; why didn't I take care of him/
her?—plays an extremely important role in the mourning work; (c)
this has led to a broader understanding of the short- and medium-
term effects of insufficiently worked-through mourning processes;
(d) a more in-depth study was performed of the metapsychology
of mourning and of the splitting it may generate; (e) difficulties
met in their mourning process by psychosomatic and borderline
patients were studied more thoroughly; (f) also studied was the loss
of significant objects during childhood, latency, puberty, and adolescence; and (h) mourning was investigated from the point of view
of its incidence in the production of gender problems, as well as
the specific features of mourning in the context of natural or social
catastrophes.

Mourning and social catastrophes

Multiple deaths, happening in situations of social catastrophes—genocides, wars, State violence, terrorist acts, and so on . . . and the fact that they are caused by violence wielded by some human beings against others, create effects that have opened a new field of research for our discipline.

Studies based on historical genocides, such as those in Turkey, Germany, and Japan, have led to the conclusion that the severe problems experienced both by survivors and the offspring of murder victims depended not on previous experiences but, rather, on social situations capable of causing tremendous trauma. They also revealed the pathogenic effects of stifled mourning and its consequences on the 1st, 2nd, 3rd, and as far as the 4th generation. What Niederland (1968) called "survivor's guilt" left significant marks on survivors and their descendants, by disorganizing or making impossible the adequate construction of their identities (Kijak, 1981; Kijak & Funto-wicz, 1982; Suárez, 1983). Repeatedly, this "massive psychic trauma" has led survivors and family members to suicide (Krystal, 1976). One particularly painful case, among many others, is that of poet Paul Celan, who committed suicide in 1970. According to some reports, from his earliest youth on this author felt utterly responsible for the murder of his parents. They had asked him to wait for them at a refuge, which he was able to reach. But he waited for them in vain: as soon as he had left their home, they were abducted and deported, and they died in an extermination camp.

Undoubtedly, the above studies helped and encouraged us when we had to face clinical situations triggered by State violence in Argentina and other countries in South America. They enabled us to become aware of the emergence of new forms of helplessness—cases that showed the mark left by trans-subjective space on subjectivity. They also enabled us to think differently about the relationship between the inner and the outer world; between the private, the inter-subjective, and the social. In the words of René Kaës, "certain events enable us to interrogate ourselves more vividly—since it is about death—about the relationship between psychic reality and social reality. The interrogation appears when the distance between these two heterogeneous orders of reality . . . seems to have vanished" . . . generating 'a confusion of boundaries between the inside and the outside'" (Kaës, 1988).

The mourning process was markedly altered, on the one hand by the State depriving citizens of the most essential of protections, such as the right to life, to be informed, the right to take care of the remains in case of death, and also by the Rule of Law being suspended in the social sphere. Not only the murders *per se*, but also the murderers' methods and the uncanny situations that preceded them, left scars on family and friends that were extremely difficult to process.

State violence

A terrorist State is considered a new form of emergency State, distinct from what the Constitution foresees in case of a threat to institutional order. Its specificity is that "the Rule of Law is suspended, in order to perpetrate unlawful actions and impose illegal practices" (Duhalde, 1997). As indicated by the historian Mariana Califano, the terrorist State is characterized by presenting two facets—a public one and a clandestine one—and in the latter all kinds of atrocities are perpetrated (Califano, 2002/2003).

These conditions, which reigned in various South American countries—in Bolivia, Chile, Paraguay, Uruguay—led in Argentina to the creation of a new signifier: the sadly world-famous "missing" [in Spanish, "*desaparecidos*"]. The term refers to people who were abducted and disappeared and were thereafter tortured and murdered. For their families and friends, this practice—the lack of confirmation of death or reliable information and the necessary symbolic elements: taking care of the remains, performing religious rituals, receiving support from the usual social practices—made it impossible to fulfil the necessary conditions to trigger and maintain the work of mourning.

As we affirmed in an earlier paper, in collaboration with Moisés Kijak, there are other situations when the remains are not found— aeroplane accidents, earthquakes, floods, even wars—but in all these circumstances official institutions supply at least some information about the event, enabling social, political, and religious practices to bring support and to contain the bereaved (Kijak & Pelento, 1985).

In the cases under consideration here, however, it was impossible to know why the persons had been abducted, where the loved ones were, what they were being submitted to, whether they were alive or dead, and, if they had been murdered, where the remains were. All this has led to the effects of the trauma component to be prolonged in time and to take precedence in the mourning process. This situation was exacerbated because public space—the plural space of opinions and dissent—also disappeared and became a threatening and persecuting field. The fact that no institution gave any account of the "missing" person added to the circulation of false and contradictory information and led to people feeling exposed to experiences of panic, confusion, and helplessness. Panic was increased because the mere fact of trying to get information about a missing person jeopardized the person making the enquiries. Whether or not one had witnessed the disappearance, anxiety flooded one's psyche so totally that it was difficult to be aware of the avalanche of feelings behind one's anxiety. Violent shock, powerlessness, despair invaded the field of consciousness. An explanation was sought for, in the dark, "through shadows" (Pontalis, 2003). For some families, wondering whether the missing person had perhaps been involved in something and if so, why she hadn't shared it with them became, for a time, a central issue: an inarticulate attempt to try to find an explanation, until it became clear that there was no explanation— "the inadmissible" had happened (Moreno—personal communication 2005—coined this term to describe any event that has never been previously recorded by the psyche), since to accept it would be almost to become non-human. What was inadmissible was that the State itself generated these facts. In any case, a moment came when it was thought that the missing person was "somehow involved" with his abduction, showing that the State had begun to disseminate the idea—still in force today in some layers of society—that some people were "innocent" and others were not. There was disavowal of the fact that the State was kidnapping people, banning information, denying the right to habeas corpus, and violating the "thou shall not kill" commandment and the social right to care for a person's remains.

How could one be convinced of the missing person's death by murder, without any news, without seeing the body, while receiving false information? How could one decide to bring to an end the search, no matter how useless, for the missing person?

I remember Sonia, a woman whose partner was missing.

... At a session, before reclining on the couch, she covered it with some newspapers she had brought and bent over them, as if trying to read them. Suddenly, as if awakening from a dream or a nightmare, she turned around and looked at me. She ruefully picked up the newspapers, lay down on the couch, and explained to me that she didn't know what had happened to her, what she was looking for in the papers. . . . Actually, a few minutes later she remembered that someone had told her that habeas corpus might be published in the dailies. . . . She also remembered how she used to criticize her mother when she was a young girl, for reading the obituaries in the paper . . . at the time she couldn't understand why her mother did that, or the value such a social practice might have. As if leaving this scene from the past and suddenly reconnecting with the present, she said, "But, what's the matter with me? don't I know the papers won't publish any habeas corpus or obituary? . . . If I go ahead with this infernal search, I'll go mad and be unable to go on with my life, but if I stop . . . it's as if I have left him alone—worse than alone, actually I'd leave him surrounded by monsters." It was extremely painful to hear Sonia speak of her search as "infernal": this term implied that words could not describe her emotions. Her allusion to "monsters" also indirectly referred to people whose behaviour was absolutely distant from any acceptable conduct. Sonia went on: "Yesterday was a terrible day: I was offered information in exchange for money . . . but I have doubts. . . . I feel it's probably one more threatening manoeuvre to humiliate me. . . . But, what if there is the slightest possibility, and I reject it . . .? I also thought, how I would I tell you this? How to tell you that they want to bribe me and perhaps I'll take their bribe . . ." The patient's ability to feel shame matched my own infuriation . . . my anger at seeing the extremes of mental pain a person is exposed to in a genocidal State.

As we pointed out in an article published with Julia Braun: "the fact of not being able to know" dominated the evolution, the vicissitudes, and the outcome of these works of mourning (Braun & Pelento, 1988). When a "possible" knowledge becomes impossible because the State needs to erase all traces of its criminal actions, the drive to know increases. And the urgent need to know replaces reality-testing. Under those circumstances, the desire to know found support in the symbolic assistance that we could sometimes offer. This symbolic support implied tolerating the "not knowing" together with the patient, but also admitting the right of the bereaved to receive information, acknowledging that this right was being violated by the State.

> At times the patient felt not only the need to continue her search, but also to fulfil a mandate of the missing person. In one of Sonia's dreams, *Raúl gave her directions on the route to follow, with one peculiarity: he was pushing her.* . . . Beyond the sexual content of this dream that we were able to understand through the patient's associations and memories, there also appeared the idea of someone "pushing her to go on looking for information without a map, she's being violated, violence is being done to her". . . .

> This does not mean that her desire to know did not fluctuate. At times Sonia felt she didn't want to know any longer. At those times she would say: "I don't want to know anything any more, why find out that he was tortured, or beaten, why learn that his body may be mutilated? There are some things that are best left unknown. . . ." Thus, she conveyed the panic she felt at being defenceless from the uncanny experiences that beleaguered her and that she received through the rumours she heard.

The support of her own subjectivity was dependent on her desperate quest for clues, and that is why Sonia felt so shaken every time doors closed on her.

> Once, after an interview with someone who, once again, after promising she would provide some information, refused to do so, the patient dreamed that *"she was driving a car, and she couldn't get out of a tunnel: each time the car seemed to get close to the exit, some sort of vines stuck to the car, trapping it, so it couldn't move. . . . She couldn't come out of the car either, because when she tried, the creepers surrounded and suffocated her. . . ."* When she awoke from this dream, which she described as causing her "terrible anxiety"—and it really did—she noticed that she was entangled in the bed sheet.

This detail of her being entangled in the bed sheet—an identification with a loved-one who, she thought, was suffering, his hands and feet painfully tied—struck me, because the same thing had happened to a 9-year-old boy whose father was missing, as I described in a paper some years ago (Kijak & Pelento, 1985).

Her dream's associations led Sonia to become aware of the fact that she felt trapped, suffocated, both by what "she didn't know" and by what she "assumed" was happening to her partner through clues she had gathered. (She had recently found out that one of the tortures they inflicted on abducted persons was to submit them to the "submarine": their head was submerged in a bucket filled with water until they almost drowned, and the sinister operation was repeated over and over again.)

> Gradually, Sonia brought to her therapy certain associations that enabled me to perceive the pressure her mind was under. "Actually"—said Sonia—"the vines are parasites, they can't stand alone, so they live as parasites on trees, they absorb all the light and they strangle them." At another session she said: "Something happens to me with time, I feel immobilized, as in the dream. . . . I can't move . . . as if I were Raúl, locked up in a prison cell, I can't see anything . . . I can't get to the other side of the bridge . . . but I'm not sure I want to get there . . . I increasingly think that I'll never see him again. . . . that they've already killed him. But I don't want to do like his sister does. . . . Some time ago, she decreed that he'd been killed, so she doesn't do anything any longer, she sees no one, she doesn't make any enquiries. . . ."

Often, this struggle came up between an aspect of the ego that looked for information, in spite of the dangers from the violent environment, and another aspect that stopped looking, terrorized by having to confront an intolerable truth. That terror led other family members of the missing to indefinitely prolong the reality test.

The term "decreed" used by the patient was extremely important at the time, in order to understand how it involved the idea that accepting that Raúl was dead was equivalent to killing him, experienced as leaving him helpless—supported by the universal fact that, for the unconscious, the issue of death is indissolubly linked to the death-wish—as well as an imaginary identification with the terrorist State, which clandestinely "decreed" those murders.

I realized that imaginary identification with the missing person and the sufferings inflicted on that person as well as with representatives of the genocidal power impregnated some images that came up in the minds of family members, both when awake and in their dreams. These images intensified when the Military Junta was brought to trial in 1985, when the voice of surviving witnesses was heard for the first time describing the tortures that had been inflicted on them. At that time, Sonia said,

"I was never particularly fearful, neither as a small girl nor as a grown-up, but this is different. . . . I don't know how to escape from some horrible images that haunt me: sometimes I see Raúl being beaten, freezing and hungry. But suddenly, these images change to a kind of monster, with a horrible grimace." . . . "Once again I was unable to sleep. . . . Yesterday I heard at the trial some people telling about the tortures they suffered at their detention place . . . it's as if everything was happening again. Images keep coming back to me."

This whirlwind of images, a mixture of extreme helpless figures and others with violent expressions, confronted Sonia with a degree of helplessness much more intense than that experienced in conventional mourning. She repeatedly mentioned her desperation at "not being able to do or to say anything at all without feeling threatened" (Puget, 1988). The "threatened state" was defined by Puget as a "state of confusion and paralysis" in which it is difficult to decide whether the danger is real or imaginary. She remembered that once, when her father was in a coma after a long and painful disease, she was able to "hold his hand, thus feeling she could do something for her father and for herself". This way of expressing the feelings of helplessness and powerlessness that overwhelmed her clearly reflected not only the abyss that had been imposed between her and her partner, but also the destruction of public space—a space that should, instead, be characterized by freedom of action and of speech, in full view of society at large.

The crimes committed against missing persons also implied, right from the beginning, an attack on people's minds. People had to confront an exceedingly difficult task: "to evaluate contradictory data coming from various sources". At first, it was data related to the fact of the disappearance itself. It was said that the missing person "isn't missing" . . . "has left the country" . . . "he was attacked by his own partisans" . . . "he's in jail" . . . "he's being tortured", and so on.

Later, it was data on the ultimate fate of the missing person, when it was said, simultaneously, that "he was moved from his clandestine detention place" . . . "he's been transferred" . . . "he escaped" . . . "he was executed" . . . "they're being thrown into the river", and so forth (Braun & Pelento, 1988).

Faced with this avalanche of contradictory data, the mind first fell into a state of confusion, for lack of reliable information.

> "I feel dizzy, confused, as if the walls shook around me," Sonia once said. "Everything moves so dizzyingly fast, one person tells me one thing, another tells me something different, but simultaneously I see scenes suspended in time, like those nightmares in which you try to run, but you can't, you're paralysed."

Rumours circulating about missing people being murdered made it possible for Sonia to include in her mind the idea that Raúl might be dead—that he too, might have been murdered. This thought increased her grief but also triggered the need to know, if he was actually dead, where his body was. Obstacles to obtaining information—still present today, thirty years later—meant that Sonia's mind, as in the case of so many other bereaved, had to endure the presence of an unburied dead person, just as it had had to endure a missing and tortured object.

Even so, by collecting clues and comparing them, the families and friends achieved some representation of what had happened, which, as a special reality test, enabled the mourning work to take place, in a unique form for each person.

In Sonia's case, this allowed another image of Raúl and another story to emerge: the story they had begun to build before the abduction: . . . they had been dating when they were very young . . . then they had parted . . . he had married someone else, and soon after, he had divorced. He and Sonia had met again by pure chance when travelling abroad, and soon after had moved in together.

Sonia couldn't get pregnant. She felt guilty for not seeking medical help when Raúl wanted so much to have a child. She remembered his sad face, each time he realized he was not going to be a father. . . . She also felt guilty because at that stage in their lives, she had felt they had time, a lot of time for that. . . . In addition, she also felt guilty for being alive and for thinking of some projects.

I would like to point out, as a conclusion to these thoughts, that it was not easy to accompany patients on this long journey. When listening to them, I often felt anxiety and horror. The anxiety had to do with the fact that I lived in the same social environment. But this experience also helped me to get rid of ideas that I had taken for granted about mourning, to listen to "that new thing" that the patients were bringing (Puget, 1988). And the "new thing" related to the acute perception of its impact on the psyche and the work of mourning for losses that were the result of social catastrophes, such as State terrorism. This implied the recognition, based on clinical observation, that this type of mourning—which we termed, together with Braun, "special mourning work"—did not have the same characteristics as ordinary mourning.

If we label it as "special", it is because it has enabled us to follow the mourning process in people affected by the loss of a love-object in an environment of State violence, basically characterized by three components: (a) people going "missing" because of acts carried out by the State; (b) the State not acknowledging such acts; and (c) the enforcement of the reign of silence and terror.

The "missing" were neither dead, nor absent: they were not absent, even though absence was involved. They were not dead either, because sooner or later each family member or friend understood that the observable fact—to be "missing"—was often linked to a specific form of death: the murder of the missing person.

This method of ideological repression was also a lethal creation in a ghost-like ontology, where the persons left behind ceaselessly struggled with a central question: was the "missing" person dead or alive? Another abominable invention was to achieve the disappearance of a person through abduction, thus eliminating any logical relationship between the consequence and its possible cause. This involved an attack on usual thought processes. This torturing ideation about how, why, where he or she, or their remains, were, was simultaneously an obstacle to the movement towards hyper-cathecting that usually takes place when we become aware that the other's absence is permanent: sparks of representations, the purpose of which is to assuage the intense grief that this awareness may generate. How is it possible to entertain such thoughts when the nature of the absence is unknown: is it temporary, or will it be irrevocable? Instead of memories, the mental space is occupied by a void, or by horrifying representations of ghosts and monsters.

In the second place, as I mentioned above, the occurrence of the disappearance generated an enormously increased drive to know. And this search for information led family members and friends to confront rumours and, in particular, the thousand-faced lies fabricated by the State. This destruction of symbolic and imaginary systems of the State and its institutions, which appeared in their lies, totally dislocated the places, the functions, the rights, and the prohibitions of subjects. It annihilated "shared representations" (Kaës, 1988). It wrecked kinship groups—family groups, groups of friends, of co-workers, of leisure-time, political, and cultural groups.

The State not only absolutely denied that it had a plan based on the production of missing people and hence denied its involvement in murders, but its answers were used to create confusion, mistrust, and guilt. Sonia was asked: "If you lived with him but were not married to him, how do you know he was not leading a double life, and perhaps he is now in hiding?"—an ambiguous message that had to be deciphered, aimed at making her suspicious and at destroying the link of trust with her partner . . . but which also tried to eliminate the distinction between private life—"a double life"—and public life: that is, the missing person's possible activism.

When long afterwards the State seemed to admit its involvement in murders, this was once again done on false terms, since it called what had happened a "war" and explained the raging violence as merely "an excess". A climax of anger and grief was attained when, before leaving power, the Military Junta passed a "self-amnesty" law—a law that was ultimately vetoed. The impunity represented by this law and others that were later repealed, the imposition of the State and its institutions, caused, as I have pointed out, the collapse of the social law that underpins human relationships. And, of course, this, in turn, dismantled the necessary support to approaching the truth and upholding the work of mourning.

The third component deserves a special comment: enforcement of the reign of silence and terror. As we know, during the era of State terrorism an attempt was made to abruptly alter the relationship between subjects and speech, either by making it dangerous so as to forbid it, or by trying to coerce people to speak through torture. To impose silence meant that the missing person's environment could not share some of their traumatic burden and their grief.

By invading the mind with terror, by proposing an indecipherable reality, by forbidding speech, the authorities actively attempted to destroy social links. If it is true that all traumatic situations, even those related to collective trauma, lead to an inclination to solitude, in this case the prohibition to speak came from the outside, against which it was almost impossible to fight, because speech might un-cover the murders that were being perpetrated. Hence the impor-tance of movements such as the Mothers and Grandmothers of the Plaza de Mayo, demanding justice and the human rights groups that helped support the quest for truth and for freedom of speech, and to locate the source of violence in the State.

In this sense, under such conditions of State violence, another issue to bear in mind is the need to help to identify the source of a violent attack. This was not social violence, organized by groups of civilians within society; neither was it a war, in which the State would have the obligation to become involved; and still less was it an outer projection of the people's own violence: this was genocide, carefully planned in all its details by the very State whose duty it was to protect its citizens. In these circumstances, all reductionism entailed sup-porting disavowal strategies about what was happening.

Individuals experiencing this particular type of mourning needed to embark on a long journey to grasp the facts covered up by the disappearance of the "missing". They also needed to escape the mad-dening demand to "de-cathect the love object because it might be dead and/or to go on cathecting it because it might be alive, operat-ing simultaneously or successively" and violently on the mind (Kijak & Pelento, 1985)—and to thus conclude that in fact the loved one had been abducted, tortured, and murdered.

Accepting this tremendously painful truth entailed a particular-ly difficult work of mourning, for various reasons: (a) the trauma burden, carried from the onset of events and the extreme anxi-ety that invaded the psyche; (b) the enormous degree of helpless-ness generated by living in a social space where speech and action were dangerous; (c) movements generated by guilt feelings, which at times reflected on the subject himself, for being unable to pro-tect the missing person. Sometimes the missing person was blamed for not having taken care of herself. This kind of movement led to a working-out of mourning that was at times melancholic, at other times paranoid; (d) increased feelings of hate awakened in subjects by the murders, their impunity, and the various laws that guaranteed that impunity; (e) uncanny fantasies generated by the facts, which erected dams that should not have been erected; (f) the breaking-up of social relationships, since the person who had a family member, a friend, or an acquaintance who was missing was considered dangerous; (g) working-out of this type of mourning is strongly dependent on social recognition of the crimes perpetration.

Finally, I would like to note that treating patients undergoing this type of "special mourning" made us aware of what goes on in the mind of a bereaved person when a genocidal State forbids both remembering and forgetting. It also enabled us to realize the enormous effort many of them had to make in order to remain human beings and to preserve their right to weep for their dead, in whom they recognized their own finitude (Viñar, 2005).

NOTE

I wish to express here my gratitude to them and to all the colleagues with whom I was able to reflect during those difficult times. In particular, I would like to mention Silvia Amati, Julia Braun, Moisés Kijak, Vicente Galli, Yolanda Gampel, Janine Puget, Maren Ulriksen de Viñar, and Marcelo Viñar, among many others.

3

The analyst, his "mourning and melancholia", analytic technique, and enactment

Roosevelt M. S. Cassorla

The aim of this chapter is to discuss current aspects of analytic technique, relating them to the ideas initially exposed by Freud in "Mourning and Melancholia".

A clinical vignette introduces the study.

A young and involved Analyst (AN) brings Mrs PT for supervision. She wants to investigate a session that has disturbed her. She had never discussed her case because the analytic work was running satisfactorily and had been pleasurable so far.

PT began the session by saying she hadn't slept well . . . she hadn't slept a wink. Her muscular pains had made her change to a new doctor again. The previous day she had been to a specialist who prescribed too many medicines for her. She had considered taking sleeping pills, but was afraid of missing the session. The doctor had recommended a physiotherapist to her. She also had pains in her legs and all over her body. She had decided not to have the recommended physiotherapy and look for another professional. She had seen his name in a women's magazine, advertising a revolutionary muscle-strengthening method.

The analyst AN intervened, pointing out that once again PT was not going to follow prescribed treatments, preferring to go after miraculous novelties. And she further added: "After all, how many doctors have you visited, and how many treatments are you getting now?"

AN immediately noticed the inadequacy of her intervention and her angry intonation. She knew that she had been aggressive. She felt disturbed, guilty, and worried about the consequences of her mistake. She anxiously tried to find ways of correcting herself. She pondered whether she should make excuses, confess her error, or share her uneasiness with PT. She hesitated, but concluded that even if she excused herself she would overburden PT.

AN observed the heavy silence that followed her intervention. She tried to cope with it as well as with her sense of guilt. But after a long while, she decided to intervene. She inquired about PT's feelings. She sadly answered that she felt awful.

AN said that PT had felt misunderstood and attacked by her. PT affirmed that she had felt that AN was annoyed and supposed that she disliked the professional whom she was about to visit.

AN agreed and said that she would have to think about the reasons for her reaction. PT tranquillized her analyst, saying that she was all right and that she shouldn't worry. PT and AN were soon reconciled, and the session proceeded. But AN remained guilty for her error and ashamed she thought about her supervisor.

Errors and losses

In the situation described above, something had presumably happened to have hampered the analyst's capacity for thinking, making her aggressive. When she noticed her error, she faced this fact, stimulating investigation.

Let us consider the situation in stages.

➤ Stage 0:   phase of analysis prior to the vignette with satisfactory work.

➤ Moment M: AN attacks PT.

> Stage 1:   AN notices she failed and feels guilty.
> Stage 2:   AN thinks of a way of mending her error.
> Stage 3:   AN gives up mending it. The dialogue is resumed.
> Stage 4:   Reconciliation between AN and PT.

Studying the stages and the sequence of the work, the analyst is surprised at failing to notice various facts. Her first impression in relation to Moment M was that she had become aggressive because PT had disobeyed her doctor. AN did not understand why this fact had disturbed her. Then, she became aware that she knew very little about PT's illnesses. She supposed that this fact had contributed to her annoyance.

After that, AN recalled that PT would constantly talk about doctors and treatments. Surprised, AN realized that she had not attributed any importance to these very uninteresting reports, and that she had considered them a medical subject. She became aware that she had followed PT's own ideas concerning somatic complaints. She felt ashamed of her blindness towards emotional factors.

The analyst went on reflecting and noticed that Stage 0, which seemed so satisfactory, also included monotonous, repetitive reports that made the atmosphere of the session aggressive and competitive. But this atmosphere was not even noticed, or it instantly faded into pleasurable relationship. AN concluded that the idealistic situation in Stage 0 concealed a sterile and destructive relationship.

After this confirmation, AN could understand Moment M much better. PT had forced her somehow to get into contact with her blindness related to psychosomatic symptoms. To avoid noticing her mistake, AN attributed the blindness to her patient, placing her self-criticism and guilt on her. Therefore, the accusation over PT *of failing to follow treatments and wishing for miraculous novelties* protected AN from noticing that she did not know how to treat the patient (and herself). The inquiry about the quantity of doctors and treatments PT had used revealed the analyst's ignorance and her unease in relation to PT's symptoms. The angry intonation indicated rivalry with other professionals and perhaps the analyst's difficulty in accepting help to deal with her diseased analytic capacity.

Only after reviewing the whole material did AN notice that she had not thought of the possibility—now obvious—that PT's dissatisfaction with treatments had revealed how she felt about *the analysis*.

It is worth emphasizing that the chronic collusion in Stage 0 was only perceived *after* AN had gone through Moment M. Also, it was soon evident that the reconciliation (Stage 4) was nothing more that a return to Stage 0.

In subsequent sessions, with the help of supervision and personal analysis, AN's analytic capacity is really recovered. Therefore, the analyst's error ended up by being productive, thanks to her understanding.

The reader might wonder how the above report differs from other similar ones, in which analytic capacity is disturbed by lack of control of countertransference (Freud, 1910d). This will be seen further on.

Melancholy and truth

If we had been aware of AN's feelings soon after Moment M, we wouldn't have been surprised if she had considered her error unjustifiable, accusing herself of being a dreadful analyst. If these ideas had not been corrected, she might also have condemned herself for other mistakes she could have made in her life, making her unworthy of being a psychoanalyst or enjoying life. The extreme punishment would be suicide.

These self-recriminations would be similar to the melancholic patient's: ". . . worthless, incapable of any achievement and morally despicable; he reproaches himself, vilifies himself and expects to be cast out and punished. He abases himself before everyone and commiserates with his own relatives for being connected with anyone so unworthy" (Freud, 1917e [1915], p. 246).

Freud states that we have no reason to contradict the patient: "he also seems to us justified . . . ; it is merely that he has a keener eye for the truth than other people who are not melancholic. When . . . he describes himself as petty, egoistic, dishonest, lacking in independence . . . , it may be, so far as we know, that he has come pretty near to understanding himself." Freud asks himself ". . . why a man has to be ill before he can be accessible to a truth of this kind" (p. 246).

In the clinical situation described here, the question could be why AN had to *fall ill* to come to the truth.

The melancholic patient has his self-criticism exacerbated, and this makes his destructive aspects more visible. He complains and criticizes himself both for his violence and for not being aware of it. It seems that he has more contact with the human being's hardships, fragile and limited in the face of destruction. He wouldn't have become melancholic if he could have *known* and *accepted* these facts by elaborating necessary mournings. But this was not possible for him.

Let us re-evaluate the clinical situation. At Moment M, AN gets into abrupt contact with her violence and fragility, which disrupts her analytic capacity. This perception activates her self-criticism and guilt (Stage 1), resulting in something transitory similar to *melancholy*. Soon afterwards, quick amendments to the error are sought, by activating *manic* defences (Stage 2) that would have rendered the error inconsequent—as if it had never occurred. If this mechanism proved to be insufficient, melancholy would be reinstalled. Then, new manic defences could be tried—and so on, resulting in a circular process.

Stage 3 indicates an attempt to get in touch with reality, by overshadowing melancholy and mania. Stage 4, presumed conciliation, is a return to manic mechanisms, showing that the possible contact with reality, with elaboration of mourning (Stage 3), was not maintained.

While she reviews her work, AN is performing mourning processes over the loss of an ideal analyst. She observes herself investigating and learning through her error. During this process AN concludes that in Stage 0 she had lived through a collusion of violence and denial. Her belief in a powerful and enjoyable relationship without dangers or pain showed that, in that stage, her capacity for thinking had been obstructed. Manic relationships avoid contact with ambivalent sorrow and destructivity of real mournings, to the extent of destructive suicidal guilt and danger of disaggregation of pathological mourning and melancholy (Freud, 1917e [1915]; Klein, 1940).

Now we know the analyst's transitory *illness*, confirming that it is similar to "circular insanity" (Freud, 1917e [1915]). (This clinical picture, which was later called "manic-depressive psychosis" in psychiatry, is today named "bipolar disorder".)

The patient's shadow falling upon the analyst

A human being has to deal with painful facts of life that always involve real or phantasized losses. Through elaboration, he will stop being Narcissus to become Oedipus, excluded from the centre of the world by the other's presence. Love and hate conflicts are exacerbated. Being able to destroy the object implies an intense sense of guilt and anxiety to re-establish goodness. Meanwhile, he has to deal with finitude, awareness of his own death, knowing that this comes from his inner self.

Becoming a separate and solitary individual indicates acceptance of reality as it is, assuming responsibility for dealing with it and with him/herself—which Klein (1935) calls the depressive position.

Problems with the elaboration of mourning, of living oedipal conflicts, impede self–object discrimination and, consequently, the formation of symbols (Segal, 1957), resulting in a precarious contact with reality, a lack of discrimination between the internal and the external world, and the creation of a private reality. This pathologic paranoid-schizoid functioning (Klein, 1946) occurs in the psychotic part of the personality (Bion, 1957) and can be found in mania and melancholy.

In melancholy the ego identifies itself with the object ambivalently loved and hated, "*the shadow of the object fell upon the ego*" (Freud, 1917e [1915], p. 249). This shadow, the introjected object, works as an exacerbated critical instance that squeezes the rest of the ego. The splitting of the ego occurs in conjunction with this introjection. This introjected instance is destructive because it contains the destructive aspects projected by the ego and later re-introjected, mingled with those from the object. Identification is strengthened by the previous narcissistic relationship with the object.

Later, the exacerbated critical instance will be considered the *superego*, a pure culture of death instinct (Freud, 1923b). Klein will deem the internal object the archaic superego, the result of cruel, destructive objects introjected in terms of initial pre-genital anxieties. Bion (1959) will describe the *ego-destructive superego*, from the psychotic part of the personality, a consequence of splitting and archaic re-introjections, and morally superior, which signals errors in everything and attacks the development of personality. In these last references these archaic, destructive aspects may make subsequent oedipal elaboration difficult, and this difficulty can prevent a reduction in the severity of these same objects.

Presumably PT's illness is a reflection of her intolerance of the oedipal situation, of reality, searching for narcissist refuges where she remains undiscriminated from the object; in other words, the impossibility of experiencing the object as something complete and separate (the depressive position) incites a return to paranoid-schizoid configurations. In the transferential re-edition, perception of separation is denied through massive projective identifications of PT's split-off parts inside AN. Thus, the analyst is conceived as PT's extension.

An important function of the analyst is to identify the patient's phantasies towards the analyst, the transference. The latter's interpretation compels the patient to differentiate what belongs to him from what belongs to the analyst, undoing the phantasy of fusion. Therefore, the patient is slowly directed towards an appropriate perception of internal and external reality.

AN would therefore hopefully be expected to show PT how she had started seeing her as her own extension, interpreting the phantasy of projective identification. But this did not happen because the analyst behaved, *in reality*, as a extension of PT. AN stopped being a *phantasy external object* (Strachey, 1934) without realizing it.

Many analysts may impute the analyst's behaviour to her uncontrolled countertransference. To others, the analyst's transitory illness, similar to the patient's, might be understandable also as *beyond her possible incompetence*. In this last proposal, *the patient's shadow falls upon the analyst*, with PT's destructive aspects inwardly attacking AN's mental functions and analytic capacity.

This last possibility raises the following recurrent problems in psychoanalysis today: (a) how a patient's aspects penetrate the analyst and attack his mental functions; (b) how the analyst permits or facilitates this identification: (c) what the role is of the analyst's own aspects in this process.

Melancholy in the analytic technique

I think Strachey (1934), when describing mutative interpretation, was the first to clearly raise the possibility of the analyst being invaded by the patient, perhaps beyond his countertransference problems. The analyst authorizes the patient to direct id impulses to him, becoming an object of the transference. The analyst starts to be seen by the patient as his *phantasy external object.* Obviously the patient is unaware of this and believes that he is in a real relationship with his analyst. The latter will avoid behaving as the patient perceives him (as the idealized or bad object), not yielding to his phantasies. The analyst's interpretation of what is happening makes the patient correct his perception of external reality and learn functioning aspects of his internal world.

An interesting aspect of mutative interpretation is the difficulty faced by the analyst in operating it. He usually does something else. "He may ask questions, or he may give reassurances or advice or discourses upon theory, or . . . interpretations that are not mutative, extra-transference interpretations, interpretations that are non-immediate, or ambiguous, or inexact . . . the giving of a mutative interpretation is a crucial act for the analyst as well as for the patient, . . . he is exposing himself to some great danger in doing so" (Strachey, 1934, p. 159).

Indeed, when the analyst makes a mutative interpretation, he forces the patient to get in contact with reality. When the analyst shows that he is separate from the patient, he destroys the good relationship between them (Caper, 1995). The analyst's belief in this good relationship shows his identification with the patient. This phenomenon corresponds to the manic aspect of the analyst's illness in the clinical vignette.

Until the end of the 1940s, analysts, with some exceptions, used to consider that their feelings towards the patient—at least those beyond their immediate comprehension—should be considered as a product of uncontrolled countertransference and repudiated (Freud, 1910d). The possibility of using countertransference as an instrument (Heimann, 1950; Racker, 1948) provoked a reversal in the development of psychoanalysis. To accept this new instrument, the analyst must accept that the patient can somehow mobilize in him intimate aspects without understanding immediately what is happening.

The development of the concept of projective identification and its varied functions (Grotstein, 1981; Klein, 1946, Ogden, 1982; Rosenfeld, 1987; Sandler, 1988) deepens the understanding of transference and countertransference processes. Money-Kyrle (1956) describes normal countertransference as the analyst feeling himself introjectively identified with the patient, understanding him on the basis of his own unconscious, and re-projecting through interpretation. The patient's material is not understood when it approaches something intimate belonging to the analyst, which has not been sufficiently elaborated. This author holds that the analyst can be a target to the patient's projective identification, that *he will do something with him*, even though this something is complementary to the analyst's aspects. At this moment projective identification ceases to be a simple phantasy of the patient, becoming something *real*.

This idea is taken to extremes by Grinberg (1957) when he makes the suggestion that the patient can do something to the analyst *beyond* the analyst's responsibility. In *projective counteridentification* the patient provokes something that is experienced as real by the analyst, and he sees himself as being at the mercy of this something. This happens independently of the analyst's personal conflicts. It can be seen that even an analyst who has been presumably well analysed is not immune to the patient's domination.

Bion (1961) describes the analyst's numbed perception of facts of this type. Elements composing the beta-screen (which cannot be thought and are expelled through pathologic projective identification) can awaken in the analyst emotions that promote the reaction unconsciously desired by the patient (Bion, 1962b). The patient's aim is to destroy the analyst's capacity for thinking.

In the last decades, various authors have emphasized the importance of interaction between the patient's and the analyst's subjectivities, prioritizing the study of projective identification functions in this interaction. Sandler (1976) described the way the analyst unconsciously performs roles stimulated by the patient (*role-responsiveness*). Joseph (1989), in detailed studies, shows how a patient recruits his analyst, inducing him to behave in such a way that the *status quo* is maintained to avoid mental pain. Caper (1995) details these mechanisms, showing that the patient uses his unconscious ability of discerning and acting upon the nuances of the analyst's personality by stimulating mental states to correspond to roles he performs in the transference.

On the basis of these, the concept of what occurs between patient and analyst has become more sophisticated. Using the concept of the analytic field (Baranger & Baranger, 1961–62), Ogden (1994) shows that a patient rejects a personal aspect that he imagines to have deposited onto the analyst, while the latter denies his own self to give way to an aspect belonging to the patient. Thus, a dialectic interaction among patient, analyst, and *a third analytic intersubjective* product from the two members of the dyad is produced. Ferro (1992), using the narrative model, shows how characters generated by the interaction of patient's and analyst's mental worlds journey through the analytic field.

By using the theatre model to describe what occurs in the analytic field, it can be observed that the analyst must perform, *simultaneously*, six roles during the scenes, product of the intersubjectivity of the members of the analytic dyad: as (a) character; (b) spectator; (c) co-author; (d) director; (e) theatre critic; (f) lighting technician (Cassorla, 2005a). Thus, he must be able to make healthy splits, taking part in and moving away from the scenes, which implies sufficient cohesion of the self. If the patient gets inside the analyst, dominating him, the latter will have his functions hampered and reduced to a simple character determined by the patient.

Therefore, the idea that the analyst can become involved by the patient to varying degrees of intensity and quality prevails in current psychoanalytic practice. The patient's mental states are transmitted in that way. But the analyst can also be recruited and controlled inwardly by some aspects of the patient that work as an internal object, capturing the professional's ego. The container–contained concept (Bion, 1962a) considers that the interaction between patient and analyst depends not only on the transforming power of the container (alpha function) but also on the intensity and quality of the projected part.

In situations in which the analyst is, without his awareness, engulfed by the patient's massive projective identifications, an unconscious collusion can be formed, and this can become chronic. This collusion can result in various types of impasse in the analytic relationship (Rosenfeld, 1987). (Although most analysts agree that a patient can *do something* with his analyst, not all of them accept that it is the phenomenon of projective identification that explains this fact. The subject is discussed by Grotstein, 2005; Mello Franco Filho, 2000; and Sandler, 1993.)

Enactment and non-dream-for-two

The situations described refer to the concept of *enactment*, which originated in ego psychology (Ellman & Moskovitz, 1998) and was soon afterward adopted by other psychoanalyst groups. It refers to situations in which the analytic dyad, under the effect of crossed massive projective identifications, becomes involved in a paralysing collusion without being aware of this. The similarity of these to bastions, recruitments, role-responsiveness, and sterile container–contained relationships is shown elsewhere (Cassorla, 2005a). Even though both members are involved, the analyst's contribution is emphasized, as his function is impaired.

Considering Bion's (1962b) theory of thinking, when the analyst's dream-work-alpha function is preserved, beta-elements, eliminated by the patient through massive projective identifications, are transformed into alpha-elements. The first mental representations of alpha-elements are shown through visual images, affective pictograms (Rocha Barros, 2000), the essence of which constitutes the dream—both waking or sleeping dreams. These pictograms are connected to each other and with words, becoming symbolic narratives that grow in complexity. In this model, the analytic session should be considered a space to dream, and the analytic process becomes a *dream-for-two* (Caper, 1995; Grotstein, 2000; Junqueira Filho, 1986; Meltzer, 1984; Ogden, 1994).

When the patient cannot symbolize or dream, he can manifest his mental state through discharges in behaviour, symptoms, speech, and other transformation into hallucinosis—hallucinations, omniscience, fanaticism, delusions, etc.—(Bion, 1965) that seize the analyst. We are dealing with the psychotic part of the personality (Bion, 1957). The analyst experiences products of these discharges, such as illnesses, mental pain, symptoms, and feelings, possibly accompanied by rough scenes. When these exist, they are poor, repetitive, stagnant, without emotional resonance. The observing analyst notices that he has come into contact with non-symbolic areas, unsuccessful sketches of symbols, symbolic equations. I proposed to call these excretions *non-dreams* (Cassorla, 2005a). The analyst's function is to dream the *non-dreams* of the patient, lending them thinkability. (In non-psychotic areas, when the patient can symbolize and dream, the analyst dreams the patient's dream again and makes new connections in the symbolic plot, expanding the capacity for thinking.)

The analyst must tolerate the *not-knowing* belonging to the *non-dream*, while he tries to dream it. This may not be feasible due to technical failures, alpha-function limitations, or because the *non-dream* has mobilized private areas, not sufficiently dreamt by the analyst. In these situations the *not-knowing* will be experienced as an internal persecutory object. That explains the appeal for the *already-known*—memories, wishes, theories, and beliefs used not because they are true, but as ways of appeasing the persecutory object. This replacement of the *not-knowing* for the *already-known* is stimulated by the non-neutralized presence of the destructive-ego superego, moralistic and omniscient, that attacks any *not-knowing*, transforming it into the *already-known*.

So, the analyst's mind is seized by the patient's *non-dream* that *falls upon the analyst's ego*, hampering his capacity for dreaming and thinking. Its replacement by the already-known resembles manic and obsessive amends.

The interaction between the patient's and the analyst's *non-dreams* will constitute a *non-dream-for-two*. *Enactment* is the product of *non-dreams-for-two*. Because they involve collusion between psychotic aspects of the personality, they do not acknowledge doubts, uncertainties, and questionings. Both patient and analyst, blind to reality, arrogantly believe that they hold the truth.

Careful observation of *enactments* or *non-dreams-for-two* shows stagnant scenes articulated in melancholic, persecutory, or manic narratives. It is possible to find between the members of the dyad ill-treatment or sadomasochistic or idealized love collusions that conceal destructivity. In sadomasochist *enactments*, the analyst denies his suffering or manically imagines it to be a necessary pain, belonging to vicissitudes of the analytic process (Cassorla, 2005b). Therefore, it is appropriate to consider that all enactment has a manic component, as there is a denial of perception of attacks occurring between both members of the analytic dyad and against the analytic process.

Freud (1917e [1915]) emphasizes the difficulty in understanding the transformation of melancholia into mania and vice-versa. This difficulty persists even today. Klein points out that, facing despair resulting from the impossibility of reparation (when the depressive position is not attainable) and terror of destruction felt by the persecutory object (in the paranoid-schizoid position), manic reparation mechanisms should be activated—jointly with obsessive defences.

Damaged objects and destructive impulses are experienced as idealized.

The question is why, in the above described material, the analyst let herself come to be involved in *chronic enactment* (Stage 0), and the possibility that this was influenced by her personal conflicts cannot be discounted. (I consider chronic enactment as one that remains concealed for a reasonable time and acute enactment as the one that appears abruptly—Cassorla, 2001.) But the power and quality of massive projective identifications can also not be excluded.

In the clinical example above, the best alternative for AN would have been to notice her discomfort and blindness, by denouncing and undoing the *chronic enactment*. The worst, in the other extreme, would have been to maintain the collusion until the analytic process had been destroyed.

However, the way the chronic enactment is undone, at Moment M, is surprising. Manic defences are roughly broken off, and the destructive component emerges as acute enactment. Its intensity makes it difficult for it to remain unnoticed. Therefore, it can be considered as a sign (as the anxiety-sign, Freud, 1926d [1925]), that something not right had been happening before, as chronic enactment. Then, the analyst could deal with the truth, elaborate necessary mournings, and regain her analytic function, disentangled from PT.

But the analyst must elaborate or re-elaborate other mournings, in addition to those entangled with PT: mourning for her idealized analysis, for the perception that she would always control her countertransference, that her destructive impulses would never overshadow her love impulses, that she would never be blind to emotional phenomena, and so on. These mournings mobilize the revival of all other mournings that the analyst has elaborated badly or well throughout her life, including oedipal mournings (Klein, 1940).

Therefore, as a last resort, the analyst can only be an analyst if he is able to obtain and preserve an insight of phenomena, acquired in the oedipal situation: to take part in a relationship and withdraw from it to observe what is happening to himself, to the other, and to the relationship between them.

Mourning work and reality

C*hronic enactment* or *non-dreams-for-two* is expected to be interrupted when the analyst resumes his analytic function. This can happen if he permits a second look (Baranger, Baranger, & Mom, 1983), possibly with the help of a colleague analyst, otherwise the analytic process can end in an impasse or it can be transformed into something that is no longer psychoanalysis. (Indeed, as the analyst believes that the process is developing "well", he is rarely interested in a "second look".)

However, as was seen in the clinical material, there is another way of perceiving *chronic enactment*: through a surge of *acute enactment*. What is it that suddenly permits the chronic collusion to be replaced by an acute manifestation of reality, hardly unnoticed by the analyst? How does the analyst suddenly regain his mental functioning and enable mourning work? Why have the situations remained frozen for such a long time in *chronic enactment?* Why has the analyst not dreamt *non-dreams-for-two* before?

Taking for granted that the patient's melancholic and manic defences resulted from the impossibility of accepting reality, of elaborating mournings for necessary losses, these defences have provoked alterations in the ego, an attack on his capacity for thinking. If the traumatic situation model were to be used (Cassorla, 2005b), the mental tissue might have been injured, disturbing its functions. In this model, PT should be considered to have experienced reality as unbearable, as traumatic, and to have done her best to respond to it.

During *chronic enactment* intense pathologic identification occurs between analyst and patient, both under the domain of damaged aspects of the mind, which prevent thinking and contact with reality. I presume that *acute enactment* occurs in a particular moment (neither before nor after), because both members of the analytic dyad unconsciously grasp that sufficient mental functions have been recovered to give symbolic meaning to reality. For a better understanding of how this recovering occurs, it is necessary to revise in detail the analyst's work during *chronic enactment* (Cassorla, 2001; 2005a, 2005b).

This revision shows that, despite being entangled in a chronic collusion, the analyst suspects that something is wrong. He seems to have some notion of reality and some defences against it in channels parallel to the obstruction, even if not totally clearly. Therefore, he frequently makes formally correct interventions that, if used, could help the patient get into contact with reality. But these interventions are not enough or are devitalized, to undo the obstructive collusion.

Therefore, while parts of the analyst's mind participate in the *chronic enactment*, other parts use alpha-function in trying to unconsciously recover damaged aspects of the mind. At a given point one or both members of the dyad unconsciously sense that there is enough recuperation to denote reality, which is no longer felt as unbearable. At this moment, the defensive obstruction is undone and the painful contact is lived as *acute enactment*.

In the clinical situation the patient compresses the traumatic lesion by *clinging* to the analyst and carrying her (as the drowning and the lifeguard). This is a symbiotic relationship, similar to mother–baby at the beginning of life, involving deep unconscious communication. This mother is permanently tested in her containing function as all life situations are potentially traumatic. The patient does the same with his analyst. The latter takes turns to scrutinize how the patient reacts to the introduction of reality, how much he profits, and how much he reverts to alpha-function (Bion, 1962a). (This process seems closely related to what Stern et al., 1998, include in the "shared implicit relationship", an intimate intersubjective engagement.)

Therefore, although the analyst fails to understand the patient during chronic enactment, the latter senses that the failure to understand is less disruptive than situations lived in the past. This occurs because, despite failures, the professional is continually trying to observe, inquire, discriminate in other mental areas, never abandoning the desire to understand. So, not even a stagnating narrative can ruin the analytic dyad.

If the above hypotheses are correct, it can be assumed that during chronic enactment the analytic dyad also prepares to face reality. Through channels parallel to the obstruction, the deeply involved analyst experiences situations similar to those occurring in the initial development of the mind. His capacity for unconscious observation makes him carefully examine the fragile injured mental tissue and the functioning of defences that try to protect him from traumatic contact with reality. During this microscopic work the analyst intuitively evaluates degrees of suffering, attempts to heal, and tries not to undo defences prematurely to avoid hurting such fragile tissue.

Meanwhile he patiently tries to find breaches to let reality in while keeping the suffering bearable.

At the same time, the patient notices that, although paralysed, his analyst is still alive and in parallel channels he is interested in observing and understanding mental functioning.

During *chronic enactment* the analyst experiences broader or narrower sketches of unconscious understanding, and this is captured by the patient. As he cannot use it, the collusion continues. This happens repeatedly while mental functions are slowly recovered. When the possibility of tolerating and symbolizing reality is unconsciously noticed, *acute enactment* takes place. Metaphorically, *the lights are put on*, because there is "enough energy for illumination" without risk of destroying the "lamp".

Now, after *acute enactment*, there are more elements to understand the analyst's guilt and embarrassment. Not only is the "good" relationship undone, but the analyst is afraid the patient may become re-traumatized by abruptly emerging reality.

The process described resembles the maternal function towards the baby. The mother patiently tries transformation in thought; never giving up when there is reversion, she keeps trying new routes. This function is predominantly unconscious, as occurs with the analyst.

I believe the patient's mental functions are slowly being reconstructed, and meaningless elements gain rough symbolization. That takes time and alternates with new attacks. During this process, each aspect of the lesion, of the painful reality, must be elaborated, in detail, similarly to mourning (Freud, 1917e [1915]). And the analyst must be patient enough to follow and diagnose the proportion and the sector in which the mind is being recovered. (I propose that the analyst should bear a *normal* masochist patience that refers to patience and capacity for suffering pain, without discouragement, as occurs in the maternal function.)

Contact with reality is finally reached when the analytic dyad unconsciously senses that, thanks to the mourning work, it is possible to support pain and suffering for separation from the object. This occurs concomitantly with symbolization and painful resumption of the capacity for thinking.

Chronic enactment must remain chronic because it also includes necessary time for mourning to be elaborated. During this time, the analyst unconsciously lives the suffering together with the patient.

Mourning for parts of the self

The hypotheses formed above are coherent with present concepts of psychoanalysis, which, as one of its main aims, emphasizes the necessity to recover projected parts of the self. Steiner (1996) discusses the difficulties in recovering and integrating elements of the self that have been spread, rejected, and attributed to other people. As there is an ego emptying and a denial of separation between subject and object, the projected parts become unavailable. In psychotic and borderline states this unavailability is condensed in a rigid defensive structure.

The reversibility of projective identification depends on the patient's capacity to elaborate mournings—that is, of entering into contact with reality, the reality of splitting with the object and, consequently, its loss. The patient can only recover projections if mourning is processed, but he can only let the object depart and recover damaged parts if he can recover projections. This occurs through a detailed mourning process, by painfully recognizing what belongs to the self and what belongs to the object. Slowly, the lost object can be seen in a more realistic way, and the parts of the self previously misappropriated are gradually recognized as such.

What, exactly, takes place to encourage detachment from the object is not known. Freud (1917e [1915]) conjectures that, when the object disappears, the ego "is persuaded by the sum of narcissistic satisfactions it derives from being alive to sever its attachment to the object that has been abolished" (p. 255). This conjecture can lead us to consider that the individual senses that only contact with reality will allow life to be enjoyed completely, even if the object remains alive. But how parts of the self are recuperated is still unknown. Steiner (1996) suggests possibilities of changes in the perception of the object. Returning to the models discussed above, this change in perception shows that capacity for thinking is presumably being regained. This recovery can be the result of what occurs in the intimate contact between analyst and patient where the former searches for ways of dreaming the patient's *non-dream*, seeking, activating, and introducing alpha-function. In other words, it is the other thinking being, who is alive, who can make the patient give up fusion and opt to live his own life.

As demonstrated, sometimes the analyst's alpha-function is hampered by identifications with the patient's projected parts that *cling* to the analyst's mental functions inwardly, impeding their functioning. The capacity for thinking and symbolizing is obstructed, as the perception of oedipal triangulation is lost, reversed into a dual undiscriminated relationship. If the analyst is unable to stand out from this relationship, he may need the help of a third person to play the role of external observer.

Being able to disengage from the dual relationship and seeing it from outside is equal to recovering alpha-function, which is the same as acquiring the capacity for using symbols, which equals thinking, which equals elaborating the depressive position, which equals elaborating mournings for the object and lost parts of the self, which equals recovering integration of the self, which equals being responsible for the self and for the object, which equals being able to get in touch with reality, which permits tolerating frustration, which enables thinking that elaborates the oedipal situation, that permits to enjoy real life, that. . . and so forth. The study and understanding of the interrelation of these aspects has been one of the tasks of psychoanalysis during the last decades, and in "Mourning and Melancholia" many of their preliminaries can be found.

Final considerations

Under no circumstances has it been suggested in this chapter that it might be good for the analyst to pathologically identify him/herself with the patient or take part in *enactments* or *non-dreams-for-two*. On the contrary, the analyst is expected to transform movements and paralysis of this type in contact with reality, elaborating the necessary mournings.

What we propose in this chapter is that, in some situations involving mainly traumatized, narcissistic, borderline, or psychotic patients, this pathological identification can be—for longer or shorter periods—a part of the analytic process.

This identification may, obviously, depend not only on the quality of elements that *have fallen upon the analyst's ego*, but also on the latter's capacity for dealing with them. When these situations are studied in detail, the converse attitude is likely to be found in analysts who have facilitated identification. In the clinical situation described, the analyst, AN, was able to perceive that the patient's somatic complaints became entangled with her own experiences related to femininity and her mother's illnesses. Other deeper articulations would be discovered by the analyst in her own personal analysis.

On the other hand, experiences of the analyst that are similar to those of the patient can also facilitate healthy identification. It is a function of our field that the distance between desirable and undesirable is fluid, and often false baits can hook the truth, as Freud (1937d) points out.

To conclude, the analyst's work requires a courageous receptivity to the patient's desperate need of doing to the analyst what he feels has happened to him (Alvarez, 1992), running the calculated risk of coming to be dominated by objects and parts of the patient's projected self. The analyst assumes this new relationship knowing that he must tolerate non-understanding. He must be aware of his own emotions towards the patient and his changes from instance to instance, while he tries to dream his non-dreams.

Situations of analytic impasse frequently derive from difficulty in elaborating mournings, setting up melancholic or manic narratives. These narratives can destroy the analytic process in cases where the analyst fails to identify them after a closer look. Sometimes the plot breaks off abruptly, in acute enactment that indicates the possibility of contact with reality, which presumes an unconscious elaboration of mourning concomitant with obstruction.

4

Not letting go:
from individual perennial mourners
to societies with entitlement ideologies

Vamık D. Volkan

For three decades my colleagues at the University of Virginia and I conducted a study of hundreds of mourning processes and their various consequences (Volkan, 1972, 1981, 1985, 2004; Volkan, Cilluffo, & Sarvay, 1975; Volkan & Josephthal, 1980; Volkan & Zintl, 1993; Zuckerman & Volkan, 1989). In this chapter I draw upon our findings, first by updating and summarizing the psychodynamics involved in an adult's mourning and depression, about which Freud's (1917e [1915]) conclusions still provide the basics. Second, I describe a condition that was not touched upon in "Mourning and Melancholia": some individuals become stuck for years—or even for a lifetime—unable to let the lost person or thing go. They utilize their various ego functions to cope with their losses, primarily to deal with the conflict between "killing" or "bringing back to life" the lost object, and they do this at the expense of using them for more adaptive purposes. They become "perennial mourners" while *not* developing depression. Third, I focus on societal mourning (Volkan, 1977, 1997, 2006), a concept that is also not mentioned in "Mourning and Melancholia", and ask this question: can a large group, such as an ethnic or religious group, become a society that suffers from perennial mourning?

Updating the psychodynamics
of grief, mourning, and depression

In "Mourning and Melancholia" Freud (1917e [1915]) focused on adults' mourning processes and not those of children who experience significant losses before they are able to keep the mental representation (a collection of many mental images) of the other in their mind—in other words, before they can establish object constancy. Obviously, a child without the capacity to maintain object constancy cannot mourn like an adult. For an adult, the mourning process refers to the sum of the mental activities the mourner performs in reviewing and psychologically dealing with the mental representation of a lost person or thing. I am in agreement with Wolfenstein (1966, 1969), who saw a parallel between adult mourning and the experience of a youngster going through an adolescent passage. An adolescent "loses" (modifies) many existing childhood self- and object images and "gains" new identifications in order to crystallize a "new" self-representation and "new" object representations (Blos, 1979). As Wolfenstein explains, going through the adolescent passage becomes a model for the adult mourning process. We can state, therefore, that Freud's model for mourning is the model of adult mourning explained by Wolfenstein, and in this chapter I refer only to the adult mourning process, as Freud did in "Mourning and Melancholia".

When a significant loss occurs, the initial reaction is "grief", which should be differentiated from the mourning process. For the mourner, experiencing the grief reaction is like hitting one's head against a wall—a wall that never opens up to allow the dead person or lost thing to come back. The mourning process—the internal reviewing and dealing with the mental images of the lost item—begins when the individual still exhibits a grief reaction and typically continues for years, until the mourner has enough life experiences with important anniversaries associated with the lost object before the object was lost. But adults are capable of keeping the mental representation of a significant object in their mind after the object is lost. Accordingly, we can say that adults' mourning processes never end during their lifetime and they can reactivate an internal relationship with various mental images of their lost object, such as during anniversaries of significant events that had been shared with the lost person or thing. A mourning process only comes to a "practical end" when the mourner is no longer preoccupied with the mental images of the lost object and when the mental representation of the lost object ceases to remain "hot". Tähkä (1984) speaks about turning a "hot" mental representation of the lost object into a "cold" one by making it "futureless". This is when the mental representation of the lost item, no longer utilized to respond to the mourner's wishes, has no future, no ongoing or perpetuating influence. A young man stops fantasizing that a wife who had been dead for some years will give him sexual pleasure, or a woman stops wishing to boss around her underlings at a job from which she had been fired years before.

Grief

The initial reaction to a significant loss includes a sense of *shock* that alternates with or is accompanied by physical reactions such as shortness of breath, tightness in the throat, a need to sigh, muscular limpness, and a loss of appetite. As shock and its physical symptoms abate, the mourner experiences a wish to have the loss reversed. He or she may deny, at least for a while, that the loss has actually taken place. A more common phenomenon is the mourner's utilization of "splitting" (Freud, 1940e [1938]). This splitting is not the same as that of borderline individuals who typically split their self-images and/or object images. The mourner utilizes an ego function so that opposing ego perceptions and experiences can take place simultaneously. For example, a man knows that his dead wife is lying in a coffin at a funeral home, but he "hears" her preparing food in the kitchen.

Grief reaction also includes the mourner's bargaining with "God", "Fate", oneself, or others in order to reverse the death of someone or undo the burning of a beloved house, as if such reversals were possible: "If I hadn't been stuck in traffic and had arrived home earlier, I would have prevented the accident that caused the death of my wife or the burning of my house." The mourner may become preoccupied with the idea of taking a different route when driving home and avoiding heavy traffic, as if this could keep his wife alive.

But in reality the lost person or thing never reappears, and the mourner feels guilty, to one degree or another, for not reversing the outcome of the tragedy and/or for continuing to live while someone else is gone or something is destroyed. The mourner's own guilt is, however, complicated because—again to one degree or another—the mourner is also angry that someone or something, by being lost, is responsible for his or her narcissistic wound. The mourner's feelings of guilt and anger may be conscious. Most often, however, such feelings are repressed or displaced onto someone or something else. A mourner may feel anger towards a physician who had taken care of his dead wife, or he may become furious with the manufacturer of the gas stove that originated the fire that burned his house. Most importantly and obviously, a mourner's grieving is accompanied by crying spells, pain, and sorrow which reflect the inability to reverse reality. Slowly a sense of manageable frustration and anger become "healthy" indications that the mourner is beginning to accept the facts.

A typical grief reaction of a "normal" adult takes some months to disappear, and it may reappear for a time on the anniversary of the event when the loss took place. In truth, there is no typical grief reaction, because the circumstances of a loss are varied and because individuals have differing degrees of internal preparedness to face significant losses.

A grief reaction itself can be complicated. There are adults who spontaneously cry and feel pain and anger whenever something in their environment reminds them of their original loss. Once I had an analysand who spent the first two and half years on my couch crying and exhibiting a grief reaction at almost every session. After grieving for a while, she would become interested in other topics that had nothing to do with her loss, until her next session, when she would grieve again. She was fixated in grief.

Mourning

As it is an internal phenomenon, reviewing the mental representation of the lost object or thing is a more silent process. It begins when the individual still exhibits a grief reaction and typically continues for years. The mourner obviously carries a mental representation of the lost person or thing in his or her mind before the loss occurs. When the mourning process starts in earnest, the mourner becomes preoccupied with the various images of this representation and accompanying and fitting emotions. The person begins at this point to deal with these images mentally and tame the emotions attached to them. While the physical burial of a dead person is typically performed in one act, "burying" the mental representation of a dead person is performed through many "burials", "reincarnations", and "reburials" of various images, until such images become "cold" and futureless (Tähkä, 1984).

More significantly, during such mental activities some images, realistic or modified by wishes and defences against them, are absorbed as *identifications*. In "Mourning and Melancholia" Freud (1917e [1915]) spoke of "narcissistic identification" in mourning in which "the object-cathexis is abandoned" (p. 250). Identifications refer to mourners making the characteristics and/or functions of a lost person or thing their own. For example, a year or so after his father's death, a footloose young man becomes a serious industrialist, just as his father used to be. Similarly, an immigrant who has lost a country may create a symbolic representation of her homeland in a painting or a song, indicating that this mourner has internalized and maintained certain images of the land she lost.

Another process in "normal" mourning that illustrates how mourners deal with the mental representation of lost objects is the depositing of the images of the lost objects into "suitable reservoirs" (Volkan, 1997, Volkan, Ast, & Greer, 2001). A mourner finds a person or thing in the external world that is capable of keeping the mourner's externalization of the images of what is lost in a secure and constant fashion, so that these images do not return and induce conflict within the mourner's psyche. For example, a woman who lost her husband and the ego functions he had provided for her "deposits" her dead husband's image and ego functions into a political leader or party and becomes a follower of this leader or party. By doing so, she withdraws her libidinal cathexis—to use Freud's term—from the object that was lost and invests it with something alive and permanent. In another example, a mother who has lost her son becomes religious and deposits her son's mental representation into that of the crucified Jesus Christ. Depositing images into "suitable reservoirs" reminds us of what is known in psychoanalysis as "projective identification" (Klein, 1946), although depositing is constant and stable. Furthermore, the "reservoirs" are shared by others within the mourner's society and the mourner's emotional investment in them is accepted as "normal". In the above examples, as long as the political leader and party are in the public eye, and as long as the existence of Jesus Christ is perceived to be timeless, both mourners can bring their work of mourning to a practical end. For the most part, identifying with the images and functions of the lost object and depositing into "suitable reservoirs" are unconscious processes.

The mourning process is considered "normal" when the mourner identifies with the images and functions of what has been lost or deposits such images and functions in "suitable reservoirs" that are selective and "healthy". The mourner, after going through the pain of grief and after spending considerable energy reviewing and deal- ing with the mental representation of the lost person or thing, gains something from these experiences. A year or so after the loss, owning the ego functions provided by the lost person enriches the mourn- er's internal world. The woman who uses a political leader and his party as a "suitable reservoir" may, for example, become an impor- tant agent in expanding the party's humane ideology. Pollock (1989) extensively studied such gains and new adaptations to external and internal worlds that followed successful mourning processes.

Depression

"In melancholia the relation to the object is no simple one: it is com- plicated by conflict due to ambivalence." This statement of Freud's (1917e [1915], p. 256) holds true today. The mourner who related to a lost object with excessive ambivalence is unable to form selec- tive and enriching identifications and assimilates, instead, the rep- resentation of the lost item into self-representations "*in toto*" (Smith, 1975). Accordingly, the love and the hate (ambivalence) that origi- nally connected the mourner to the lost person or thing now turns the mourner's self-representation into a battleground. The mourner now feels the struggle between love and hate within the self-repre- sentation that assimilated the ambivalently related mental repre- sentation of the lost item through a total identification with it. This results in depression, which has its own typical physical symptoms, such as disturbances in appetite, sleep, sexual desire, and the expe- rience of pleasure. The individual feels tired and may experience cardiac arrhythmias. Such physical symptoms may also appear in "normal" mourning, although in much milder forms.

When hate towards the assimilated mental representation of the lost object becomes dominant, some mourners may even attempt to kill themselves (suicide) in order to "kill" the assimilated mental representation. In other words, they want to psychologically blast or choke off the mental representation of the lost object, which is located within their self-representations and so, accordingly, they shoot or hang themselves. Such psychodynamics can best be observed, of course, if the depressed mourner does not succeed in the suicide attempt and is willing to undergo a psychoanalytic investigation. Some can clearly verbalize who it is they really wanted to get rid of by trying to kill themselves.

The mourner who is incapable of forming healthy identifications with the mental representation of the lost person or thing is also incapable of finding "suitable reservoirs" for externalization. The mourner who will become depressed deposits the mental images of the lost person or thing in unstable and maladaptive reservoirs. For example, instead of depositing the lost object's mental representation into a socially acceptable religious organization, the mourner deposits it into a fanatical religious cult, joins this cult, and becomes involved in maladaptive activities while experiencing low self-esteem.

Trauma

In addition to relating to the lost object with ambivalence or depositing the mental representation of the lost person or thing in unstable reservoirs, a mourner may encounter other factors that lead to depression following an object loss. Although Freud did not mention it in "Mourning and Melancholia" (1917e [1915]), trauma also complicates the work of mourning and sometimes turns it into depression. A loss may be traumatic in its own right, especially when it is sudden and unexpected, but the combination of loss with actual trauma associated with the mourner's helplessness, shame, humiliation, and survival guilt seriously complicates the mourning process. Imagine a boat accident in which a man loses his wife and child after a failed effort to rescue them. In such a situation the work of mourning is contaminated with the mourner's attempts to reverse helplessness, shame, and humiliation and tame survival guilt. The mental representations of the lost ones remain within the mourner as constant reminders of guilt feelings, shame, and humiliation causing narcissistic hurt and low self-esteem that result in depression.

When a loss occurs due to murder, suicide, or other tragedies where rage was expressed by those who caused the loss, the mourner may also experience depression. In a grief reaction there is a "normal" degree of aggression directed towards the lost object as well as during the work of mourning because, by its very act of disappearing, the lost object initiates a narcissistic wound in the mourner: "How dare you leave me?" During grief the mourner experiences anger because he or she cannot reverse the reality of the loss. During mourning the mourner also experiences anger because he or she is forced to reactivate, to some extent, childhood "developmental losses", especially the "oral" ones (Abraham, 1924a) such as losing mother's breast or mother's love due to the birth of a sibling (Volkan & Ast, 1997). The mourner also reactivates the childhood "separation–individuation" anxiety (Mahler, 1968). The rage expressed through murder, suicide, or other such tragedies may unconsciously become connected with the mourner's "normal" anger level while grieving or mourning. The struggle with the mental representation of the lost object may then increase, causing depression.

Neurobiology

Since after experiencing a significant loss a person exhibits physical symptoms during grief, mourning, or depression, there is a need to understand the meaning of disturbances in many organ functions, especially during depression. Can neurobiological findings concerning depression be integrated with psychoanalysis and give support to Freud's basic theories on depression? Neurobiologist and psychoanalyst Johannes Lehtonen and his colleagues at Finland's Kuopio University have made significant contributions to the neurobiology of depression (Laasonen-Balk et al., 2004; Lehtonen, 2006; Saarinen et al., 2005) and have attempted to answer this question. Kuopio studies have illustrated that nursing experiences change the bodily state of the infant (Lehtonen et al., 2002). According to Lehtonen (2006), such experiences create a matrix-like structure within the body ego (body self) where bodily consciousness of emotions—not yet available through verbal communication due to the immaturity of the infant—are present. Lehtonen states that we have an opportunity "to recognize similarities that exist in early ego formation and the psychobiology of symptoms of depression, which concern sleep and appetite regulation, and the capacity to experience affects, which basically consist of feelings of well-being or malaise, regulation of the pain–pleasure axis, and general vitality versus fatigue and exhaustion." Thus the Kuopio studies are trying to illustrate a similarity between the "affective cry signal" of an infant that expresses a need for care and the signs of sadness or feeling of despair experienced by a mourner in grief or depression. Lehtonen concludes: "The pathogenic meaning of object loss and its typical consequences thus have an impact on primordial early oral personality layer that is so intensely connected to the general well-being of the individual, as Karl Abraham (1924a) already pointed out in his elaboration of Freud's view of depression as a pathogenic internalization of object loss and mourning."

Perennial mourners

Complications in one's mourning process do not always lead to depression, but may result in another outcome not described in "Mourning and Melancholia": some adults, who are unable to bring their mourning to a practical conclusion, become "perennial mourners", a condition that can manifest varying degrees of severity. Some perennial mourners live miserable lives while others express their unending mourning in more creative ways. Even most of these people, however, when not obsessed with their creative work, feel uncomfortable.

A perennial mourner, to a large extent, cannot identify with the enriching aspects of the mental representation of the lost object and the adaptive ego functions associated with this mental representation. This kind of mourner cannot find "suitable reservoirs" for externalizing the representation of the lost person or thing. On the other hand, the mourner does not end up identifying totally with the lost object representation and does not, in other words, go through a "normal" mourning process or develop depression. Instead, these mourners keep the object representation of the lost person or thing within their self-representation as a specific and unassimilated "foreign body". In the psychoanalytic literature such an unassimilated object representation or object image is known as an "introject".

An introject is an object representation or a special object image with which the individual who has it wishes to identify. But the identification does not take place, and the object representation or the special object image, with its own "boundaries", remains in the individual's self-representation as an unassimilated mental construct. An introject excessively influences the self-representation of the person who has it. A perennial mourner constantly utilizes ego mechanisms to deal with an introject. Although nowadays the term "introject" is seldom used in psychoanalytic writings, I suggest that we keep it as it is most useful in explaining the internal world of a perennial mourner.

A man came to see me complaining that his younger brother had been disturbing him daily, and, not knowing how to deal with the situation, he sought treatment in order to free himself from his brother's influence. He explained that while driving to work, his brother constantly talked with him, giving him advice about everything, even when my patient wanted some time for himself or when he wanted to listen to the car radio. For example, the brother made suggestions as to how my patient should behave when meeting his boss or when talking to a particular secretary at work. My patient did not like his brother's advice and occasionally told his brother to shut up, but the younger man continued to talk and irritate him. I also learned that when both men were young, my patient had experienced considerable sibling rivalry. In my mind, I pictured my patient in his car with his brother sitting next to him. I even imagined that my patient and his brother lived together in the same house or at least nearby, which would explain their riding together each workday to the downtown business area. Therefore, I was really surprised when my patient, in his sixth therapeutic session, informed me that his younger brother had died in an accident six years earlier. The "brother" with whom he had conversations while driving to work was actually his brother's unassimilated object representation. This patient felt the lost person's mental representation to be lodged in his chest. Sometimes he experienced this object representation as a puppet-sized younger brother sitting on one of his shoulders, literally a symbolized weight on his shoulder. But most of the time, the "brother" was inside my patient's body image.

Having an "introject" of a lost person or thing brings about its own unpleasant consequences for the perennial mourner who is preoccupied with an ambivalent internal struggle with it. This is reflected in the perennial mourner's subjective experience in that the person is torn between a strong yearning for the restored presence of the lost person or thing and an equally deep dread that the lost item might be confronted. The presence of the introject provides an illusion of choice but not a solution. A perennial mourner daily expends energy to "kill" or to "bring back to life" the lost person or thing. The severity of this preoccupation varies from individual to individual, and in severe cases the struggle renders the mourner's adaptation to daily life very difficult. Perennial mourners are compulsive about reading obituary notices, betraying not only anxiety over their own death but an attempt to deny the death of the one they mourn because they find no current mention of it in the papers. Some such mourners fancy they recognize their lost ones in someone alive whom they encounter at a distance. For example, a man in his mid-twenties was very well aware that his father had died three years before, but often he would "see" his father walking in front of him on a crowded street. He would run and overtake the man whom he considered to be his father and then turn back to be sure that the man was not really his father. Perennial mourners make daily references to death, tombs, or graveyards in a ritualistic way and talk about the dead in the present tense. The listener gets the impression that the speaker's daily life includes some actual relationship with the deceased who continues to watch over him or her. If the lost item is a thing, the perennial mourner thinks about scenarios that involve finding and losing this object again and again. Sometimes the preoccupation with "losing" and "finding" become generalized. For example, friends might know the perennial mourner as an individual who very often loses car keys and who then finds them in unexpected places.

Many perennial mourners spontaneously use the term "frozen" when they speak of their dreams. I think that this word reflects their internal sense that they are stuck in their mourning processes. It also reflects lifelessness. Frozen dreams are often composed of what appears to be one slide after another, with no motion taking place upon any of them. Such individuals also typically dream of the one who has died or is lost as still living or existing, but engaged in a life-and-death struggle. The dreamer then tries to rescue the person or thing—or to finish him, her, or it, off. The outcome remains uncertain because the dreamer invariably awakens before the situation in the dream can be resolved. For example, one perennial mourner had repeating dreams of trying to rescue the lost person from a small burning car. Each time he would wake up before learning the outcome of his efforts. The perennial mourner also dreams of seeing the dead body but noticing something about it—like sweat—that denies the reality of death.

The above characteristics of perennial mourning do not make the perennial mourner a psychotic individual. For example, apart from conversing with his dead younger brother's object representation while driving to work, the patient I described above was simply a neurotic. He did not experience any break with reality except when communicating with his introject. A perennial mourning may imitate a psychotic condition, and a clinician needs to be alert and not confuse it with schizophrenia or related, excessively regressed conditions.

Linking objects and phenomena

In order to further study the psychodynamics of individuals I call "perennial mourners", let us return to the patient who had conversations with the object representation of his dead brother while driving to work. It will be recalled that sometimes he felt that a little "figure" had been sitting on his shoulder. This imagined figure was an externalized version of his brother's introject. In 1972 I coined the terms "linking object" and "linking phenomenon" to describe externalized versions of introjects of lost persons or things. My patient "created" this imaginary figure, and it was his linking phenomenon. Through experiencing a figure on his shoulder, my patient connected himself with his dead brother. For a perennial mourner, sometimes a song, a hand gesture, or even a certain type of weather condition functions as a linking phenomenon. For example, a mourner notices certain types of clouds during a funeral. Later in life, whenever similarly shaped clouds appear in the sky, the mourner emotionally links to the object representation of the dead person.

Most perennial mourners, however, utilize certain concrete inanimate or animate objects such as a special photograph that symbolizes a meeting ground between the mental representation of a lost person or thing and the mourner's corresponding self-representation. I call such objects "linking objects". Perennial mourners "choose" an inanimate linking object from various items available in their environment. A linking object may be a personal possession of the deceased—often something the deceased wore or used routinely, like a watch. A gift the deceased made to the mourner before death, or a letter written by a soldier in the battlefield before being killed, may evolve into a linking object. A realistic representation of the lost person, such as a photograph, can also function as a linking object. The same is true for what I call "last-minute objects"—something at hand when a mourner first learned of the death or saw the dead body, objects that relate to the last moment in which the deceased was regarded as a living person.

Sometimes objects that are connected with the psychodynamics of mourning are "selected" soon after the loss occurs, but such items become crystallized as linking objects when the individual who has one becomes a perennial mourner. Once an item truly evolves into a linking object, the perennial mourner experiences it as "magical" and may hide it, while needing to know its whereabouts, as it must be protected and controlled. Since a person can control an inanimate thing more easily than an animate thing, most linking objects are inanimate items. If a linking object is lost, the perennial mourner will experience anxiety, which is often severe. But there are animate linking objects too, such as a pet. I worked with a refugee family in the Republic of Georgia that used a dog as their linking object. When they were forced from their home, their dog Charlie was left behind, and they later learned of his death. One day in their miserable new location they noticed a dog that looked like Charlie. The family adopted this dog as their new pet, named him "Charlie", and utilized the dog as a linking object—a story I have detailed in other writing (Volkan, 2006).

Through the creation of a linking object or phenomenon, the perennial mourner makes an "adjustment" to the complication within the mourning process; the mourner makes the mourning process "unending" so as not to face their conflicted relationship with the object representation of the deceased or the lost thing. By controlling the linking object, perennial mourners control their wish to "bring back" (love) or "kill" (hate) the lost person, and thus they avoid the psychological consequences of either of these two wishes. If the dead person comes back to life or the lost item is found, the mourner will feel obliged to depend on it forever. If the dead person or the lost thing is "killed", the mourner's existing anger will cause feelings of guilt.

The linking object in the external world contains the tension caused by ambivalence and anger pertaining to the narcissistic hurt the loss has inflicted on the mourner. Since the linking object or phenomenon is "out there", the mourner's mourning process is externalized. When a photograph that has become a linking object is locked into a drawer, the mourner has, in essence, "hidden" the complicated mourning process in the same drawer. All such a person needs is to know is where the photograph is, and that it is safely tucked away. The drawer may be unlocked during an anniversary of the loss, the photograph looked at and touched, but as soon as the mourner feels anxious, the photograph is locked up again.

Linking objects and phenomena should not be confused with childhood transitional objects and phenomena (Winnicott, 1953) that are reactivated in adulthood. Certainly there are some severely regressed adults, such as some with schizophrenia, who reactivate the transitional relatedness of their childhoods and may "recreate" transitional objects. A transitional object represents the first not-me, but it is never totally not-me. It links not-me with mother-me and it is a temporary construction towards a sense of reality (Greenacre, 1969). Linking objects contain high-level symbolism. They must be thought of as tightly packed symbols whose significance is bound up in the conscious and unconscious nuances of the relationship that preceded the loss. Not every keepsake or memento cherished by a mourner should be considered as a linking object possessing a significant investment of symbolism and magic. A linking object or phenomenon is an external bridge between the representations of the mourner and that of the lost person or thing, just as the introject serves as an internal bridge.

Initially in my decades-long study on grief and mourning I focused on the pathological aspects of linking objects and linking phenomena, and I considered their existence only as a sign of a mourner's "freezing" the mourning process. Later I wrote about the linking object or the linking phenomenon as a source of inspiration that gave direction to creativity in some individuals (Volkan & Zintl, 1993). Complicated mourning still remains in these people, but now it is expressed in art forms. It is not proper, I think, to refer to someone who created such a thing as the "Taj Mahal" as "pathological".

I also understood that under some favourable conditions linking objects can be used to reactivate a "normal" mourning process long after the loss has occurred. My interviews with over 100 members of the American Network of World War II Orphans (AWON), now in their fifties or sixties, illustrated this finding. These are individuals who lost their fathers during World War II, when they were small children or even before they were born, and as a result they became perennial mourners. In 1991 they formed AWON and began to share their stories. As they focused on their losses, they restarted their grieving and mourning process as adult mourners by using an existing linking object or by finding or creating linking objects (see Volkan, 2006). I was with many of them when they participated in the opening of the World War II Memorial in Washington, DC on Memorial Day 2004. This memorial became their shared linking object.

Societal mourning: shared linking objects, transgenerational transmissions, and entitlement ideologies

An examination of memorials as shared linking objects is one way to begin to understand what is called "societal mourning". Manmade or natural calamities result in major losses and changes that are shared by hundreds, thousands, or millions of people, whether or not they are relatives, or whether or not they ever meet during their lifetimes. Persons living in the same town or country or persons belonging to a particular ethnic, national, or religious group may be involved in "societal mourning" or "large-group mourning". Natural or man-made accidental disasters do not deliberately shame, humiliate, dehumanize, kill, or destroy physical environments. But in wars and war-like conditions losses are accompanied by a shared sense of humiliation and a helpless wish for revenge. A massive trauma at the hands of the enemy can never remain a regional trauma. The feeling of humiliation and helplessness of the people of the affected sector is automatically felt by almost all those who belong to the same large-group identity, such as one defined by ethnicity or nationality. The society then starts behaving like an individual who suffers from perennial mourning. Here I am referring to societies composed of thousands or millions of people who share some deep sentiments and a permanent sense of sameness (Erikson, 1956) and are connected emotionally by a "large-group identity" (Volkan, 2006). Obviously, since such a society is comprised of individuals, large-group processes reflect individual psychology. But shared responses to what enemies have done to a society take on their own specific characteristics by becoming recognizable societal expressions and even political ideologies. In this section I examine *only three* societal processes—in a sense, symptoms—that may accompany a societal mourning process: building monuments, the evolution of "chosen traumas", and the establishment of entitlement ideologies.

Monuments

A common societal expression of societal mourning is the building of memorials. Young (1993) treats all memory-sites as memorials. He states that a memorial can be a day or conference, for example, and need not be a monument; but a monument, he adds, is always a kind of memorial. By building a monument, societies—like the individual who finds a "suitable reservoir" to deposit the image of the lost item—create an externalized location that becomes involved in the shared mourning process. Architect Jeffrey Ochsner states: "[W]e do not intend to build linking objects, although objects we do make clearly can serve us in this way. Indeed, the role played by linking objects does not require that they be objects intentionally created to serve this purpose (although they can be) or that they be objects that we personally shared with those remembered (again, they can be)" (1997, p. 168).

An examination of a monument that is dedicated to an event that created a disaster in which significant losses took place often gives an indication of the way a society has handled the shared mourning process and its complications. Sometimes a monument as a shared linking object externally absorbs unfinished elements of incomplete mourning and helps the group to adjust to its current situation without re-experiencing the impact of the past trauma and its disturbing emotions. The marble or the metal structure suggests a sense of indestructibility. This makes the monument a "psycho-logical container" in which the remaining unpleasant feelings of a society's shared mourning can be sealed. For example, many studies show that building the Vietnam Veterans Memorial helped to bring the American shared mourning process from that war to a practical end (Campbell, 1983; Ochsner, 1997; Scruggs & Swerdlow, 1985; K. Volkan, 1992).

A memorial like Yad Vashem in Jerusalem is a place where mourning is "stored" and affects pertaining to it are experienced.

Yad Vashem is associated not with a sense of revenge, but with the determination to keep the Jewish state safe. On the other hand, a monument can be built in order to reactivate a society's perennial mourning in the hope of recovering what was lost, a motivation that fuels feelings of revenge. An illustration of this comes from Serbia under Slobodan Milosevic. The shared mental representation of the Battle of Kosovo, which took place in 1389, and the losses associated with it have remained influential in the Serbian large-group identity (Volkan, 1997). After the collapse of the former Yugoslavia, a huge monument was built on a hill overlooking the Kosovo battlefield. Made of red stone symbolizing blood, it stands a hundred feet high. On 28 June 1989, the day marking the 600th anniversary of the Battle of Kosovo, Milosevic used this monument in a ceremony to reactivate Serbian perennial mourning. I will return to the story of the reactivation of the "memory" of the Battle of Kosovo later.

As decades and centuries pass, a society performs certain rituals around a monument, which becomes a shared linking object. The healing power of lapsed time brings changes in the function of monuments. They may become tourist attractions or artistically prized works of art; others come to symbolize a myriad of shared perceptions.

Chosen trauma

A chosen trauma is the shared mental representation of an event in a large group's history in which the group has suffered a catastrophic loss, humiliation, and helplessness at the hands of enemies (Volkan, 1991, 2006). When members of a victim group are unable to mourn such losses and reverse their humiliation and helplessness, they pass on to their offspring the images of their injured selves and psychological tasks that need to be completed. These inherited images and tasks contain references to the same historical event, and as decades pass, the mental representation of this event links all the individuals in the large group. This process is known as the "transgenerational transmission of trauma" (Volkan, Ast, & Greer, 2001). Although it is beyond the purpose of this chapter to examine how transgenerational transmissions take place, it is relevant to note that the mental representations of such events can emerge as significant large-group identity markers.

A chosen trauma reflects the existence of "perennial mourning" within the society, whether it is actively experienced or whether it is "hidden". Sometimes political leaders inflame chosen traumas in order to promote new massive societal movements, some of them deadly and malignant.

For the Serbian people, the Battle of Kosovo is their chosen trauma. On 28 June 1389, Serbian Prince Lazar (Lazar Hrebeljanovic) and his army clashed at Kosovo Polje, the Field of Blackbirds, with the army of the Ottoman Turkish sultan, Murat I. Since we have no eyewitness reports, the historical truth about the Battle of Kosovo remains unknown (Emmert, 1990), but what is known is that Lazar was beheaded and Murat also lost his life. About 70 years later the Ottomans began conquering Serbia, and as Turkish rule settled over the area, many Serbs migrated north. In 1690 the few remaining monks at the monastery of Ravanica (in Kosovo) where Lazar was originally buried, joined the northern migrations, taking the corpse of Lazar with them. Lazar, reburied at a location in the Fruka Gora region northwest of Belgrade, then became an "exile". The shared mental representation of the Battle of Kosovo followed the Serbs throughout history, becoming the Serbian chosen trauma.

As time passed, events and characters of this battle mingled with elements and characters of the Christian religion. According to legend, Saint Ilya, in the shape of a grey falcon, appeared before Lazar on the eve of the battle with a message from the Virgin Mary. She gave the prince two choices: he could win the battle and find a kingdom on earth, or he could find a kingdom in heaven through death and martyrdom. Lazar chose the latter, and the Serbs subsequently associated his image with the image of Jesus Christ. This chosen trauma, like a "psychological DNA", has passed from generation to generation.

Milosevic was already an established political leader in 1989, the time of the 600th anniversary of the Battle of Kosovo, and he and his associates were determined to bring Lazar's body out of "exile". In preparation for the coming anniversary, Lazar's remains were placed in a coffin and taken on a year-long tour to every Serbian village and town, where they were received by huge crowds of mourners dressed in black. Every night Lazar was symbolically buried and every morning he was reincarnated, and eventually he was taken back to Kosovo Polje for a final burial. This created what I call a "time collapse". This term denotes the conscious and unconscious connections between

a large-group's historical trauma and contemporary threats, threats
that typically emerge when a chosen trauma is dramatically reactivated. The reactivation of shared anxieties, expectations, fantasies,
and defences associated with the chosen trauma magnifies the image
of current enemies and current conflicts. If the large group is now
in a powerful position, the sense of revenge may become exagger-
ated, even ennobled. (If the large group is in a powerless position, a
current event may reanimate a shared sense of victimization.) Time
collapse may lead to irrational and sadistic or masochistic decision-
making by the leaders of a large group; in turn, members of the
large group may become psychologically prepared for sadistic or
masochistic acts and, in worst case scenarios, perpetrate monstrous
cruelty against "others".

Political "entitlement ideologies"

Another sign of a "perennial mourning" that spans generations in
a society is the evolution of political entitlement ideologies. Such
ideologies are known by various names, such as "irredentism" or the
"Megali Idea" (Volkan, 2006). In simple terms, they refer to regain-
ing all the lands that a large ethnic, religious, or national group
considers "lost" and now occupied by others. The inflammation of
these ideologies in a society is usually accompanied by the reactivation of a chosen trauma. Milosevic and his associates created an
entitlement ideology in Serbia by reactivating the chosen trauma of
the Battle of Kosovo just before massive atrocities took place in that
part of the world (Volkan, 1997). By utilizing an entitlement ideology and propagandizing the desire for a greater Serbia, the Serbian
leadership turned a "memory" of an historical event—associated as
it was with losses, inability to mourn, and the difficulty of shared
mourning—into a tool of revenge.

Last remarks

"Mourning and Melancholia", one of Freud's most significant contributions to psychoanalysis, furthered his ideas on narcissism and
identification and became one of the stepping stones for the evolution of the superego concept. Today we also consider this paper as

a forerunner of modern theories on internalized object relations. In this chapter I attempted to add to Freud's thoughts concerning significant losses by describing "perennial mourning" in individuals and societies. When referring to societal mourning, we should recall that a society is not a living organism with one brain, but once large-group processes following massive losses associated with humiliation, helplessness, and complications in mourning begin, they take on a life of their own, sometimes causing new tragedies and making their mark on history.

5

Mourning and creativity

María Cristina Melgar

Jorge Luis Borges writes that after Socrates' death, Plato invented the Platonic dialogue so as to hear his master's voice once again. He adds: "Some of these dialogues do not reach any conclusion because Plato thought as he was writing them. . . . I imagine that his main purpose was to have the illusion that, in spite of Socrates having taken hemlock, he was still accompanying him" (Borges, 1967–68, pp. 22–23).

In "Mourning and Melancholia" (1917e [1915]) Freud did not probe into the relationship between mourning and creativity, but dealt with inhibition in melancholia. However, mourning as well as trauma has negative effects, as is the case with unresolved mournings, but it may also have positive ones that stimulate creativity. In this text he did not answer the question of how the psychic pain produced by the loss of a person or an ideal, of something concrete or abstract, can trigger creativity. Notwithstanding this, the complex metapsychology that pervades "Mourning and Melancholia", with its obscurities and confrontations and without the theories he would develop later on, advances some ideas and opens new paths related to the ways and mechanisms with which man creates so as to be able to retain what death makes him lose.

In Borges' Plato, out of the heart of mourning there emerges an amazing novelty, a creation by the psyche in mourning, and with this an innovatory work for Greek thought: the dialogue. Plato is among those geniuses whom mourning leads to produce outstanding creative works in the world and in themselves. Nostalgia for the object, remembrance, and fantasy, Borges remarks, are in charge of revealing that the past is not a burden without life but, rather, a potential to keep on living.

The genesis of psychoanalysis is somehow related to Freud's mournings. Didier Anzieu (1974) pointed out the temporal relationship between Freud's moments of creative inspiration and his mournings that reawakened symptoms, reactivated memories and traumas, and led to the conquest of the unconscious—a relationship that he himself discovered in the mourning for his father's death, which was emblematic in the development of his psychoanalytic production.

Memories and fantasy

Remembrance and memories—sources of knowledge, elaboration, and inspiration—play a fundamental role in working through mourning. Freud states this clearly in "Mourning and Melancholia": "Each single one of the memories and expectations in which the libido is bound to the object is brought up and hypercathected, and detachment of the libido is accomplished in respect of it." Piece by piece. It is a particular confrontation of the intensity of memories with the distressing operation of being free from the object. This is more painful when "the reaction to the loss of someone who is loved, contains the same painful frame of mind, the same loss of interest in the outside world—in so far as it does not recall him—the same loss of capacity to adopt any new object of love (which would mean replacing him) and the same turning away from any activity that is not connected with thoughts of him. . . ." "In mourning it is the world which has become poor and empty."

The past arrives with memories and forgetfulness, with short-circuits of memory and with day-dreaming, which try to transform the story into a new narrative. Memories and day-dreaming stir the preconscious, reviving its unconscious roots and awakening old con-

flicts. Unlike melancholia and the theoretical and clinical ambigui-
ties of depression, mourning does not necessarily mean the sadness
of a dull mental life, the litanies for the loss, or the manic glorifica-
tion of pleasures experienced in the past or to have in the future.

Day-dreaming, which evokes the object, has a bearing on working
through mourning. Harold Blum (1999, p. 54) articulates a significant relationship that goes from present depressive moments to the
regressive capture of past experiences and to the imaginative creation of giving future representation to the realization of an erotic desire. In a movement towards the primal, Janine Chasseguet-Smirgel
(1999), on a Kleinian line of thought, stresses the creative function
of the unconscious fantasy and calls "somatic matrix" the connection
of these fantasies with the body and sensoriality.

Regression by the process of mourning reaches the body. Sensory
and affect traces that had not achieved representation emerge from
the soma, thus adding something new to the path that goes from
image to thought. So the most archaic and obscure layers of the psyche arise from the body, now aching and excited by the economy of
mourning, to contribute to the creative construction of the psychic
scenes of pain.

André Green (2000) speaks of a primary pole placed at the beginning of the history, which is of utmost importance for regression. Madeleine Baranger (2004) thinks that at every encounter of
the subject with the unknown (mourning plunges the ego into the
unknown of death) the drive takes both a regressive turn towards
the secrets of the past—even up to what cannot have representation, being originary, archaic, or traumatic—and a prospective turn
towards metaphoric metonymical objects of the future. In mourning the creativity of the psyche straddles the border between the
unknown and what is known, between what is lost and what is about
to be resumed.

In my opinion, there is in mourning something else that arouses
different resonances when we are concerned with creativity, which
Freud suggests by the word "puzzling". We try here to elucidate (without overlooking the ideas in "Mourning and Melancholia") what is
enigmatic in the unconscious pattern of the absorbing memory or
in the traumatic factor corresponding to the economy when the
drive begins to lose its object or in the enigmatic area available for
the drive when, during the struggle between the structure and the

death drive, disaffection from the object erases the place occupied by specular identifications of narcissistic structures. In other words, mourning sets in motion along different paths and processes the creative potential of an enigmatic absence.

Jean Laplanche's (1992) ideas about the enigmatic are fundamental to an examination of creativity and can also be extended to deal with the process of mourning. The prototypical enigmatic message—that is, the primal seduction at the early stages of psychic life, which is unfathomed for the infant as well as, to a great extent, for the adult, lays the enigma. What is enigmatic in other distressing yet not devastating mournings and traumas remains as potential stimulation for the representational power of the psyche, even the enigmatic of the archaic past where symbiosis was first a space of need and then one of enclosure. During the psychic evolution of the body, what remains as traces of the exciting–excited body of the infant and of the exciting–excited body of the adult in symbiosis, when both are lost to the other, finds absence and freedom. Even so, the real loss of the object reactivates, in the various oedipal and pre-oedipal stratifications, the archaic antecedent.

It is true that a new mourning reactivates previous mournings and traumatic situations, and it is also true that each new mourning bears the mark of the moment. Memories and resignification, the phantasms that made up for the traumatic void, the interior–exterior void produced by the economy of mourning, disinvestment, bodily and psychic pain, what was and what could not be done, all travel along the time spiral, which Enrique Pichon Rivière set against linear time.

The most amazing aspect of the work of mourning is the violence of the unleashed movements, which bring together a host of past sensations and images. Past and present meet and are reconstructed and deconstructed in an attempt by the ego to rehabilitate the attractive and loving characteristics of the object, the pleasure of what has been lost. Also with regression towards the archaic, with "the ego's original reaction to objects in the external world" in the hostility that Freud identifies and which he will resignify in his work on denial (1925h), something of the object is left out and alien to the ego. The enigmatic inside and the enigmatic outside, good and evil, are open to the pursuits of a creativity that does not relinquish representation.

The dead person captures the imagination, and imagination invents the scenes of mourning. Death defies representation. However, metaphors and scenes of death, which the suffering man is able to invent through the experience of his mourning, are present in literature and art, in mathematics and physics, in Freud's theoretical thinking about the wooden spool. Mourning brings us closer to the enjoyable pain of constructing what we will never know and what we never knew about the mysteries of death and what has been lost.

Identification and transformation

Julia Kristeva (1994, p. 224) defines mourning as "a loss that throws me into time and into the search for the past which is delightfully destructive of my present identity". A time irremediably lost and encounters that will not take place lead to "tempting a presence in the Being".

The correction of poignant reality through an identification that turns object-seeking into a modification of the being is Freud's discovery and alters the notion of structure for that of an identity in movement. Granted that during the evolution of mourning identification varies according to the traumatic intensity or the hermeneutic hidden in the history. Massive identification with a person, with a quality, or with mental functioning cannot be equated with identification with the psychic potential of the force of beneficial fragments of the lost being. I believe the idea of transformation is appropriate if we are referring to the creative side of the identification processes during mourning.

Massive identification points to the quality of the previous relationship and failure in its evolution. Van Gogh's paintings done in Ambers some months after his father's death bear witness to this kind of identification. During the three months he stayed there, he lost some teeth, suffered gastric and cardiac discomfort, had fits of rage, caught venereal disease, and neglected his body to an extreme. At the same time he first became interested in self-portraits, to which he would return with each crisis and with renewed creative impulse. In his famous *Self-Portrait with a Pipe* and in his drawings— *Skull with Cigarette* and *Skeleton with Cat at the Window*—he shows identification with his father's destroyed and destructive persecutory and depressive aspects. The shadow of the object had fallen on the ego, and through identification without discrimination between the dead father's positive and the negative aspects, which his works reveal, Van Gogh must have been able to detach from the object and obtain his liberation. Certainly, Van Gogh ventured into unexplored territory, going to the very depths of experiences of pleasure and pain as the condition for creating the artistic signs of a melancholic mourning.

What, then, does identification offer to make up for a loss for which remembrance failed to compensate? It might be something incarnate, more concrete than the stuff of dreams, something alive from an interrupted intersubjectivity, which can make uncertain things continue constructing history and reality. This is the identification with Socrates that Borges finds in Plato's Dialogues—that is, a non-mimetic identification that maintains internalized the transforming potential of intersubjectivity.

Identification grounded in the subject by bonds of blood, love, sex, or admiration will contain multiple and different sensations from pre-oedipal and oedipal stratifications and from topologic density attained through the work of mourning, which reconstructs the memory, the vision of the subjectivity and of the world from various angles.

Identification with some aspects of the object and of the relationship, which are still alive, does not have a fixed quality frozen in time. I agree with Madeleine Baranger (2004) that it is a starting point, a first step for the development in the psyche of something different, which can keep on growing and changing with life experiences. Carlos Aslan (2006) thinks that one of the functions of identification is to be "structure-making". The psychoanalytic clinical approach to mourning often describes this functioning when absence and identification produce movements of caesura and reconstruction in the structure so that identification is not equivalent to what has been lost. One of the paradoxes of mourning is that a loss becomes a gain.

Memories and drive charge coming from the body and from what had no representation in the past merge in the scenic construction of what is lost. This is, to my mind, the contribution of memories, unconscious fantasy, and imagination to creativity in mourning, thus allowing mental space for a poiesis of death.

Identification is another source of creation during mourning, provided the object had a separate existence and was not a narcissistic object.

If because the impossible is so fervently desired, desire consumes itself and with it the pleasure that needs an object to maintain the balance of the structure, then identification plays an active part in saving the ego from atony. When dealing with regression in mourning, Freud turned to narcissism for identification to occur but stated that a structuring identification needs a separate—not a fused—object.

A previous symbiotic relationship with the object often leads to unresolved mournings and to non-structuring identifications. This is the dead–alive—described by Willy Baranger (1961)—who identifies with an object that can neither live again nor die completely. On a Kleinian line of thought that defines psychic evolution as normal or pathological depending on how someone deals with mourning and depression, Baranger thought that the dead–alive belongs to the universal stage of overcoming the infantile depressive position—that is, to accept that our objects die. The antecedent is unresolved early symbiosis caught between the weak, fragile, vulnerable aspects of the ego and an idealized persecutory object.

For the theory of narcissism, the dead–alive is an imaginary construction that keeps narcissistic passion secret and split in a fantasy of specular eternity. Every new mourning reawakens narcissistic passion that often avoids the work of present mournings and even draws towards the subject the idealized and persecutory aspects of the object. Frankenstein, the frightening character Mary Shelley created at the age of 19 during a stormy night, in Byron's and Shelley's romantic atmosphere and in the modern enthusiasm of the science of the time, can help the reader to figure out the horror of a living spectre constructed with fragments, with parts of unresolved mournings. Like Frankenstein, the dead–alive is made up of dead parts left from other mournings. Psychiatric clinical work yields a psychopathological example of an ego absorbed and identified with a phantasm, which is character and hero of the melancholic drama in the denial of the existence of body and mind, together with the omnipotent idea of grandiosity that characterizes Cotard's melancholy (also present in neurotic expressions of the syndrome) (Cotard, 1882).

However, more often than not the analyst finds that the reactivation of the dead–alive during the analysis of a present mourning finally kills what had not completely died. Detachment from the object is achieved by identification, and its phantasmatic components find a place in the chain of resignifications or else join new sublimations. On this occasion the positive side of mourning is not to construct something new but to take out of their defensive enclosure the narcissistic and oedipal components caught in the narcissistic passion (Melgar, 1999) and give them representation—perhaps the one they had when they were formed—and psychic scene.

In structuring identifications, the absent object of the drive pleasure is actively discriminated and transformed during mourning, and the drive follows the way to an encounter that can be adequate and possible only through metaphors of creativity. The semiotic power of the *madeleine* in "A la recherche du temps perdu" comes immediately to my mind. After going through different changes in the choice of a word, of bringing forth memories and associations, of gathering affects and thoughts about people, love, and hate, after his mother's death, and after retrieving extremely pleasant sensorial memories, Proust found the meaningful metaphor in the unforgettable, musical, delicious *madeleine*.

Identifications established from the narcissism of the primary objects that have as referent of the narcissistic specular enjoyment (*jouissance* for Lacan) the existence of the object, on the other hand, are quite different. Norberto Marucco (1999, p. 70) called passive primary identifications those narcissistic identifications that entailed an archaic sacrifice of the ego and of the drives and that appear again with new objects from the narcissistic structure. The relief of depressive suffering after a person's death or after the loss of an ideal led me to think that with the death of the object some part of it that was split in the narcissistic structure also dies. Primary identification, which restrains the drive charge and repeats in the near present the archaic sacrifice, finds in the work of mourning the possibility of being deconstructed. On this line, death drive during libidinal disinvestment kills specular pleasure, and this takes place in narcissism.

The feeling of rebirth experienced at the end of mourning is close to the deliverance from symbiotic and narcissistic identifications, and this moment endows the ego with prospective illumination. The recovery of sensorial pleasure present in being able to feel, perceive, and vibrate with retrieved sensuality is one of the contributions of mourning to new sublimation formations of the enigmatic in primal sexuality, of the enigma that identification with the other's desire erases from the subject's creativity.

From mourning and trauma to creative solitude

Mourning and trauma join when faced with a loss that breaks the symbolic alliance between image, word, and the external world. Confronted with disorganization, disinvestment, and traumatic void, phantasmagorization emerges to lessen the negative effects (Baranger, Baranger, & Mom, 1987). With mourning, a second relationship of causality, now between absence-emptiness and memory-phantasmagorization, generates psychic creativity, although there is always something enigmatic that has no resignification. The reactivation of other mournings and traumatic situations during the present mourning has both positive and negative aspects. Among the first of these is when the absence left by death becomes a place for meeting the unknown again.

The loss of mourning is not the same as the void of trauma. The subject in mourning knows whom he has lost, although he does not know much about what he has lost, whereas the ego of trauma repeats the emptiness and the misery. The working through of mourning leads to the principle of reality and to a desire to go on living, but separation from the object does not mean total detachment in psychic reality: there is suffering to be re-experienced and the nostalgic desire to create something of the past in future time. When this resolution achieves its most positive form, experience stirs the power of the unconscious capable of playing creatively between traumatic nonsense and the unknown of death.

It is no wonder that art gives us a glimpse into one of the creative transformations of mourning, thus revealing or suggesting the aesthetic sublimation of a silence of representations (Melgar, 2005). In Carpaccio's *Saint Augustine's Vision* the saint is interrupted in his writing by the vision of Saint Jerome, who announces his death. Carpaccio does not portray the vision but illuminates the empty space in the room, and this light renders an effect of reality. The narrow window is the point through which invisible death comes into the scene, and Saint Augustine's expression reveals astonishment as something unexpected interrupts the action and leaves the text awaiting. Carpaccio, with talent and deep thought, has depicted the void that death leaves behind.

To my mind, sublimated void prompts one of the creative mechanisms of mourning. This mechanism does not consist in filling the void with baroque imaginings that do not renounce completeness nor does it rely on negative hallucination. Instead, it subordinates the history and the events to a moment when the meaning of the loss is absorbed by what is sensorial in the experience.

George Pollock (1975), in his studies on music and psychoanalysis, advanced the idea that mourning can be experienced through musical works. He admits the influence of old mournings but he stresses that in funeral music the composer is mourning his own death—a mourning constructed by music. Drawing on the theory of self, Pollock believes that the vision of the physical and psychical disintegration or decay of the self gives rise to a musical work that actually means the mourning for his own death. Mozart said explicitly that the Requiem (which he left unfinished) was for his own death. Therefore, music would not be merely a product but, rather, mourning itself and the pain for the loss of the body and soul is present in the language of the work.

Of all the arts, music in particular assembles the existence of a work and its conclusion during the time of the performance. The musical genius who is able to put together memory and abstraction may have the talent to subtract sonority, like algebra does, to reach the ultimate sonority of one's own disappearance. Although it expresses the Pythagorean ideal of interaction between music and mathematics that provides beauty and freedom, we should not forget the devastating effect of mourning when it absorbs the ego.

From another point of view, when we are confronted with the finitude of the body, of knowledge and of representation, the desire to create seems to focus on the essential. To give shape and sound to death, or rather, to the mourning for dying, is part of life, of erotism, and—why not?—of the narcissistic desire for immortality. The paradox of reaching mourning through creativity, which is not limited to music, should include what there is of the musical in words as well as in other different external and internal forms of creativity. Poets have also written their requiem. Borges draws our attention to the musicality and poetic worth of an accepted and joyful mourning in Robert Louis Stevenson's *Requiem*:

Under the wild and starry sky
Dig the grave and let me lie.
Glad did I live and gladly die,
And I laid me down with a will.

The acceptance of loss during mourning enables the drives to reach
for the unknown in the past and in the future, by all possible paths:
seeking other love objects, in epistemophilia trying to discover something new, in the conquest of unknown worlds, and also in the unexpected encounters of the body with image and thought.

The body feels, and the traces that did not attain psychic inscrip-
tion strive for it. If there was not a pathological arrest of mourning,
sensoriality of the pained body and the evanescence of the object
awaken creativity in the psyche. Affects that cannot be reached, hallucinatory and delirious phenomena, depersonalization and alien-
ation, psychosomatic or neurotic symptoms are a potential cauldron.
This is negative for the melancholic enclosure or for psychosis and
positive for figurability (Botella & Botella, 1990, pp. 61–67) and for
the symbol-making exercise of the thought that tries to tame what
is traumatic in mourning with the *language of perceptions* (Freud,
1940a[1938]). To overcome the moment in which the world is dis-
mal and empty and there is no interest other than that connected
with what was lost, it is necessary to accept detachment from the
object. Even when mourning fails to overcome the rejection of everyday pleasure and the desire for the object is frustrated and turns
to sadomasochism, inner solitude begins to be enjoyable. Loss that is
worked through without destructive bitterness is considered by those
authors, specially Winnicott, who remarked on the care-taking role
of the mother and of primary objects that ensures the capacity for
being alone.

Guy Rosolato (1996) states that painful loneliness lies at the core
of mourning and melancholia. It may appear either as defensive isolation before guilt and persecution or as an attempt to avoid painful
affects. Rosolato also stresses the evolutionary force present in the
serene and creative seclusion that keeps the subject away from other
satisfactions and provides the internal–external framework of the exercise of silence. A silence placed on the border between what there
is and what there is not, between what was said and what was not said,
between words and affects. This creative solitude of the resolution
of mourning does not exclude the recovery of ideals necessary for
sublimation or the creative flapping of poiesis.

The work of mourning

Psychoanalysis discovered that for the construction of the psychic apparatus and of language, of the functions of the ego and of the freedom of the subject to feel, imagine, think, and create, it is necessary to lose the objects of need and love. The evolution of the psyche bears the mark of mourning and trauma. In "Mourning and Melancholia" the object, the drives, and identification are at the centre of the present mourning, but the outcome of the processes involved are beyond any lineal logic. Psychoanalytic thinking about creativity should consider the complexity and contradictions of mourning.

It may seem paradoxical that the loss of an object, perhaps unique and irreplaceable, does not weaken creativity and might even enhance it; that a traumatic void or an absence that sacrifices the ego becomes an appeal to the drive, no matter the vicissitudes of the investment; that non-existence is compensated for by identification that rouses identity; that narcissistic pain disentangles the narcissistic structure of previous ties and specular prisons.

The work of mourning can lead to possible paths of creativity—the kind that produces transformations in the psyche as well as the one that is the germ of future works. Mourning is a process of working through that leads to the acceptance of what has been lost. Each moment carries a prospective potential. However, working through and creation may not coincide, creativity does not share the specific mechanisms of mourning and may turn away from and even omit working through.

The works of great creators who underwent traumatic mourning in early childhood testify to the way in which the ego creatively came out of catastrophe, although the value and originality of the product sometimes failed to block the wild force of destructiveness. André Green (1983a) related the moment the child is disinvested ruthlessly by the mother (and more tragically so if there is physical death during infancy) to creativity. When the attempt to gather the fragments of a torn ego takes place in the area of the phantasm, art cannot protect the ego from traumatic effects. Isidore Ducasse, Comte de Lautréamont, inspired herald of surrealism, lost his mother at the age of eighteen months. The genial blasphemy of *The Songs of Maldoror* seems to suggest the plunging into the hell of appalling mourning. Let us remember the second canto: "*Le fantôme fait claquer sa langue, comme pour se dire à lui-même qu'il va cesser la poursuite. . . . Sa voix de condamné s'entend jusque dans les couches les plus lointaines de l'espace, et, lorsque son hurlement épouvantable pénètre dans le cœur humain, celui-ci préférerait avoir, dit-on, la mort pour mère que le remords pour fils."* ["The phantom clicks its tongue, as if to say to itself that it would cease its pursuit. . . . Its voice of the condemned can be heard even in the remotest reaches of space, and when its terrible howl penetrates the human heart, the latter would prefer, it is said, the death of the mother over the remorse of the son."] Lautréamont died in Paris at 24 years of age, but he had already staged and embodied an early mourning in a persecutory and guilt-ridden phantasm.

Works created with material from present mourning show some characteristics that prompt us to explore the work of mourning to pinpoint its contribution to creativity in the psyche and in cultural life.

Whenever the phantasmagorization of the trauma mingles with memories and fantasies of what was lost, scenes of death—cause and effect of pain in mourning—contribute to enrich the limited knowledge of its enigmas. Identification with the positive traits of the lost object is important for the mobility of identity. Moreover, it is an important step towards the construction of a prospective dialogue with what has been lost. Acceptance of the loss leads to idealization and sublimation of the void, and this encourages the potentiality of the enigmatic. Lastly, detachment of representation from sensoriality acquires another value: it invites the body to take again the path of the senses towards the psyche, paving the way for metaphor and metonymy.

To conclude, the evolution of the creative side of mourning depends on the capacity to maintain the desire for the unknown.

NOTE

Translated by Haydee F. de Breyter.

6

A new reading
of the origins of object relations theory

Thomas H. Ogden

Some authors write what they think; others think what they write. The latter seem to do their thinking in the very act of writing, as if thoughts arise from the conjunction of pen and paper, the work unfolding by surprise as it goes. Freud in many of his most important books and articles, including "Mourning and Melancholia" (1917e [1915]), was a writer of this latter sort. In these writings, Freud made no attempt to cover his tracks, for example, his false starts, his un-certainties, his reversals of thinking (often done mid-sentence), his shelving of compelling ideas for the time being because they seemed to him too speculative or lacking adequate clinical foundation.

The legacy that Freud left was not simply a set of ideas but, as important, and inseparable from those ideas, a new way of thinking about human experience that gave rise to nothing less than a new form of human subjectivity. Each of his psychoanalytic writings, from this point of view, is simultaneously an explication of a set of con-cepts and a demonstration of a newly created way of thinking about and experiencing ourselves. I have chosen to look closely at Freud's "Mourning and Melancholia" for two reasons: First, I consider this paper to be one of Freud's most important contributions in that it develops for the first time, in a systematic way, a line of thought that would later be termed "object-relations theory"[1] (Fairbairn, 1952).

This line of thought has played a major role in shaping psychoanalysis from 1917 onwards. Second, I have found that attending closely to Freud's writing *as writing* in "Mourning and Melancholia" provides an extraordinary opportunity not only to listen to Freud think, but also, through the writing, to enter into that thinking process with him. In this way, the reader may learn a good deal about what is distinctive to the new form of thinking (and its attendant subjectivity) that Freud was in the process of creating in this article.[2]

Freud wrote "Mourning and Melancholia" in less than three months in early 1915 during a period that was, for him, filled with great intellectual and emotional upheaval. Europe was in the throes of World War I. Despite his protestations, two of Freud's sons volunteered for military service and fought at the front lines. Freud was at the same time in the grip of intense intellectual foment. In the years 1914 and 1915, Freud wrote a series of twelve essays, which represented his first major revision of psychoanalytic theory since the publication of *The Interpretation of Dreams* (1900a). Freud's intent was to publish these papers as a book to be titled *Preliminaries to a Metapsychology*. He hoped that this collection would "provide a stable theoretical foundation for psycho-analysis" (Freud, quoted by Strachey, 1957a, p. 105).

In the summer of 1915, Freud wrote to Ferenczi, "The twelve articles are, as it were, ready" (Gay, 1988, p. 367). As the phrase "as it were" suggests, Freud had misgivings about what he had written. Only five of the essays—all of which are ground-breaking papers—were ever published: "Instincts and Their Vicissitudes", "Repression", and "The Unconscious" were published as journal articles in 1915. "A Metapsychological Supplement to the Theory of Dreams" and "Mourning and Melancholia", although completed in 1915, were not published until 1917. Freud destroyed the other seven articles, which papers, he told Ferenczi, "deserved suppression and silence" (Gay, 1988, p. 373). None of these articles was shown to even his innermost circle of friends. Freud's reasons for "silencing" these essays remain a mystery in the history of psychoanalysis.

In the discussion that follows, I take up five portions of the text of "Mourning and Melancholia", each of which contains a pivotal contribution to the analytic understanding of the unconscious work of mourning and of melancholia; at the same time, I look at the way Freud made use of this seemingly focal exploration of these two psychological states as a vehicle for introducing—as much implicitly as explicitly—the foundations of his theory of unconscious internal object relations.[3]

I

Freud's unique voice resounds in the opening sentence of "Mourning and Melancholia": "Dreams having served us as the prototype in normal life of narcissistic mental disorders, we will now try to throw some light on the nature of melancholia by comparing it with the normal affect of mourning" (p. 243).

The voice we hear in Freud's writing is remarkably constant through the twenty-three volumes of the *Standard Edition*. It is a voice with which no other psychoanalyst has written because no other analyst has had the right to do so. The voice Freud creates is that of the founding father of a new discipline.[4] Already in this opening sentence, something quite remarkable can be heard which we regularly take for granted in reading Freud: in the course of the twenty years preceding the writing of this sentence, Freud had not only created a revolutionary conceptual system, he had altered language itself. It is, for me, astounding to observe that virtually every word in the opening sentence has acquired, in Freud's hands, new meanings and a new set of relationships, not only to practically every other word in the sentence, but also to innumerable words in language as a whole. For example, the word "dreams" that begins the sentence is a word that conveys rich layers of meaning and mystery that did not exist prior to the publication of *The Interpretation of Dreams* (1900a). Concentrated in this word newly created by Freud are allusions to (a) a conception of a repressed unconscious inner world that powerfully, but obliquely, exerts force on conscious experience, and vice versa; (b) a view that sexual desire is present from birth onwards and is rooted in bodily instincts that manifest themselves in universal unconscious incestuous wishes, parricidal fantasies, and fears of retaliation in the form of genital mutilation; (c) a recognition of the role of dreaming as an essential conversation between unconscious and preconscious aspects of ourselves; and (d) a radical reconceptualization of human symbology—at once universal and exquisitely idiosyncratic to the life history of each individual. Of course, this list is only a sampling of the meanings that the word "dream"—newly made by Freud—invokes. Similarly, the words "normal life", "mental disorders", and "narcissistic" speak to one another and to the word "dream" in ways that simply could not have occurred twenty years earlier. The second half of the sentence suggests that two other words denoting aspects of human experience will be made anew in this paper: "mourning" and "melancholia".[5]

The logic of the central argument of "Mourning and Melancholia" begins to unfold as Freud compares the psychological features of mourning to those of melancholia: both are responses to loss and involve "grave departures from the normal attitude to life" (p. 243).[6] In melancholia, one finds

> a profoundly painful dejection, cessation of interest in the out-
> side world, loss of the capacity to love, inhibition of all activity,
> and a lowering of the self-regarding feelings to a degree that
> finds utterance in self-reproaches and self-revilings, and culmi-
> nates in a delusional expectation of punishment. [p. 244]

Freud points out that the same traits characterize mourning—with one exception: "the disturbance of self-regard". Only in retrospect will the reader realize that the full weight of the thesis that Freud develops in this paper rests on this simple observation made almost in passing: "The disturbance of self-regard is absent in mourning; but otherwise the features are the same" (p. 243). As in every good detective novel, all clues necessary for solving the crime are laid out in plain view practically from the outset.

With the background of the discussion of the similarities and differences—there is only one symptomatic difference—between mourning and melancholia, the paper seems abruptly to plunge into the exploration of the unconscious. In melancholia, the patient and the analyst may not even know what the patient has lost—a remarkable idea from the point of view of common sense in 1915. Even when the melancholic is aware that he has suffered the loss of a person, "he knows *whom* he has lost but not *what* he has lost in him" (p. 245). There is ambiguity in Freud's language here: is the melancholic unaware of the sort of importance the tie to the object held for him: "*what* [it is that the melancholic] has lost in [losing] him". Or is the melancholic unaware of what he has lost in *himself* as a consequence of losing the object? The ambiguity—whether or not Freud intended it—subtly introduces the important notion of the simultaneity and interdependence of two unconscious aspects of object loss in melancholia. One involves the nature of the melancholic's tie to the object, and the other involves an alteration of the self in response to the loss of the object.

> This [lack of awareness on the part of the melancholic of what he has lost] would suggest that melancholia is in some way related to an object-loss which is withdrawn from consciousness, in contradistinction to mourning, in which there is nothing about the loss that is unconscious. [p. 245]

In his effort to understand the nature of the unconscious object loss in melancholia, Freud returns to the sole observable symptomatic difference between mourning and melancholia: the melancholic's diminished self-esteem.

> In mourning it is the world which has become poor and empty; in melancholia it is the ego itself. The patient represents his ego to us as worthless, incapable of any achievement and morally despicable; he reproaches himself, vilifies himself and expects to be cast out and punished. He abases himself before everyone and commiserates with his own relatives for being connected with anyone so unworthy. He is not of the opinion that a change has taken place in him, but extends his self-criticism back over the past; he declares that he was never any better. [p. 246]

More in his use of language than in explicit theoretical statements, Freud's model of the mind is being reworked here. There is a steady flow of subject–object, I–me pairings in this passage: the patient as object reproaches, abases, vilifies himself as object (and extends the reproaches backwards and forwards in time). What is being suggested—and only suggested—is that these subject–object pairings extend beyond consciousness into the timeless unconscious and constitute what is going on unconsciously in melancholia that is not occurring in mourning. The unconscious is in this sense a metaphorical place in which the "I–me" pairings are unconscious psychological contents that actively engage in a continuous timeless attack of the subject (I) upon the object (me) which depletes the ego (a concept in transition here) to the point that it becomes "poor and empty" in the process.

The melancholic is ill in that he stands in a different relationship to his failings than does the mourner. The melancholic does not evidence the shame one would expect of a person who experiences himself as "petty, egoistic, [and] dishonest" (p. 246) and instead demonstrates an "insistent communicativeness which finds satisfaction in self-exposure" (p. 247). Each time Freud returns to the observation of the melancholic's diminished self-regard, he makes use of it to illuminate a different aspect of the unconscious "internal work" (p. 245) of melancholia. This time the observation, with its accrued set of meanings, becomes an important underpinning for a new conception of the ego, which to this point has only been hinted at:

> . . . the melancholic's disorder affords [a view] of the constitution of the human ego. We see how in [the melancholic] one part of the ego sets itself over against the other, judges it critically, and, as it were, takes it as its object. What we are here becoming acquainted with is the agency commonly called "conscience" . . . and we shall come upon evidence to show that it can become diseased on its own account. [p. 247]

Here, Freud is reconceiving the ego in several important ways. These revisions, taken together, constitute the first of a set of tenets underlying Freud's emerging psychoanalytic theory of unconscious internal object relations: first, the ego, now a psychic structure with conscious and unconscious components ("parts"), can be split; second, an unconscious split-off aspect of the ego has the capacity to generate thoughts and feelings independently—in the case of the critical agency these thoughts and feelings are of a self-observing moralistic, judgemental sort; third, a split-off part of the ego may enter into an unconscious relationship to another part of the ego; and, fourth, a split-off aspect of the ego may be either healthy or pathological.

II

The paper becomes positively fugue-like in its structure as Freud takes up again—yet in a new way—the sole symptomatic difference between mourning and melancholia:

> If one listens patiently to a melancholic's many and various self-accusations, one cannot in the end avoid the impression that often the most violent of them are hardly at all applicable to the patient himself, but that with insignificant modifications they do fit someone else, someone whom the patient loves or has loved or should love. . . . So we find the key to the clinical picture: we perceive that the self-reproaches are reproaches against a loved object which have been shifted away from it on to the patient's own ego. [p. 248]

Thus, Freud, as if developing enhanced observational acuity as he writes, sees something he previously had not noticed: that the accusations the melancholic heaps upon himself represent unconsciously displaced attacks on the loved object. This observation serves as a starting point from which Freud goes on to posit a second set of elements of his object relations theory.

In considering the melancholic's unconscious reproaches of the loved object, Freud picks up a thread that he had introduced earlier in the discussion. Melancholia often entails a psychological struggle involving ambivalent feelings for the loved object, as "in the case of a betrothed girl who has been jilted" (p. 245). Freud elaborates on the role of ambivalence in melancholia by observing that melancholics show not the slightest humility despite their insistence on their own worthlessness "and always seem as though they felt slighted and had been treated with great injustice" (p. 248). Their intense sense of entitlement and injustice "is possible only because the reactions expressed in their behaviour still proceed from a mental constellation of revolt, which has then, by a certain process, passed over into the crushed state of melancholia" (p. 248).

It seems to me that Freud is suggesting that the melancholic experiences outrage (as opposed to anger of other sorts) at the object for disappointing him and doing him a "great injustice". This emotional protest/revolt is crushed in melancholia as a consequence of "a certain process". It is the delineation of that "certain process" in theoretical terms that will occupy much of the remainder of "Mourning and Melancholia".

The reader can hear unmistakable excitement in Freud's voice in the sentence that follows: "There is no difficulty in reconstructing this [transformative] process" (p. 248). Ideas are falling into place. A certain clarity is emerging from the tangle of seemingly contradictory observations—for example, the melancholic's combination of severe self-condemnation and vociferous self-righteous outrage. In spelling out the psychological process mediating the melancholic's movement from revolt (against injustices he has suffered) to a crushed state, Freud, with extraordinary dexterity, presents a radically new conception of the structure of the unconscious:

An object-choice, an attachment of the libido to a particular person, had at one time existed [for the melancholic]; then, owing to a real slight or disappointment coming from this loved person, the object-relationship was shattered. The result was not

the normal one of a withdrawal of the libido [loving emotional
energy] from this object and a displacement of it on to a new
one. . . . [Instead,] the object-cathexis [the emotional investment
in the object] proved to have little power of resistance [little capacity to maintain the tie to the object], and was brought to an
end. But the free libido was not displaced on to another object;
it was withdrawn into the ego. There . . . it [the loving emotional
investment which has been withdrawn from the object] served
to establish an *identification* of [a part of] the ego with the abandoned object. Thus the shadow of the object fell upon [a part of]
the ego, and the latter could henceforth be judged by a special
agency [another part of the ego], as though it were an object, the
forsaken object. In this way an object-loss was transformed into an
ego-loss and the conflict between the ego and the loved person
[was transformed] into a cleavage between the critical activity of
[a part of] the ego [later to be called the superego] and [another
part of] the ego as altered by identification. [pp. 248–249]

These sentences represent a powerfully succinct demonstration of
the way Freud in this paper was beginning to write/think theoretically and clinically in terms of relationships between unconscious,
paired, split-off aspects of the ego (i.e. about unconscious internal
object relations).[7] Freud, for the first time, is gathering together into
a coherent narrative expressed in higher order theoretical terms his
newly conceived revised model of the mind.

There is so much going on in this passage that it is difficult to
know where to start in discussing it. Freud's use of language seems
to me to afford a port of entry into this critical moment in the development of psychoanalytic thought. There is an important shift in
the language Freud is using that serves to convey a rethinking of an
important aspect of his conception of melancholia. The words "object-loss", "lost object", and even "lost as an object of love" are, without comment on Freud's part, replaced by the words "abandoned
object" and "forsaken object". The melancholic's "abandonment" of
the object (as opposed to the mourner's loss of the object) involves a
paradoxical psychological event: the abandoned object, for the melancholic, is preserved in the form of an identification with it: "Thus
[in identifying with the object] the shadow of the object fell upon
the ego . . ." (p. 249). In melancholia, the ego is altered not by the
glow of the object, but (more darkly) by "the shadow of the object".
The shadow metaphor suggests that the melancholic's experience of
identifying with the abandoned object has a thin, two-dimensional

quality as opposed to a lively, robust feeling tone. The painful experience of loss is short-circuited by the melancholic's identification with
the object, thus denying the separateness of the object: the object
is me and I am the object. There is no loss; an external object (the
abandoned object) is omnipotently replaced by an internal one (the
ego-identified-with-the-object).

So, in response to the pain of loss, the ego is twice split forming
an internal object relationship in which one split-off part of the ego
(the critical agency) angrily (with outrage) turns on another split-off
part of the ego (the ego-identified-with-the-object). Although Freud
does not speak in these terms, it could be said that the internal object
relationship is created for purposes of evading the painful feeling of
object loss. This avoidance is achieved by means of an unconscious
"deal with the devil": in exchange for the evasion of the pain of
object loss, the melancholic is doomed to experience the sense of
lifelessness that comes as a consequence of disconnecting oneself
from large portions of external reality. In this sense, the melancholic
forfeits a substantial part of his own life—the three-dimensional
emotional life lived in the world of real external objects. The internal world of the melancholic is powerfully shaped by the wish to hold
captive the object in the form of an imaginary substitute for it—the
ego-identified-with-the-object. In a sense, the internalization of the
object renders the object forever captive to the melancholic and at
the same time renders the melancholic endlessly captive to it.

A dream of one of my patients comes to mind as a particularly
poignant expression of the frozen quality of the melancholic's unconscious internal object world.

The patient, Mr K, began analysis a year after the death of his
wife of twenty-two years. In a dream that Mr K reported several years
into the analysis,

*he was attending a gathering in which a tribute was to be paid to someone
whose identity was unclear to him. Just as the proceedings were getting
under way, a man in the audience rose to his feet and spoke glowingly
of Mr K's fine character and important accomplishments. When the man
finished, the patient stood and expressed his gratitude for the high praise,
but said that the purpose of the meeting was to pay tribute to the guest of
honour, so the group's attention should be directed to him. Immediately
upon Mr K's sitting down, another person stood and again praised the
patient at great length. Mr K again stood and, after briefly repeating his*

statement of gratitude for the adulation, he redirected the attention of the gathering to the honoured guest. This sequence was repeated again and again until the patient had the terrifying realization that this sequence would go on forever.

Mr K awoke from the dream with his heart racing in a state of panic.

The patient had told me in the sessions preceding the dream that he had become increasingly despairing of ever being able to love another woman and "resume life". He said he has never ceased expecting his wife to return home after work each evening at six-thirty. He added that every family event after her death has been for him nothing more than another occasion at which his wife is missing. He apologized for his lugubrious, self-pitying tones.

I told Mr K that I thought that the dream captured a sense of the way he feels imprisoned in his inability genuinely to be interested in, much less honour, new experiences with people. In the dream, he, in the form of the guests paying endless homage to him, directed to himself what might have been interest paid to someone outside himself, someone outside his internally frozen relationship with his wife. I went on to say that it was striking that the honoured guest in the dream was not given a name, much less an identity and human qualities that might have stirred curiosity, puzzlement, anger, jealousy, envy, compassion, love, admiration, or any other set of feeling responses to another person. I added that the horror he felt at the end of the dream seemed to reflect his awareness that the static state of self-imprisonment in which he lives is potentially endless. (A good deal of this interpretation referred back to many discussions Mr K and I had had concerning his state of being "stuck" in a world that no longer existed.) Mr K responded by telling me that as I was speaking he remembered another part of the dream made up of *a single still image of himself wrapped in heavy chains unable to move even a single muscle of his body.* He said he felt repelled by the extreme passivity of the image.

The dreams and the discussion that followed represented something of a turning point in the analysis. The patient's response to separations from me between sessions and during weekend and holiday breaks became less frighteningly bleak for him. In the period following this session, Mr K found that he could sometimes go for hours without experiencing the heavy bodily sensation in his chest that he had lived with unremittingly since his wife's death.

While the idea of the melancholic's unconscious identification with the lost/abandoned object for Freud held "the key to the clinical picture" (p. 248) of melancholia, Freud believed that the key to the theoretical problem of melancholia would have to satisfactorily resolve an important contradiction:

> On the one hand, a strong fixation [an intense, yet static emotional tie] to the loved object must have been present; on the other hand, in contradiction to this, the object-cathexis must have had little power of resistance [i.e. little power to maintain that tie to the object in the face of actual or feared death of the object or object-loss as a consequence of disappointment]. [p. 249]

The "key" to a psychoanalytic theory of melancholia that resolves the contradiction of the coexisting strong fixation to the object and the lack of tenacity of that object-tie lies, for Freud, in the concept of narcissism:

> this contradiction seems to imply that the object-choice has been effected on a narcissistic basis, so that the object-cathexis, when obstacles come in its way, can regress to narcissism. [p. 249]

Freud's theory of narcissism, which he had introduced only months earlier in his paper, "On Narcissism: An Introduction" (1914c), provided an important part of the context for the object relations theory of melancholia that Freud was developing in "Mourning and Melancholia". In his narcissism paper, Freud proposed that the normal infant begins in a state of "original" or "primary narcissism" (p. 75)—a state in which all emotional energy is ego-libido, a form of emotional investment that takes the ego (oneself) as its sole object. The infant's initial step towards the world outside himself is in the form of narcissistic identification—a type of object-tie that treats the external object as an extension of oneself.

From the psychological position of narcissistic identification, the healthy infant, in time, develops sufficient psychological stability to engage in a narcissistic form of relatedness to objects in which the tie to the object is largely comprised of a displacement of ego-libido from the ego on to the object (Freud, 1914c). In other words, a narcissistic object-tie is one in which the object is invested with emotional energy that originally was directed at oneself (and, in that sense, the object is a stand-in for the self). The movement from

narcissistic identification to narcissistic object-tie is a matter of a shift
in the degree of recognition of, and emotional investment in, the
otherness of the object.[8]

The healthy infant is able to achieve progressive differentiation
of, and complementarity between, ego-libido and object-libido. In
this process of differentiation, he is beginning to engage in a form
of object love that is not simply a displacement of love of oneself
onto the object. Instead, a more mature form of object love evolves
in which the infant achieves relatedness to objects that are experienced as external to himself outside the realm of the infant's omnipotence.

Herein lies, for Freud, the key to the theoretical problem—the
"contradiction"—posed by melancholia: melancholia is a disease of
narcissism. A necessary "precondition" (p. 249) for melancholia is
a disturbance in early narcissistic development. The melancholic
patient in infancy and childhood was unable to move successfully
from narcissistic object love to mature object love involving a person
who is experienced as separate from himself. Consequently, in the
face of object loss or disappointment, the melancholic is incapable
of mourning—that is, unable to face the full impact of the reality
of the loss of the object and, over time, to enter into mature object
love with another person. The melancholic does not have the capacity to disengage from the lost object and, instead, evades the pain
of loss through regression from narcissistic object relatedness to
narcissistic identification: "the result of which is that in spite of the
conflict [disappointment leading to outrage] with the loved person,
the love relation need not be given up" (p. 249). As Freud put it in
a summary statement near the end of the paper, "So by taking flight
into the ego [by means of a powerful narcissistic identification] love
escapes extinction" (p. 257).

A misreading of "Mourning and Melancholia" has, to my mind,
become entrenched in what is commonly held to be Freud's view
of melancholia (see, for example, Gay, 1988, pp. 372–373). What
I am referring to is the misconception that melancholia, according to Freud, involves an identification with the hated aspect of an
ambivalently loved object that has been lost. Such a reading, while
accurate so far as it goes, misses the central point of Freud's thesis.
What differentiates the melancholic from the mourner is the fact
that the melancholic has all along been able to engage only in nar-

cissistic forms of object relatedness. The narcissistic nature of the melancholic's personality renders him incapable of maintaining a firm connection with the painful reality of the irrevocable loss of the object that is necessary for mourning. Melancholia involves ready, reflexive recourse to regression to narcissistic identification as a way of not experiencing the hard edge of recognition of one's inability to undo the fact of the loss of the object. Object relations theory, as it is taking shape in the course of Freud's writing this paper, now includes an early developmental axis. The world of unconscious internal object relations is being viewed by Freud as a defensive regression to very early forms of object relatedness in response to psychological pain—in the case of the melancholic, the pain is the pain of loss. The individual replaces what might have become a three-dimensional relatedness to the mortal and at times disappointing external object with a two-dimensional (shadow-like) relationship to an internal object that exists in a psychological domain outside time (and consequently sheltered from the reality of death). In so doing, the melancholic evades the pain of loss and, by extension, other forms of psychological pain, but does so at an enormous cost—the loss of a good deal of his own (emotional) vitality.

III

Having hypothesized the melancholic's substitution of an unconscious internal object relationship for an external one and having wed this to a conception of defensive regression to narcissistic identification, Freud turns to a third defining feature of melancholia, which, as will be seen, provides the basis for another important feature of his psychoanalytic theory of unconscious internal object relationships:

> In melancholia, the occasions which give rise to the illness extend for the most part beyond the clear case of a loss by death, and include all those situations of being slighted, neglected or disappointed, which can import opposed feelings of love and hate into the relationship or reinforce an already existing ambivalence. . . . The melancholic's erotic cathexis [erotic emotional investment in the object] . . . has thus undergone a double vicissitude: part of it has regressed to [narcissistic] identification, but the other

136 Thomas H. Ogden

part, under the influence of the conflict due to ambivalence, has
been carried back to the stage of sadism. . . . [pp. 251–252]

Sadism is a form of object-tie in which hate (the melancholic's outrage at the object) becomes inextricably intertwined with erotic love
and can, in this combined state, be an even more powerful binding
force (in a suffocating, subjugating, tyrannizing way) than the ties
of love alone. The sadism in melancholia (generated in response to
the loss of or disappointment by a loved object) gives rise to a special
form of torment for both the subject and the object—that particular
mixture of love and hate encountered in stalking. In this sense, the
sadistic aspect of the relationship of the critical agency to the split-
off ego-identified-with-the-object might be thought of as a relentless,
crazed stalking of one split-off aspect of the ego by another—what
Fairbairn (1944) would later view as the love/hate bond between the
libidinal ego and the exciting object.

This conception of the enormous binding force of combined love
and hate is an integral part of the psychoanalytic understanding of
the astounding durability of pathological internal object relations.
Such allegiance to the bad (hated and hating) internal object is
often the source both for the stability of the pathological structure of the patient's personality organization and for some of the
most intractable transference–countertransference impasses that we
encounter in analytic work. In addition, the bonds of love mixed
with hate account for such forms of pathological relationships as
the ferocious ties of the abused child and the battered spouse to
their abusers (and the tie of the abusers to the abused). The abuse
is unconsciously experienced by both abused and abuser as loving
hate and hateful love—both of which are far preferable to no object
relationship at all (Fairbairn, 1944).

IV

Employing one of his favourite extended metaphors—the analyst
as detective—Freud creates in his writing a sense of adventure, risk-
taking, and even suspense as he takes on "the most remarkable
characteristic of melancholia . . . its tendency to change round into
mania—a state which is the opposite of it in its symptoms" (p. 253).
Freud's use of language in his discussion of mania—which is insepa-

rable from the ideas he presents—creates for the reader a sense of the fundamental differences between mourning and melancholia, and between healthy (internal and external) object relationships and pathological ones.

> I cannot promise that this attempt [to explain mania] will prove entirely satisfactory. It hardly carries us much beyond the possibility of taking one's initial bearings. We have two things to go upon: the first is a psycho-analytic impression, and the second what we may perhaps call a matter of general economic experience. The [psycho-analytic] impression . . . [is] that . . . both disorders [mania and melancholia] are wrestling with the same [unconscious] "complex", but that probably in melancholia the ego has succumbed to the complex [in the form of a painful feeling of having been crushed] whereas in mania it has mastered it [the pain of loss] or pushed it aside. [pp. 253–254]

The second of the two things "we have . . . to go upon" is "general economic experience". In attempting to account for the feelings of exuberance and triumph in mania, Freud hypothesized that the economics of mania—the quantitative distribution and play of psychological forces—may be similar to those seen when

> some poor wretch, by winning a large sum of money, is suddenly relieved from chronic worry about his daily bread, or when a long and arduous struggle is finally crowned with success, or when a man finds himself in a position to throw off at a single blow some oppressive compulsion, some false position which he has long had to keep up, and so on. [p. 254]

Beginning with the pun on "economic conditions" in the description of the poor wretch who wins a great deal of money, the sentence goes on to capture something of the feel of mania in its succession of images, which are unlike any other set of images in the article. These dramatic cameos suggest to me Freud's own understandable magical wishes to have his own "arduous struggle . . . finally crowned with success" or to be able "to throw off at a single blow [his own] . . . oppressive compulsion" to write prodigious numbers of books and articles in his efforts to attain for himself and psychoanalysis the stature they deserve. And, like the inevitable end of the expanding bubble of mania, the driving force of the succession of images seems to collapse into the sentences that immediately follow:

This explanation [of mania by analogy to other forms of sudden release from pain] certainly sounds plausible, but in the first place it is too indefinite, and, secondly, it gives rise to more new problems and doubts than we can answer. We will not evade a discussion of them, even though we cannot expect it to lead us to a clear understanding. [p. 255]

Freud—whether or not he was aware of it—is doing more than alerting the reader to his uncertainties regarding how to understand mania and its relation to melancholia: he is showing the reader, in his use of language, in the structure of his thinking and writing, what it sounds like and feels like to think and write in a way that does not attempt to confuse what is omnipotently, self-deceptively wished for with what is real; words are used in an effort to simply, accurately, clearly give ideas and situations their proper names.

Bion's work provides a useful context for understanding more fully the significance of Freud's comment that he will not "evade" the new problems and doubts to which his hypothesis gives rise. Bion (1962a) uses the idea of evasion to refer to what he believes to be a hallmark of psychosis: eluding pain rather than attempting to symbolize it for oneself (for example, in dreaming), live with it and do genuine psychological work with it over time. The latter response to pain—living with it, symbolizing it for oneself, and doing psychological work with it—lies at the heart of the experience of mourning. In contrast, the manic patient who "master[s] the [pain of loss] . . . or push[es] it aside" (Freud, 1917e [1915], p. 254) transforms what might become a feeling of a terrible disappointment, aloneness and impotent rage into a state resembling "joy, exultation or triumph" (p. 254).

I believe that Freud here, without explicit acknowledgement—and perhaps without conscious awareness—begins to address the psychotic edge of mania and melancholia. The psychotic aspect of both mania and melancholia involve the evasion of grief as well as a good deal of external reality. This is effected by means of multiple splittings of the ego in conjunction with the creation of a timeless imaginary internal object relationship that omnipotently substitutes for the loss of a real external object relationship. More broadly speaking, a fantasied unconscious internal object world replaces an actual external one; omnipotence replaces helplessness; immortality substitutes for the uncompromising realities of the passage of time and of death; triumph replaces despair; contempt substitutes for love.

Thus Freud (in part explicitly, in part implicitly, and perhaps in part unknowingly) through his discussion of mania adds another important element to his evolving object relations theory. The reader can hear in Freud's use of language (for example, in his comments on the manic patient's triumphantly pushing aside the pain of loss and exulting in his imaginary victory over the lost object) the idea that the unconscious internal object world of the manic patient is constructed for the purpose of evading, "taking flight" (p. 257) from, the external reality of loss and death. This act of taking flight from external reality has the effect of plunging the patient into a sphere of omnipotent thinking cut off from life lived in relation to actual external objects. The world of external object relations becomes depleted as a consequence of its having been disconnected from the individual's unconscious internal object world. The patient's experience in the world of external objects is disconnected from the enlivening "fire" (Loewald, 1978, p. 189) of the unconscious internal object world. Conversely, the unconscious internal object world, having been cut off from the world of external objects, cannot grow, cannot "learn from experience" (Bion, 1962a), and cannot enter (in more than a very limited way) into generative "conversations" between unconscious and preconscious aspects of oneself "at the frontier of dreaming" (Ogden, 2001a).

V

Freud concludes the paper with a series of thoughts on a wide range of topics related to mourning and melancholia. Of these, Freud's expansion of the concept of ambivalence is, I believe, the one that represents the most important contribution both to the understanding of melancholia and to the development of his object relations theory. Freud had discussed on many previous occasions, beginning as early as 1900, a view of ambivalence as an unconscious conflict of love and hate in which the individual unconsciously loves the same person he hates—for example, in the distressing ambivalence of healthy oedipal experience or in the paralysing torments of the ambivalence of the obsessional neurotic. In "Mourning and

Melancholia" Freud uses the term "ambivalence" in a strikingly different way: he uses it to refer to a struggle between the wish to live
with the living and the wish to be at one with the dead:

> . . . hate and love contend with each other [in melancholia]; the
> one seeks to detach the libido from the object [thus allowing the
> subject to live and the object to die], the other to maintain this
> position of the libido [which is bonded to the immortal internal
> version of the object]. [p. 256]

Thus, the melancholic experiences a conflict between, on the one
hand, the wish to be alive with the pain of irreversible loss and the
reality of death and, on the other hand, the wish to deaden himself to the pain of loss and the knowledge of death. The individual
capable of mourning succeeds in freeing himself from the struggle
between life and death that freezes the melancholic: "mourning
impels the ego to give up the object by declaring the object to be
dead and offering the ego the inducement of continuing to live . . ."
(p. 257). So the mourner's painful acceptance of the reality of the
death of the object is achieved in part because the mourner knows
(unconsciously and at times consciously) that his own life, his own
capacity for "continuing to live", is at stake.

I am reminded of a patient who began analysis with me almost
twenty years after the death of her husband. Ms G told me that, not
long after her husband's death, she had spent a weekend alone at a
lake where, for each of the fifteen years before his death, she and her
husband had rented a cabin. She told me that during a trip to the
lake soon after his death, she had set out alone in a motorboat and
headed towards a labyrinth of small islands and tortuous waterways
that she and her husband had explored many times. Ms G said that
the idea had come to her with a sense of absolute certainty that her
husband was in that set of waterways and that, if she were to have
entered that part of the lake, she would never have come out because
she would not have been able to "tear" herself away from him. She
told me that she had had to fight with all her might not to go to be
with her husband.

That decision not to follow her husband into death became an
important symbol in the analysis of the patient's choosing to live her
life in a world filled with the pain of grief and her living memories of
her husband. As the analysis proceeded, that same event at the lake
came to symbolize something quite different: the incompleteness of

her act of "tearing" herself away from her husband after his death. It became increasingly clear in the transference–countertransference that, in an important sense, a part of herself had gone with her husband into death—that is, an aspect of herself had been deadened and that that had been "all right" with her until that juncture in the analysis.

In the course of the subsequent year of analysis, Ms G experienced a sense of enormous loss—not only the loss of her husband, but also the loss of her own life. She confronted for the first time the pain and sadness of the recognition of the ways she had for decades unconsciously limited herself with regard to utilizing her intelligence and artistic talents as well as her capacities to be fully alive in her everyday experience (including her analysis). (I do not view Ms G as manic, or even as relying heavily on manic defences, but I believe that she holds in common with the manic patient a form of ambivalence that involves a tension between, on the one hand the wish to live life among the living—internally and externally—and, on the other hand, the wish to exist with the dead in a timeless dead and deadening internal object world.)

Returning to Freud's discussion of mania, the manic patient is engaged in a "struggle of ambivalence [in a desperate unconscious effort to come to life through] loosen[ing] the fixation of the libido to the [internal] object by disparaging it, denigrating it and even as it were killing it" (p. 257).[9] This sentence is surprising: mania represents not only the patient's effort to evade the pain of grief by disparaging and denigrating the object: it also represents the patient's (often unsuccessful) attempts *to achieve grief* by freeing himself from the mutual captivity involved in the unconscious internal relationship with the lost object. In order to grieve for the loss of the object, one must first kill it—that is, one must do the psychological work of allowing the object to be irrevocably dead, both in one's own mind and in the external world.

By introducing the notion of a form of ambivalence involving the struggle between the wish to go on living and the wish to deaden oneself in an effort to be with the dead, Freud added a critical dimension to his object relations theory: the notion that unconscious internal object relations may have either a living and enlivening quality or a dead and deadening quality (and, by extension, every possible combination of the two). Such a way of conceiving the internal object world has been central to recent developments in psychoanalytic theory pioneered by Winnicott (1971) and Green (1983a). These authors have placed emphasis on the importance of the analyst's and the patient's experiences of the aliveness and deadness of the patient's internal object world. The sense of alive- ness and deadness of the transference–countertransference is, to my mind, perhaps the single most important measure of the status of the analytic process on a moment-to-moment basis (Ogden, 1995, 1997). The sound of much of current analytic thinking—and, I suspect, the sound of psychoanalytic thinking yet to come—can be heard in Freud's "Mourning and Melancholia", if we know how to listen.

Freud closes the paper with a voice of genuine humility, breaking off his enquiry mid-thought:

> But here once again, it will be well to call a halt and to postpone any further explanation of mania. . . . As we already know, the in- terdependence of the complicated problems of the mind forces us to break off every enquiry before it is completed—till the out- come of some other enquiry can come to its assistance. [p. 259]

How better to end a paper on the pain of facing reality and the consequences of attempts to evade it? The solipsistic world of a psy- choanalytic theorist who is not firmly grounded in the reality of his lived experience with patients is very similar to the self-imprisoned melancholic who survives in a timeless, deathless (and yet deadened and deadening) internal object world.

NOTES

1. I use the term object relations theory to refer to a group of psycho- analytic theories holding in common a loosely knit set of metaphors that address the intrapsychic and interpersonal effects of relationships among unconscious "internal" objects (i.e. among unconscious split-off parts of the personality). This group of theories coexists in Freudian psychoana- lytic theory as a whole with many other overlapping, complementary often contradictory lines of thought (each utilizing somewhat different sets of metaphors).
2. I have previously discussed (Ogden, 2001b) the interdependence of the vitality of the ideas and the life of the writing in a very different, but no less significant, psychoanalytic contribution: Winnicott's "Primitive Emo- tional Development" (1945).

3. I am using Strachey's 1957 translation of "Mourning and Melancholia" in the *Standard Edition* as the text for my discussion. It is beyond the scope of this paper to address questions relating to the quality of that translation.

4. Less than a year before writing "Mourning and Melancholia", Freud remarked that no one need wonder about his role in the history of psycho-analysis: "Psycho-analysis is my creation; for ten years I was the only person who concerned himself with it" (1914d, p. 7).

5. Freud's term *melancholia* is roughly synonymous with *depression* as the latter term is currently used.

6. Freud comments that "it never occurs to us to regard . . . [mourning] as a pathological condition and to refer it to medical treatment. . . . We rely on its being overcome after a certain lapse of time, and we look upon any interference with it as useless or even harmful" (pp. 243–244). This observation is offered as a statement of the self-evident and may have been so in Vienna in 1915. But, to my mind, that understanding today is paid lip service far more often than it is genuinely honoured.

7. While Freud made use of the idea of "an internal world" in "Mourning and Melancholia", it was Klein (1935, 1940, 1952b) who transformed the idea into a systematic theory of the structure of the unconscious and of the interplay between the internal object world and the world of external objects. In developing her conception of the unconscious, Klein richly contributed to a critical alteration of analytic theory. She shifted the dominant metaphors from those associated with Freud's topographic and structural models to a set of spatial metaphors (some stated, some only suggested in "Mourning and Melancholia"). These spatial metaphors depict an unconscious inner world inhabited by "internal objects"—split-off aspects of the ego—that are bound together in "internal object relationships" by powerful affective ties. (For a discussion of the concepts of "internal objects" and "internal object relations" as these ideas evolved in the work of Freud, Abraham, Klein, Fairbairn, and Winnicott, see Ogden, 1983.)

8. At the same time as the infant is engaged in the movement from narcissistic identification to narcissistic object-tie, he is simultaneously engaged in the development of a "type . . . of object-choice [driven by object-libido], which may be called the 'analytic' or 'attachment type'" (Freud, 1914c, p. 87). The latter form of object relatedness has its "source" (p. 87) in the infant's "original attachment . . . [to] the persons who are concerned with a child's feeding, care, and protection . . ." (p. 87). In health, the two forms of object relatedness—narcissistic and attachment-type—develop "side by side" (p. 87). Under less than optimal environmental or biological circumstances, the infant may develop psychopathology characterized by an almost exclusive reliance on narcissistic object relatedness (as opposed to relatedness of an attachment sort).

9. The reader can hear the voice of Melanie Klein (1935, 1940) in this part of Freud's comments on mania. All three elements of Klein's (1935) well-known clinical triad characterizing mania and the manic defence—control, contempt, and triumph—can be found in nascent form in Freud's

conception of mania. The object never will be lost or missed because it is, in unconscious fantasy, under one's omnipotent control, so there is no danger of losing it; even if the object were to be lost, it would not matter because the contemptible object is "valueless" (p. 257) and one is better off without it; moreover, being without the object is a "triumph" (p. 254), an occasion for "enjoy[ing]" (p. 257) one's emancipation from the burdensome albatross that has been hanging from one's neck.

7

Mourning and mental development

Florence Guignard

In this chapter I attempt to redraw the contours of some basic psychoanalytic concepts concerning mental development as opposed to mere adaptation, particularly with regard to Western society as we know it today. From this point of view, the question of the object and its loss in the external world and/or in the internal (psychic) world seems to me to be a crucial one, as is that of symbolization, compared to the extraordinary development in modern times of virtual reality. I shall therefore discuss the disappearance—recent, but now widespread in Western society—of the latency period, and the impact this may have on repression and on the model of the neuroses as the prototype of how the human mind works.

Mourning:
an intersection for the mind

Mourning lies at the intersection of several domains that themselves link together various components of mental functioning. It is the outcome of "relationships of relationships", which, in an earlier paper, I have called a "concept of the third kind" (Guignard, 2001):

▷ relationships between the pleasure/unpleasure principle and the reality principle (Freud, 1911b);

▷ relationships between certain drives:

—sexual drives and self-preservative ones, to use the terms employed by Freud in his topographic model and first theory of the instincts (1915c);

—object drives and ego drives in the movement that led Freud from his topographic to his structural model of the mind and second theory of the instincts;

—life and death drives, in Freud's structural model and second theory of the instincts (1923b);

▷ relationships between objects the loss of which has to be processed by the mental apparatus:

—external and internal objects (Klein, 1921);
—part-objects and whole objects (Klein, 1921);

▷ relationships between:

—thing-presentations and word-presentations, to use Freud's terms;

—ego, object, and symbol, in Kleinian terminology (Klein, 1930);

—beta-elements and their transformation into alpha-elements by means of the alpha-function, as Bion (1962b) put it;

▷ identification—and, more specifically, modes of identification with lost objects (on this important issue see, for example, Freud, 1914c; Klein, 1955).

The pleasure/unpleasure principle
and the reality principle

In "Mourning and Melancholia", Freud attempted to follow the economic perspective of his topographic model, with the emphasis on the functional role of the external object, in the service of the pleasure/unpleasure principle. As such, however, the pleasure/unpleasure principle contradicts the whole idea of mental growth. Indeed, it was the tendency to repeat linked to the pleasure principle that led Freud to take things further in *Beyond the Pleasure Principle* (1920g). That said, the introduction of the death drive does not in itself solve the mystery of what makes a mourning process "successful"—nor does the representation we may have of the latter's role in mental development.

If we follow Freud's reasoning in "Formulations on the Two Principles of Mental Functioning", the term "development" is linked only to "education", while the aim of the reality-ego—in contrast to the pleasure-ego—has to do with how the individual adjusts to reality. Freud writes: "A general tendency of our mental apparatus, which can be traced back to the economic principle of saving expenditure [of energy], seems to find expression in the tenacity with which we hold on to the sources of pleasure at our disposal, and in the difficulty with which we renounce them. With the introduction of the reality principle one species of thought-activity was split off; it was kept free from reality-testing and remained subordinated to the pleasure principle alone. This activity is *phantasying*, which begins already in children's play, and later, continued as day-dreaming, abandons dependence on real objects . . ." (Freud, 1911b, p. 222).

As in *The Interpretation of Dreams* (Freud, 1900a), internal mental life is conceived of exclusively in terms of phantasying, functioning under the sole aegis of the pleasure principle, with a solution of continuity between the "real" object and its trace in unconscious functioning.

Freud goes on to invoke a form of causality that owes more to phenomenology than to metapsychology: "These two factors—auto-erotism and the latency period—have as their result that the sexual instinct is held up in its psychical development and remains far longer under the dominance of the pleasure principle, from which in many people it is never able to withdraw" (1911b, p. 222). That is an important development, because it underpins Freud's whole conception of the neuroses and of deferred action: "An essential part of the psychical disposition to neurosis thus lies in the delay in educating the sexual instincts to pay regard to reality and, as a corollary, in the conditions which make this delay possible" (p. 223).

It is true, of course, that the development of Freud's thinking took him from these views he expressed in 1911 first to "On Narcissism: An Introduction" (1914c) and to his papers on metapsychology (1917d [1915]), and then, beyond these, to the upheaval that was his structural model of the mind and his second theory of the drives. I must, all the same, emphasize the fact that Freud stood by this view in all of his writings, making that delay the very condition of neurotic organizations.

It has to be said that this whole metapsychological construction includes basic assumptions that must nowadays be called into question, given the changes that modern society imposes on us. The value system of the Western world has changed significantly: mental growth comes far behind criteria of efficiency and adjustment to an environment that has undergone considerable change in recent years. The reality principle is just as difficult to accept today as it was in Freud's time, but what is substituted for it no longer stops at individual phantasying, even when this is relayed through works of art, literature, theatre, or even the cinema.

The extraordinary growth of techniques of immediate exchange of information—and disinformation—about what is happening, perhaps not the whole world over, but certainly in the greater part of it, means that individuals have to deal with new demands on their drive economy and, as a result, with new forms of anxiety. The sheer rapidity of technological advance and means of communication—the Internet is a notable example—puts people more easily in contact with each other, whatever the geographical distance that separates them, outside their everyday environment. In the field of human relationships, however, this instrument reduces only very slightly—and even then in an illusory manner—the isolation that so many people experience nowadays, whatever the generation to which they belong. This expansion in modes of communication only rarely leads to a true encounter. The main reason for this lies in its virtual quality. Virtual reality has made for incomparable advances in science and technology; on a human level it can, of course, get the imagination going, but the gap between, on the one hand, a photograph, a film, or words and, on the other, the reality of an encounter between two human beings remains as wide as ever. The immediate nature of virtual contact only rarely involves the expression of a certain depth of emotion and therefore of thinking.

Virtual reality has a completely different relationship to the pleasure/unpleasure principle and to the reality principle from that of fantasy. Confusing fantasy and reality requires an extremely intense—not to say pathological—projective organization, whereas virtual reality offers an illusion of what is real, thus circumventing the need for mentally processing the links and transformations on which is based a positive relationship between the inner mental world and external reality.

Thus the reality of loss can be avoided by means of some interaction or other at the virtual level—I am thinking in particular here of the so-called "interactive" games in which human life, reduced to a mere virtuality, has no deeper meaning than that of an obstacle to be shot down in order to win the game. Quite clearly, then, it is the reality principle that is demolished in this manner, and it is on children that the impact of virtual reality will be at its most violent, given their psychological immaturity.

The relationship between drives

Drive economy implies a continued reworking of the equilibrium between sexual drives and self-preservative drives—in other words, between sexual drives and ego-drives. That equilibrium in turn depends upon a proper interconnection between life and death drives (Guignard, 1997). Both of these states of equilibrium depend on the individual's capacity to accept a certain degree of loss as far as his or her drive satisfaction is concerned. It is for this reason that the drives have to do with the problem-complex surrounding mourning processes.

I would like to place my hypotheses on this issue under the aegis of the fundamental comments made by Strachey in his Editor's Note to "Instincts and Their Vicissitudes" (Strachey, 1957b, 111–116).

Strachey notes that the word "instinct" is hardly to be found in Freud's work until the *Three Essays* (1905d). The place of the instincts, he writes, "was taken to a great extent by such things as 'excitations', 'affective ideas', 'wishful impulses', 'endogenous stimuli', and so on." It is important to note that the distinction made here by Freud between a "stimulus", which operates as a force giving a single impact, and an "instinct", which always operates as a constant one, is almost identical to the one he had made twenty years earlier between "exogenous" and "endogenous excitations" (1895b). In the *Project* (1950 [1895]) Freud adds that these endogenous stimuli "have their origin in the cells of the body and give rise to the major needs: hunger, respiration and sexuality", but nowhere here is the actual word 'instinct' to be found.

Strachey points out that, at this early period, the underlying conflict in psychoneuroses was described as being between "the ego" and "sexuality". The word "libido" was used as a manifestation of "somatic sexual tension"—a "chemical event". Strachey writes: "Only in the *Three Essays* was libido explicitly established as an expression of the sexual instinct." As for "the ego", Strachey notes that it remained undefined for a very long time in Freud's writings, mainly discussed in connection with its functions, but not so much with its structure or dynamics. The "self-preservative" instincts were only referred to indirectly as those to which the libido attached itself in the early phases of its development, not in connection with the part played by the ego as the repressive agent in neurotic conflicts.

Strachey writes:

> Then, with apparent suddenness, in a short paper on psychogenic disturbance of vision (1910i), Freud introduced the term "ego-instincts" and identified these on the one hand with the self-preservative instincts and on the other with the repressive function. From this time forward the conflict was regularly represented as being between two sets of instincts—the libido and the ego-instincts.

Strachey notes how the introduction of the concept of "narcissism" raised a complication:

> In his paper on that theory (1914c), Freud advanced the notion of "ego-libido" (or "narcissistic libido") which cathects the ego, as contrasted with "object-libido" which cathects objects (p. 76 . . .). A passage in that paper (loc. cit.) as well as a remark in the present one (p. 124) show that he was already feeling uneasy as to whether his "dualistic" classification of the instincts would hold. It is true that in the Schreber analysis (1911c) he insisted on the difference between "ego-cathexes" and "libido" and between "interest emanating from erotic sources" and "interest in general"—a distinction which re-appears in the rejoinder to Jung in the paper on narcissism (p. 80–1 . . .). The term "interest" is used again in the present paper (p. 135); and in Lecture XXVI of the *Introductory Lectures* (1916–17) "ego-interest" or simply "interest" is regularly contrasted with "libido". Nevertheless, the exact nature of these non-libidinal instincts was obscure.

Strachey goes on:

> The turning-point in Freud's classification of the instincts was reached in *Beyond the Pleasure Principle* (1920g). In Chapter VI of that work he frankly recognized the difficulty of the position that had been reached, and explicitly declared that "narcissistic

libido was of course a manifestation of the force of the sexual instinct" and that "it had to be identified with the 'self-preservative
instincts'" (*S.E.*, *18*, 50 ff.). He still held, however, that there were
ego-instincts and object-instincts other than libidinal ones; and it
was here that, still adhering to a dualistic view, he introduced his
hypothesis of the death-instinct.

An account of the development of his views on the classifica-
tion of the instincts up to that point was given in the long footnote at the end of Chapter VI of *Beyond the Pleasure Principle*, and
a further discussion of the subject, in the light of his newly completed picture of the structure of the mind, occupied Chapter
IV of *The Ego and the Id* (1923b). He traversed the whole ground
once again in much detail in Chapter VI of *Civilization and its
Discontents* (1930a), and he there for the first time gave especial
consideration to the aggressive and destructive instincts. He had
earlier paid little attention to these except where (as in sadism
and masochism) they were fused with libidinal elements; but he
now discussed them in their pure form and explained them as
derivatives of the death-instinct. A still later review of the subject
will be found in the second half of Lecture XXXII of the *New
Introductory Lectures* (1933a) and a final summary in Chapter II of
the posthumous *Outline of Psycho-Analysis.* [1940a (1938)]

It was Melanie Klein who expanded psychoanalytic thinking on the
fundamental importance, for normal mental growth, of the mixing together of the drives in "primary sadism" (Klein, 1927). She
described the patience that the analyst must have in order to help
the child patient to progress beyond play scenarios dominated by
the almost tireless repetition of oral-sadistic and anal-sadistic situations which, from the end of the first year of life, "interlink with
Oedipal tendencies and are therefore aimed at objects around which
the Oedipus complex develops, i.e. the parents" (Klein, 1927). She
recommends that the child's sadistic fantasies be taken in, without
in any way being judgemental, in order to analyse them; Klein emphasizes the importance for later development of the relationship
between these fantasies and the child's sexuality. She argues that "the
principal factor in criminality is not the absence of a superego, but
a different development of the superego—probably its fixation at a
very early phase" (1927).

It is on children that the nowadays unavoidable "virtual reality"
will make its impact felt most brutally. There may be no adult figure
to help the child through these experiences of sadistic games by

taking on board the child's unconscious guilt feelings—yet we cannot expect young children to deal with these by themselves. Given their emotional and intellectual immaturity, they already have difficulty—an inherent feature of development—in establishing a capacity for symbolization. As we know, that capacity requires a tripartite relationship: the ego, the symbol, and the object symbolized (Klein, 1930; Segal, 1957).

According to Klein (1930),

> if the child is too terrified by his own sadism, if he defends himself against it in an exaggerated and premature manner, the infant's Ego will not be able to develop a harmonious fantasy life nor will he be able to establish an appropriate relationship to reality. Under conditions such as these, he will not be able to possess, in fantasy, the contents of the mother's body without being attacked, in return, by a threatening metamorphosis of the maternal body, now that it has become dangerous as a result of being taken over by his own sadistic drives. Consequently, exploration of the outside world—which is always experienced an extension of the mother's body—will be inhibited.

This situation, Klein goes on to say,

> causes the more or less complete suspension of the symbolic relation to the things and objects representing the contents of the mother's body and, hence, of the relation to the subject's environment and to reality. This withdrawal becomes the basis of the lack of affect and anxiety, which is one of the symptoms of dementia praecox. [Klein, 1930, p. 39].

Every child is influenced by preceding generations, above all by that of his or her parents. There has been a serious drift in the infantile dimension (Guignard, 1996) of the present generation of adults who, theoretically responsible for taking care of and educating the upcoming generation, in reality use their children for projecting and satisfying their own infantile hedonism. The priority that present-day adults give to the immediate satisfaction of their own infantile desires—utilizing the younger generation to do this—results in serious failures in an essential feature of all mental development: the necessary delay between the formulation of a wish and its satisfaction.

Relationships between objects involved in the mourning process

In discussing the issues raised by the mourning process, Freud obviously could not ignore the object, but he does treat it in a somewhat vague manner: its status as the aim-object of the drive hardly leaves it with any constancy inside the mind once it disappears from the external world. The dialectic relationship between ego and object implies that the ego is already established, so that the lost object no longer has any part to play in its construction; it also regards the object that is cathected as being exclusively external.

In his attempt to shore up his positivist *Weltanschauung* by invoking the reality principle, Freud tried to describe the work of mourning as aiming to remove one by one all the cathexes from the lost object in order to displace them onto another object, able to satisfy the pleasure principle. It is tempting to think that this process thus has no developmental power, since the reality principle acts in this case only to make the ego acknowledge that it will have to look for a new object of satisfaction in a new reality.

However, the very idea of narcissism, which Freud had studied the year before writing "Mourning and Melancholia", makes for an unsteady equilibrium—marked as it was by the basic assumptions of the scientific theories of the time—because of the components that identify with the lost object. Freud therefore argued that these components should be thought of as equivalent to a primary agency: the ideal ego. This meant, too, that the ego and superego would have to be looked at from an identificatory angle—a process that Freud would go on to develop in his structural model of the mind. As Strachey points out in his Editor's Note to "Mourning and Melancholia", that paper and the one on narcissism describe, under the name "critical agency", how the concept of the superego took shape in what was to be the cornerstone of Freud's structural model: *The Ego and the Id* (1923b). Strachey goes on to point out that, for Freud, the most significant feature of "Mourning and Melancholia" is his discussion of how an object cathexis is replaced in melancholia by narcissistic identification. As is well known, Freud turned his attention several times to the topic of identification, without managing to construct a unified theory of the process.

Although the text gives a remarkable description of that pathology of mourning we call melancholia, Freud himself says that he is not particularly satisfied by what he understands of normal mourning processes. In his discussion of the intensity of the pain felt by someone in mourning, he writes: "We shall probably see the justification for this when we are in a position to give a characterization of the economics of pain" (Freud, 1917e [1915], p. 244). Freud therefore considers the survival of the lost object only with respect to pathology—melancholia—and in the form of a hallucination, which he likens to a psychosis. He does, of course, mention hallucination in dreams, but even there equates it with psychotic functioning. In his description of the melancholic, Freud says that such patients are particularly perceptive with respect to their self-image:

> When, in his heightened self-criticism, he describes himself as petty, egoistic, dishonest, lacking in independence, one whose sole aim has been to hide the weaknesses of his own nature, it may be, so far as we know, that he has come pretty near to understanding himself; *we only wonder why a man has to be ill before he can be accessible to a truth of this kind.* [p. 246; italics added]

It was Melanie Klein who investigated the introjection of cathected external objects and explored what became of them in fantasy once they become internal objects. This introjection is obviously very closely linked to the idea of loss of the object and mourning for it. In the two key papers in which she discusses these topics (Klein, 1935, 1940), Klein refers to two concepts she had discovered in her earlier work—part-object and whole object—and adds a new one: that of the depressive position.

In her 1940 paper, Klein quotes some of the essential ideas Freud had put forward in "Mourning and Melancholia".

> We found . . . that in mourning time is needed for the command of reality-testing to be carried out in detail, and that when this work has been accomplished the ego will have succeeded in freeing its libido from the lost object. [Freud, 1917e [1915], p. 252]

Freud continues:

> Each single one of the memories and expectations in which the libido is bound to the object is brought up and hyper-cathected, and detachment of the libido is accomplished in respect of it. Why this compromise by which the command of reality is carried out piecemeal should be so extraordinarily painful is not at all easy to explain in terms of economics. It is remarkable that this painful unpleasure is taken as a matter of course by us. [p. 245]

He then goes on to say:

> ... We do not even know the economic means by which mourn-
> ing carries out its task. Possibly, however, a conjecture will help us
> here. Each single one of the memories and situations of expect-
> ancy which demonstrate the libido's attachment to the lost object
> is met by the verdict of reality that the object no longer exists;
> and the ego, confronted as it were with the question whether it
> shall share this fate, is persuaded by the sum of the narcissistic
> satisfactions it derives from being alive to sever its attachment to
> the object that has been abolished. We may perhaps suppose that
> this work of severance is so slow and gradual that by the time it
> has been finished the expenditure of energy necessary for it is
> also dissipated. [p. 255]

Klein writes:

> In my view there is a close connection between the testing of
> reality in normal mourning and early processes of the mind. My
> contention is that the child goes through states of mind compara-
> ble to the mourning of the adult, or rather, that this early mourn-
> ing is revived whenever grief is experienced in later life. The
> most important of the methods by which the child overcomes
> his states of mourning, is, in my view, the testing of reality; this
> process, however, as Freud stresses, is part of the work of mourn-
> ing. [Klein, 1940, p. 344]

As is clear from the above quotation, Klein immediately displaces
the issue, moving from the physical death of a person cathected as
an object to the psychological death of a quality of the object that is
no longer available for cathexis by the subject.

She describes the constant interaction between external and internal objects, saying:

> The fact that by being internalized, people, things, situations
> and happenings—the whole inner world which is being built
> up—become inaccessible to the child's accurate observation and
> judgement, and cannot be verified by the means of perception
> which are available in connection with the tangible and palpable
> object-world, has an important bearing on the phantastic nature
> of this inner world. [Klein, 1940, p. 346].

Klein emphasizes the importance of a sufficiently loving and secure environment to enable the infant to adjust his or her splitting (of ego and objects) to reality, and she describes two defensive

modalities aimed at overcoming the distress experienced in the depressive position: manic and obsessional defences.

> obsessional defences—including the compulsion to repeat—aim to isolate and deny the infant's helplessness and the loss of the object; they do this by means of omnipotence
> manic defences aim at the manic—and therefore illusory—reparation of both ego and objects.

Klein notes that "fluctuations between the depressive and the manic position are an essential part of normal development" (1940, p. 349), drawing our attention at the same time to the fact that, if they are too powerful, manic defences will hinder the reparation of the internal world and the creativity of the individual—whereas a successful mourning process often leads to creative and sublimated activity (painting, writing, etc.). She goes on to say: "Omnipotence, however, is so closely bound up in the unconscious with the sadistic impulses with which it was first associated that the child feels again and again that his attempts at reparation have not succeeded, or will not succeed" (Klein, 1940, p. 350).

Symbolization, identification, and virtual reality

In constructing his "theory of thinking", W. R. Bion (1962b) took as his basis "A Project for a Scientific Psychology" (Freud, 1950 [1895]), "Formulations on the Two Principles of Mental Functioning" (Freud, 1911b) and the developments by Melanie Klein (1930) and Hanna Segal (1957) in the field of symbol-formation. In his model, Bion deconstructed symbolic thinking in order to reveal its sensory elements—beta-elements—and examine their transformation into thought-components—alpha-elements—by means of the normal version of projective identification discovered by Klein in 1946; this is what Bion called alpha-function, the prototype of which is the mother's capacity for reverie. For Bion, then, the infant's earliest object relations have an oedipal structure such as we find in adult mental functioning.

As regards the issue of mourning, Bion brings together all the parameters involved in mental functioning into a dynamic and metaphorical basic entity, mother-and-infant: the pleasure/unpleasure principle (infant) and the reality principle (mother); cathexis of the real object (mother and infant) and its loss (infant); introjection of the lost object (infant); projective identification with the other's internal world (mother and infant).

If we are to examine the impact of virtual reality on ourselves, on our contemporaries in general and, above all, on present-day children and adolescents, the most effective psychoanalytic instrument we have at our disposal is probably that of Bion's theory of thinking. Virtual reality cannot be accounted for by Freud's idea of transforming thing-presentations into word-presentations; nor is symbol-formation as developed by Klein an appropriate instrument in that it demands a triangular relationship: the ego, the symbol, and the thing symbolized. If we were to consider virtual reality as a symbolic equation (Segal, 1957)—the closest we have to a proper description—we would have to say that, for those who use it, virtual reality is not virtual at all: it is quite simply a substitute for the real world. That would imply entry into a wholly schizophrenic and delusional universe. . . .

In spite of the dangerous excesses of virtual reality, it would be more sensible to see it as a new metamorphosis of thing-presentations, different from that of word-presentations (cf. the development Freud proposes in Appendix C to "The Unconscious" [Freud, 1915e]).

Mourning and identification:
what the future holds for Western society

What consequences will this inflation of virtual reality have on psychic economy, and on the future of drive economics, object relations, and symbolization in Western society?

Freud's papers on social issues (1912–13, 1915b, 1921c, 1927c, 1930a), like Bion's (1961), draw our attention to the fact that, in reflecting on this wide-ranging question, we have to keep in mind the group-aspect that exists in each of us. That element, which ranges from gregariousness to the ability to participate in a work-group and includes such phenomena as messianic tendencies, racism, and attacks on creativity, may amount to a real trivialization (Bion) of human drives, which, dislocated from one another, are expressed in a most inhuman and perverse manner. The globalization of virtual

communication cannot take place without increasing the risk of seeing basic assumption group mentality take precedence over thinking
for oneself.

Children nowadays in the Western world begin life in society at
a very early age: day nursery at three months, infant school at three
or even two years of age. Immersion in the fabric of family life is reduced to a minimum for two main reasons: first, children spend little
time at home and, second, the very structure of families is increasingly being transformed. In addition, children are having to split
their parental cathexes at a very early age, given the way in which
family life has evolved. Often nowadays the child's birth parents live
together for only a very short period; they separate, with each of
them restructuring his or her love life in what have come to be called
"reconstituted" families, either homo- or heterosexual—or, indeed,
the mother may, as is more and more often the case, bring up the
child on her own. The paternal third-party role, which is essential
if the infant is to break free of symbiosis (Bleger, 1990) and set up
a proper oedipal configuration, nowadays adopts some very vague
and variable forms in which the social group and its basic assumption mentality are substituted for the contribution that the original
parental couple could have made.

When they subject their children to such drastic—and often repeated—changes in their life, parents cannot avoid having strong
guilt feelings, although these may be more or less conscious. They
often try to offset these feelings by offering their children a great
deal in the way of material goods, in the hope of easing the emotional deprivation they are inflicting on their offspring. More than
ever before, children are able to obtain immediate satisfaction of
whatever they may want from a material point of view—and they
learn quickly to express that kind of wish rather than their need to
be listened to and contained. They soon learn to take advantage of
the splitting that has been forced upon them and shamelessly play
one side of their divided birth family off against the other.

I would suggest at this point that the endemic growth in com-
munications technology over the past twenty or so years has brought
about tremendous changes in the model of mental functioning that
the environment proposes to children. This is a second-generation
phenomenon, and it is beginning to have long-term effects: psychoanalysts who are asked to treat children are becoming increasingly
aware of this issue.

Freud's models—Oedipus complex, castration complex, infantile neurosis as the prototype of transference neurosis—were based
on his discovery that infantile sexuality developed in two phases
separated by what he called the latency period. During this period,
children's drive-related interests move away from the quest for direct
satisfaction and turn towards the world of learning. Acknowledging
the difference between the sexes and between generations represents a landmark in the growing organization of the child's mind
and results from the construction of an ideal superego via identification with the parental couple and with representatives of previous
generations. Acknowledging these differences also implies that this
identification with the parents guarantees the future supremacy of
the reality principle over the pleasure/unpleasure principle. From
this perspective, puberty occurs in a domain that is already "culti-
vated"—in every sense of the word—thereby establishing limits to
the deferred effect of the adolescent's identity crisis.

However, contemporary society in Western countries makes that
description all but obsolete. In my day-to-day work I deal not only with
children and adolescents but also with their carers—adult patients,
parents, child psychotherapists—and I would say without hesitation
that the psychological development of children in our society has
changed more in the past ten years than it ever did in the thirty-year
"boom" period that preceded it. I have discovered that there is a—to
me unexpected—consensus of opinion shared by all practitioners of
child and adolescent psychoanalysis whom I have questioned over
the past two years in several European cities: they are unanimous in
saying that the latency period as defined by Freud in 1905 is fast disappearing in contemporary society (1905d). There is no longer any
"cooling down" of drive-related manifestations in children between
six and twelve years of age; instead of deflecting their sexual drives
towards sublimated activities, they are just as excitable as three- to
five-year-olds in their "Oedipal" phase—and at the same time they
imitate at every possible opportunity the attitudes and sexual behaviour of pubertal youngsters, adolescents, and young adults.

The epistemophilic drives are no longer structured essentially
around a primal-scene fantasy that turns the child's curiosity and
wish to understand in the direction of the knowledge that—in fantasy or in reality—the parental couple is deemed to possess, as the
ultimate vehicle of the history of human thought. Siphoned off by
the extraordinary development of virtual reality as an offshoot of

artificial intelligence, these drives are mainly attracted to a binary-logic system rather than oriented in the direction of development with the establishment of a capacity for symbol-formation.

Binary logic, however, leads directly to the enactment of whatever solution is adopted. The individual is thus drawn back to the primary level of the pleasure/unpleasure principle as Freud described it: "'I should like to eat this', or 'I should like to spit it out'" (Freud, 1925h, p. 237).

This split, which bypasses anxiety concerning what is unfamiliar and anxiety over death, can have several consequences, among which are:

> De-cathecting the enigma of the Sphinx—linear time and the finite nature of human life—and replacing it with hyper-cathexis of immediate action experienced as timeless.

> Increased denial of the reality principle with, at its apex, denial of the reality of one's own death.

> Myths about transformation and rebirth tend to give more importance to the technological aspect of change, to the detriment of developing mental capacities.

This new defensive equilibrium that incorporates the virtual dimension is, of course, not particularly effective. Children who run away from reality and take refuge in "Game-Boy" adventures or combat are soon back in touch with their anxiety once "game over" is announced.

De-cathexis of inner mental life goes hand-in-hand with a pathology of repression and, consequently, with the disorganization of the two-stage development described by Freud in his model of infantile neurosis. What he called the deferred reaction is not built up in the same way, because infantile modes of sexuality remain active from the normal oedipal age until puberty. There is, in particular, an unrestrained arousing of infantile genitality characterized by imitation of adult sexuality: this is a direct expression of the denial of the difference between generations. In a sense, children no longer have any childhood; what appears as hyper-maturity is in fact nothing but pseudo-maturity.

These oedipal elements do not in themselves constitute an Oedipus complex, just as those aspects that have to do with castration are

not organized into a proper castration complex. As a result no intimate relationship—the cornerstone of a mental organization that
could truly be called genital—can be set up in later adolescence or
at the beginning of adult sexual life. It is replaced by the continuation of phallic and group values—always in pursuit of some exploit
or other, in a voyeuristic/exhibitionistic mind-set.

Conclusion

In the world in which children and adolescents live today, virtual
reality is expressed more easily than is true fantasy; a binary system
of meaning replaces tripartite symbol-formation. The binary-logic
universe of virtual reality is such a powerful attractor for our young
patients that they no longer need to accomplish the mental work
of symbol-formation linked to the interiorization of the object and,
ultimately, to processing the work of mourning for that object.

It is up to contemporary psychoanalysts—and to those who come
after us—to learn how to listen long enough to what is going on in
the virtual reality scenario that their patients communicate, in order
for the "inanimate objects" of which that scenario is composed to
acquire a "soul" (In Lamartine's 1826 poem, *Milly*: "*Objets inanimés,
avez-vous donc une âme Qui s'attache à notre âme et la force d'aimer?*"
[Inanimate objects, have you then a soul / That attaches itself to
our own and forces it to love?]). It is only on that condition that the
words of the "talking cure" will regain their status as representatives
of the emotions rather than remaining mere evacuations that have
recourse to enactment.

8

"Mourning and Melancholia": a Freudian metapsychological updating

Carlos Mario Aslan

> And I hope that you will soon find consolation from my death
> and that you will allow me to continue living in your friendly
> thoughts—the only limited immortality that I acknowledge.
>
> Freud's letter to Marie Bonaparte, 1937 (in Jones, 1957, p. 465)

"Mourning and Melancholia", *fons et origo*, fount and origin of any psychoanalytic reflection on depression, is a relatively short but very important paper, considered by many authors as a hinge—an articulation—between the first, "topographic" theory of the mind, and the second, "structural" theory.

Besides opening the way to a psychoanalytic, metapsychological conception of both normal and pathological mourning—melancholia—this paper introduces, among other important ideas, an advancement of the concept of the "critical instance" (the future superego) and of forms of structuring internalizations such as the introjection of objects and of secondary identifications.

Mourning is a phenomenon belonging to everyday life. We all have experienced it, together with its consequent mourning processes, through either our own or other people's losses

Object loss and mourning are painful and unpleasurable aspects of normal life, and perhaps because of this, its study and consideration have somehow been relatively neglected when compared to other psychic processes. It was Freud, in his paper "Mourning and Melancholia" (1917e [1915]), who with his usual courage opened the path for the understanding and description of its psychodynamics. But I must observe that, important and even fundamental though it is, this paper was not revised nor updated by Freud, as he did with other works—as for instance: *The Interpretation of Dreams* (1900a) or the Three Essays (1905d)—with regard to his subsequent and pertinent metapsychological concepts, such as the destructive or death drive, the structural theory, signal anxiety, and so on.

Some post-Freudian clarifications and additions must also be included so as to have a clearer and more complete picture of the metapsychological concepts that underlie the different observable clinical pictures that both normal and pathological mourning present to our clinical observation.

Some observations on "Mourning and Melancholia"

A.   It is important to have a clear differentiation between external objects and their psychic representation—or, as I would prefer, their corresponding internal objects.

I agree with Strachey (1957c, p. 240) that "Mourning and Melancholia" may "be regarded as an extension of the one on narcissism which Freud had written a year before". I will add the hypothesis that Freud's idea about the mechanism of the introjection of the (external) object in melancholia was based on the behaviour of the "narcissistic amoeba" (Freud, 1940a [1938], pp. 150–151) with respect to external foreign bodies—the extension of pseudopod, the engulfing of the foreign body, and the withdrawal of the pseudopod containing the foreign body to include it inside the amoeba—to explain the mechanism of *melancholia*, whereby the lost object (external) is internalized into the ego, together with the withdrawal of libido into it.

In Freud's impressive formulation: "The shadow of the object fell upon the ego."

In *normal mourning*, on the other hand, the loss of the object (external) would only cause the slow and painful withdrawal of the libido cathexis into the ego. (In Addendum C of "Inhibitions, Symptoms and Anxiety", 1926d [1925], Freud advanced the idea these libidinal cathexes—"longing cathexes"—accumulated in the ego, were the cause of psychic pain in mourning).

It is evident that in these formulations there are unclear ideas, a certain confusion, or at least a marked ambiguity between the concepts of external object and psychic (internal) representation of the external object. Which one receives the libidinal cathexis? From which one is the libido withdrawn in the mourning process and in the melancholic process? Strachey (1953, p. 217), in a note in another of Freud's papers (Freud, 1905d), clearly expressed *his own* opinion:

> . . . it is scarcely necessary that here, as in every other part, when speaking of libido concentrating in objects, withdrawing from objects, etc., Freud had in mind the mental representations— Vorstellungen—of objects, and not, of course objects of the external world.

Strachey says it is scarcely necessary, but he nevertheless finds it necessary, and when explicating *his own* interpretation of Freud's ideas, he is at the same time pointing to Freud's ambiguity. I would add that Strachey had, of course, read Freud's later writings. For instance, in the "Outline of Psychoanalysis" (1940a [1938]), Freud had written:

> . . . We call this state absolute, primary narcissism. It lasts until the ego begins to *cathect the ideas of object with libido,* to transform narcissistic libido into object-libido. [Italics added].

B. *Distinction between introjection and identification.* In 1909 Ferenczi introduced introjection as the process whereby aspects of the external world were "taken in" into the psyche. Freud often used this word, and employed it as a synonym to identification. I consider it useful to differentiate the two concepts. I would define *introjection* as the psychic process by which an external object and all its relations with the ego (the self) are internalized into the psyche, *keeping their identity and characteristics as object,* as subjectively perceived. It should be stressed that this is a rather complex and active psychical structure, and many analysts prefer referring to it as "*internal* object" (some also refer to it as "introject") instead of the more classic "object *representation*".

I am aware that these terms originate in different frames of reference; *object representation* stems from Freud (thing representation plus word representation form an object representation) and *internal object* stems from various object relations theories. I think that both terms refer to the same psychic structure, but that "internal object" reflects more accurately its "vivid", "active", character. Nevertheless I shall not distinguish between them in this paper.

In *identifications* the ego (the self) acquires, as an integral part of it, some or all of the characteristics of the *external* object (as in primary identifications) or part or all of the characteristics of the *internal* object (as in secondary identifications).

We, from our selves, from us as subjects, relate to our internal objects, we "talk" with them (Sandler, personal communication 1991), and we receive "their" comments, criticisms, or praise, depending, on whether they are functioning as ego, superego, or ego ideal, respectively.

To sum up: in a logical and chronological order, we would have, as structuring internalizations: primary identifications, introjections that create object representations/internal objects, and secondary identifications. These psychic structures are recognized by their functions and their way of functioning (perceiving stimuli and information, processing them, and responding to them), and they have a degree of permanence that fleeting or transitory internalizations (imitation, adolescent identifications with fictional heroes, partial identifications of the analyst with the patient such as in empathy, etc.) do not.

Since they are functional structures, as I have remarked, a given identification or internal object can function as ego, superego, or ideal, and are recognized by their way of functioning.

C. Freud described how in melancholia the object is "introduced" in the ego, and a dissociated or differentiated part of the ego criticizes the object, or the part of the ego that contained it (this is an example of Freud's lack of distinction between the—supposedly— internalized object and identification with it). The more ambivalent the previous relation with the object, the harsher the criticism, which takes the form of self-reproaches ("Klagen sind Anklagen": reproaches are accusations). But in 1924, one year after *The Ego and the Id* (1923b), Abraham (1924b) clearly demonstrated that the internalization of the object also occurred in the superego, with the logical consequence that the internalized object criticized the rest of the ego. The contemporary psychoanalytic concept of the dynamic psychic structure offers the less cumbersome idea that an internal object or identification can function as ego or as superego.

* * *

These clarifications serve as a preamble to one of the main theses of this paper: the differentiation between normal mourning and melancholia does not rest upon the supposed introjection of the lost object in melancholia, whereas this would not happen in normal mourning. In both cases the object was already present in the psyche, as an object representation (or internal object). So Freud's impressive phrase, "The shadow of the object fell upon the ego", should be understood nowadays as reflecting the process whereby in object loss the object representation (internal object) undergoes a process in which parts—or all—of it turn into an identification. In this process, the internal object loses (totally or partially) his character of object within the ego, and functions as part of the ego (or as part of the superego). This process is known as secondary identification. It is secondary to primary identification, and also secondary to a previous object relation.

Mourning:
definitions and characteristics

Mourning is the sum of psychic events, a process produced as a consequence of the loss of an important and significant "*object*", for a given person.

▷ In this context, "object" means a person or an ideal; something concrete or an abstraction; a symbolic or an intrinsic value; a "something" meaningful and relevant. Since the list of objects that can be lost is infinite, we generally use, as a "*princeps*" example, the unexpected death of a beloved person. From this model all the different varieties and shapes of mourning can be deduced.

▷ By loss I mean its psychic reality, which could be related to a real, a symbolic, or a fantasized loss.

▷ The mourning process requires a given time span, which cannot be shortened. It can, however, be protracted, or it can be interrupted, because of diverse causes. The mourning time span oscillates within short limits, according to different authors and in relation to cultural considerations: Freud speaks of one to two years (in the "Rat Man" case—1909d) and Engel (1962) of six to eighteen months; Josef Karo (1557) establishes "twelve months and one day".

▷ The mourning process *is not voluntary: it is an automatic process*, such as Freud considered many psychic processes to be:

This may be because dealing with a conflict by forming symptoms is after all an *automatic process* which cannot prove adequate to meeting the demands of life and in which the subject has abandoned the use of his best and highest powers. If there was a choice, it would be preferable to go down in an honorable struggle with fate. [Freud, 1917e [1915]; italics added]

▷ In my opinion, this implies that many expressions, such as "the object is internalized to keep him alive", are *post-hoc* attributions of sense, secondary to the occurrence of the fact.

Mourning as disease

As the mourning process develops the subject in mourning presents transitory symptoms that could coincide with or resemble different clinical pictures. Freud remarked: ". . . truly, if his conduct [the subject in mourning's] does not seem pathological to us, it is because we can explain it very well".

In his paper "Is Grief a Disease?" Engel (1961) argues that there is a known etiological factor, a "normal" evolution, painful psychical symptoms, sometimes organic components, difficulties in the ability to function—for days, weeks, or months—an evolution relatively marked in time, possibility of complications, and, finally, a "healing" or "cicatrization" more or less accomplished.

Sense of mourning

The unconscious sense of mourning is not unique. As can be inferred from different psychoanalytic authors and can be observed by ourselves, we can differentiate in every mourning process two main senses, not mutually exclusive but varying in their proportions.

A. Mourning as the detachment from a love object with which acts of love can no longer be exchanged. It is along this line that Freud developed "Mourning and Melancholia". Pollock also considers it in this sense. Perhaps this is a more mature sense, closer to the reality principle, and it is the cause of sadness, longing, grief.

B   Mourning as a process to get rid of a persecutory, anti-hedonic, anti-erotic psychic structure. For instance, Lagache (1956) says: "The sense of the work of mourning . . . is the destruction of a moral authority that does not permit living" (my translation). And Engel (1962): "During all this period [the mourning process] the mourner imposes on himself a ban against pleasure and enjoyment." That is to say, two contemporary analysts, one coming from the French school and the other from the American, concur in giving this sense to mourning.

Freud had already anticipated this sense, although not in "Mourning . . ." but in *Totem and Taboo*. In the section called "The Taboo of the Dead", he wrote:

> This theory is based on a supposition so extraordinary that it seems at first sight incredible: the supposition, namely that a dearly loved relative at the moment of his death changes into a demon, from whom his survivors can expect nothing but hostility and against whose evil desires they must protect themselves by every possible means. Nevertheless, almost all the authorities are at one in attributing these views to primitive peoples. [Freud, 1912–13, p. 58]

And he adds:

> . . . Rudolph Kleinpaul (1898) has used *the remnants among civilized races* of the ancient belief in spirits to throw light on the relation between the living and the dead. He too, reaches the final conclusion that the dead, filled with a lust for murder, sought to drag the living in to their train, etc. [pp. 58–59; italics added]

The word "mourning" translates into Spanish as *duelo*, derived from Latin, and in this latter language it has two etymologies: (a) from *dolus* [pain], and (b) from *duellum* [duel; combat between two persons: *due*: two and *llum*, from *bellum*, war].

As can be seen, Latin etymology reflects the two senses.

Both varieties of meaning, of sense, can be found in every mourning; however, the second variety, the most persecutory, has been less considered in relation to mourning. Clinical and life experiences, however, demonstrate, with the force of evidence, the general predominance of the latter.

One of the main purposes of the present chapter is to propose and to sustain a metapsychological explanation of this view.

Summing up

1. The difference between the psychodynamics of mourning and of melancholia, cannot be, as Freud holds, that in melancholia the lost external object is introjected, and this is not the case in normal mourning. For an external object to have psychic life in the soul of a person, the external object must have a psychic representation, in the form of an internal object. This psychic existence of the object is the precondition of the possibility of registering its loss in the external world.

2. The difference between mourning and melancholia resides elsewhere, in the differences between the intervening factors, in the previous characteristics of the main psychical structures, in the kind of narcissistic object choice, in the degree of the previous ambivalence towards the lost object, the personal and cultural circumstances in which the loss takes place, and so forth. So,

    . . . it is not difficult to perceive an essential analogy between *the work of* melancholia and of mourning. [Freud, 1917e [1915], p. 257; italics added]

3. Mourning processes have two main purposes: to work through the loss of a love object and to get rid of an internal persecutory thanatic object that is opposed to pleasure and to life.

And I would add:

4. Any mourning process that is interrupted in any given moment of its evolution is a pathological mourning and is the cause of a depressive disturbance.

5. Not all pathological mournings are caused by an interruption in their evolution.

6. Not all depressive–melancholic disease is caused by pathological mourning.

7. These assertions must be sustained in metapsychological terms.

The psychic scene prior to the loss

"All the world's a stage,
And all the men and women merely players."

Shakespeare, *As You Like It*, Act II, Scene 7, ll. 139–140

I shall refer to this psychic stage or scene from the Freudian structural theory and from some post-Freudian concepts: it should be understood as psychic structure, a *functional* structure—that is, a group of functions and models of functioning directed to one or several common goals, and with a much lower rate of change than the rest of psychic processes.

Thus ego, superego, id, are not places, *topoi*, but psychic structures, as previously defined. This means that the different types of internalizations do not *go to* the ego, or superego, or ideal, but *function as* ego, superego, or ideal.

We find in this stage, prior to the loss, the great structures: ego, id, superego, and ideal, with their intra and interstructural relations and conflicts, and also those with their internal objects (internal objects relations). All these cathect with the life and destructive drives, always with a certain degree of quantitative and qualitative mixture [*Mischung* in Freud's original German].

From this internal world, interacting with himself and with the external world, there sprouts early the notion and the feeling of oneself—of the self. It is known that Freud always used only one German word: *Ich* ("I" in English, but usually translated as the Latin "ego") to name that which in different contexts are the functions ego, the ego of identifications, the structural ego, the *Selbst* (self) (the more subjective ego), and so on.

In that psychic stage, the sudden and unexpected loss of an important external object, as prototypical example, will initiate the mourning process—the "plot".

The plot: the process of mourning

The drama begins with denial, disavowal [*Verleugnung*] of the fact: No! It's impossible! I can't believe it! and so on. This stage can go on for a relatively long time, with fleeting periods of accepting the fact and more intense periods of disavowal; such periods coexist and often alternate rapidly. Finally the reality principle prevails, and the individual accepts the loss.

> Reality-testing has shown that the loved object no longer exists, and *it proceeds to demand* that *all libido shall be withdrawn from its attachments to that object.* This demand arouses *understandable opposition*—it is a matter of general observation that people never willingly abandon a libidinal position, not even, indeed, when a substitute is already beckoning to them. . . . Normally, respect for reality gains the day. Nevertheless its orders *cannot be obeyed at once* . . . and in the meantime the existence of the lost object is psychically prolonged. [Freud, 1917e [1915]; italics added]

I remark that: "*understandable opposition—it is a matter of general observation that people never willingly abandon a libidinal position, not even, indeed, when a substitute is already beckoning to them*", and "*Nevertheless its orders cannot be obeyed at once*" are not psychoanalytic explanations of unconscious process, but phenomenological or clinical observations.

I believe that the process is more complicated than Freud describes it, and, in the light of present developments, I can provide a more precise metapsychological description that is more appropriate to the clinical and phenomenological facts.

Here is my hypothesis: The ego, accepting its judgement, which derives from reality-testing, withdraws its libidinal investment from the internal object that represents the lost external object. With difference to what Freud points out, I hold that such withdrawal begins immediately and tends rapidly to become massive. This would lead to a de-neutralization, an extrication, or an "unmixing" [*Entmischung*] of the destructive or death drive, in the internal object representing the lost object.

By destructive or death drive I refer here to the tendency of undoing complex structures and leading them to a simpler structural state, to the inorganic: ". . . we assume a death instinct, in charge of reconducting the living organic being to the inert state . . ." (Freud, 1923b). The internal object involved does not merely

remain "without life" when libidinal investments are withdrawn from
it but, rather, it undergoes a rapid process of deterioration, disorganization, and self-destructiveness. This process would be expressed
and perceived through corresponding affects and ideas. To quote a
classic author: "The presence of death and the disruption of a libidinal tie liberates Thanatos in its original form which manifests itself in
the self-mortification of the mourners" (Roheim, 1945, p. 69).

The processes I am describing represent a dangerous situation
for the ego that contains this actively self-destructive and threatening
"dead object". In the face of this intensely dangerous situation, the
ego produces its signal anxiety and puts its defences into action. The
most important defence is the erotic libidinal and massive recathect-
ing of the internal representative of the lost external object, as an
attempt to neutralize its destructivity. This defence is of the same
kind as Freud described in *Beyond the Pleasure Principle* when there is
a breach in the protective shield:

> . . . cathectic energy is summoned from all sides to provide suf-
> ficiently high cathexis of energy in the environs of the breach.
> An "anticathexis" on a grand scale is set up, for whose benefit all
> the other psychical systems are impoverished . . . [Freud, 1920g,
> p. 30]

Since all these processes do not occur simultaneously, it is difficult
to describe their exact correspondence with the individual's mental
conscious states. Yet I shall say that the "No! No!—I can't believe it!"
corresponds to the phase of initial disavowal. The state of stupor or
shock, immobility and disconnection would correspond to the massive withdrawal of libidinal investment, along with the "liberation" of
the destructive drive. The next step would correspond to a transitory
identification with the dead, also expressed by wishes and/or ideas
of dying like the object. Also, the individual in mourning may experience in this stage an acute sensation of psychical pain and anxiety,
and/or a painful sense of emptiness.

Together with the start of the activation of the defences (mainly
the libidinal recathexis) against this internal danger, there appears
the fear of death (fear to a massive identification). And the important libidinal recathexis of the internal representative of the lost
object has the subject having his mind almost permanently occupied
in his thinking and feelings with the lost object: "I can't think about
anything else", "I can't get it out of my mind", and so forth.

This situation had been described by Freud in "Mourning and Melancholia" in a quite similar manner, although in that work Freud held that it only occurred in melancholia and not in normal mourning. This I consider a mistake.

> The complex of melancholia behaves like an open wound, drawing to himself cathectic energies—which in the transference neurosis we have called "anticathexis"—from all directions, and emptying the ego until it is totally impoverished. [Freud, 1917e [1915], p. 253]

We can here perceive a subtle difference: in this formulation it is the "melancholic complex" that "behaves like an open wound" and *attracts* towards itself the energy of the investments. In the hypothesis I have proposed, it is the ego (the self) who *sends* defensive counterinvestments. (At this point my description agrees with Freud's in *Beyond the Pleasure Principle* [1920g]). I believe that the difference derives from whether we first take into account the subjective experience or the metapsychological description. From the latter, things are as I have described, *both in mourning and in melancholia*. From the experience of the subject in mourning, things are as Freud has described them. This has led me to describe the subjective sensation of the mourner as if the "internal dead–alive object" were as a "black hole", as described by astronomers. All this can be clearly seen when the defensive erotic countercathexes are already active, and consequently a defence against the massive identification with the dead is set.

> Example 1:   In Ingmar Bergman's film *Cries and Whispers* a woman is holding a wake over her dead elder sister. At one point the dead woman sits up and grabs her sister, as if she wanted to drag her along with her. The living sister manages to get away in horror after a brief struggle.
>
> Example 2:   A patient in acute mourning due to the recent death of a beloved father-figure dreams: "*Sergio was ill and in a hospital. I was walking down a hospital corridor. From a dark room a bell could be heard, as if someone was calling. I was very scared, and ran away.*" Then she associates: "Here in my bosom I have a huge hole through which things go down."

At this point of the mourning process, and because of persecutory fears, there appear typical appeasement ideas. "*De mortuis nil nisi bonum"* [of the dead, nothing except good things], goes the Latin saying. And that is the rule in obituaries and funeral eulogies. Pious rituals of soldiers keeping guard around the coffin, heavy grave-stones, monuments over graves can be traced to very old measures designed to prevent the return of the dead.

The denial of the negative aspects and the often excessive praise of the positive aspects, endeavours, and character traits of the lost object often lead to a more-or-less important *idealization* of the object. However, this idealization produces a certain distance between the subject and the object, which facilitates the separation between them and consequently also facilitates the mourning process.

A short digression on the death or destructive drive

In 1920 Freud presented the death or destructive drive as an specula-tion. But just a few years later he clearly stated that it was a hypothesis he could not do without. I know this aspect of Freud's theorization does not find general acceptance in the psychoanalytic world, and that those analysts who do accept it do not share a common idea about it. In this short digression, since I find the destructive–death hypothesis both theoretically and clinically useful and since I have used it in the present chapter, I would like to add some pertinent comments:

a. Many misunderstandings arise from simultaneous arguments about different levels of the theory. I consider that it might be helpful to differentiate three different levels in scientific contro-versies: the biological, the psychological, and the social.

b. The death-drive, in its purity, has no purpose, no signification, no meaningful finality. It is only through its unavoidable mixing [*Mischung*] with the life drive (Freud, 1940a [1938]) that mean-ing, sense, and finality appears.

Digression: the internal lost object in mourning

Melanie Klein has described it eloquently: "In my experience the paranoiac conception of a dead object within, is one of a secret and uncanny persecutor. He is felt as not being fully dead, and may re-appear at any time in cunning and plotting ways" (1950, p. 304).

Willy Baranger (1961) has described variations of this object in great detail: the dead–alive object, the dying object, the dead object, also within a predominantly Kleinian frame of reference.

I would observe that the expression "dead–alive object" implies that part of the object is dead. This is a half-truth. The problem is that the object is felt as alive in psychic reality, and, specially in the first stages, alive with malignity and presenting some of his worst previous features and traits. It is here that Lagache's (1956) dictum: "The purpose of the work of mourning is to kill the dead", acquires its maximum validity.

A schematic chronology
of the origin of the aggressivity in mourning

Freud postulated that the aggressivity towards the internalized object had most of its origin in the ambivalence previously felt towards it.

Abraham (1924b) described that the internalization of the lost object occurs not only in the ego, but in the superego as well, so that the internalized object now also attacks and reproaches the ego of the subject.

According to the hypothesis I am now presenting, the persecution and aggressivity of the internal "lost" or "dead" object depends on the de-neutralization of the destructive drive in it, as a consequence of the withdrawal of libido from it. As already remarked, this (functional) structure can function as ego or superego.

Identifications

Classical theory holds that the mourning process *ends* with structural and partial identifications with the lost object. In my experience there are *early*, mostly transitory and partial identifications with the lost object, but with the characteristic of reflecting negative aspects of it: its symptoms, failures, weaknesses. I have denominated thanatic identifications these partial and often—but not always—fleeting identifications (Aslan, 1978a).

There are manifold versions of these "thanatic identifications". Perhaps the most common example would be mourning clothes: white, purple, black are mourning colours in different cultures, and they imitate paleness, cyanosis, and corruption.

So far I have emphasized predominantly persecutory situations, ideas, and aspects of the mourning processes. I must now again insist on the more mature and very important realistic and rational reactions to object loss: sadness, psychic pain, anxiety, helplessness, loneliness. As Engel (1962) has pointed out, crying with tears is typical in these states, and it implies a relief of an internal need, a certain degree of regression, and also a communication to others.

A transversal midway view of the process

It is a heterogeneous view.

1. Parts of the object have undergone the process of secondary identifications. At the beginning of mourning, they are mostly "thanatic", but under the continuous pressure of libidinal cathexis they slowly turn into "erotic" identifications.

2. Parts of the object have suffered a process of idealization. Even though this implies a degree of denial, it also creates a certain "distance" that facilitates the withdrawal from the object, and at the same time acts as countercathexis to the action of:

3. parts of the object still charged with hate, destructiveness, and aggression towards the self. To quote Freud (1912–13) again at this point: "We know that the dead are powerful rulers; but we may perhaps be surprised that they are treated as enemies."

As I have previously said, these objects, and also the secondary identifications they produce, can function as ego or superego. A banal and frequent situation can illustrate this, as in the following vignette: If a relatively recent widower intends to have sexual relations with someone and reacts with impotence, we can speculate that: (a) the internal object that represents his dead/alive wife, or its subsequent identification, both acting as superego, and in conflict with his sexual desires, will make the widow feel guilty and pained, and these feelings interfere with the sexual performance. (b) If the dead wife is identified as ego, the widower may not even feel desire: he will be "dead" to sexuality, and/or so, also, will be his genitals. (c) Most frequently, there is a combination of both.

The plot: evolution

In a favourable evolution of mourning—that is, towards its resolution—my basic assumption is that through the continuous flow of life drive, libido, to the psychic representative of the lost object is effected the neutralization of the deadly/persecutory object, and the final separation from it.

Which is the intimate process in this metaphoric description?

We arc without any physiological understanding of the ways and means by which this taming [*Bändigung*] of the death-instinct by the libido may be effected. So far as the psycho-analytic field of ideas is concerned, we can only assume that a very extensive fusion and amalgamation, in diverse proportions of the two classes of instincts takes place . . . [Freud, 1924c, p. 164]

What we can observe, in a favourable evolution is the following:

1. The identifications with the lost object become identifications with its most positive features, with its achievements, and with its ideals. ("I shall now become an architect, as mother wished.")

2. The painful affects evolve from a predominant concern with the subject in mourning (psychic pain, fear, anxiety) towards a predominant preoccupation for the lost object (sadness, grief, longing); then they diminish and eventually disappear.

3. Memories become more truthful, complete, and adequate. Idealizations of the lost object tend to disappear, and a more realistic picture of the human being appears instead.

4. At the end of the process, the ego is enriched with positive, "erotic", identifications, the libido is free for new objects and relationships, and the subject is capable to remember realistically both the pleasures and the unpleasantness of the lost relationship.

Mourning, pathological mourning, and melancholia

Under the heading "Mourning as disease" I have quoted Freud and Engel, both considering normal mourning to be comparable with a pathological process. I would like to add that, in my opinion, in its evolution, normal mourning passes through different and successive ideative and affective psychic states that reproduce or resemble, for hours, days, weeks, or even months, depressive–melancholic conditions. These run the whole gamut of depressive illness, starting with psychotic denial and stuporous depression and continuing through major depressions and neurotic depressions, to simple depressions and "common unhappiness" (Freud).

If, because of internal or external factors (or both) the mourning process stops or is severely protracted and remains "fixated" in a given stage, the person will exhibit a melancholic–depressive condition corresponding to the degree of evolution reached by the mourning process. The earlier the stop, the worse the depressive condition.

Among the more frequent factors that interfere and stop the evolution of the process are: narcissistic object choice; narcissistic character disorders, without a clear subject–object differentiation; extreme previous ambivalence towards and from the lost object; extremely harsh previous superego (excessive guilt, masochism, etc.); multiple or massive losses; losses in extremely traumatic circumstances; and so on. In general, we meet a combination of these factors.

To end, I would like to stress the following conclusions:

▷ Every mourning process that is interrupted in its evolution turns into a pathological mourning and is the cause of depressive–melancholic pathology.

▷ Not all depressive–melancholic pathology is caused by pathological mourning.

▷ There are a variety of pathological mournings, whose origin and clinical features are not those cited above: for instance: "absence of grief", "mourning by proxy", and so forth and are beyond the scope of this chapter.

9

Teaching Freud's "Mourning and Melancholia"

Jean-Michel Quinodoz

Many ways of teaching Freud's works

"Mourning and Melancholia" constitutes one of Freud's major contributions to psychoanalysis. But, like most of his writings, this contribution cannot be read as an isolated piece of work. As Freud continuously revised his ideas, we need to take into account the evolution of his thinking over more than four decades. This is the reason why I have simultaneously used a selective and a chrono-logical approach to teaching Freud's psychoanalytic texts, especially "Mourning and Melancholia". These two approaches do not stand in opposition to each other: in fact they are complementary, for each in its own way illustrates how Freud himself kept uncertainty to advantage and taking his clinical experience into account in order to develop further what he had discovered.

For didactic reasons, I have divided this chapter into four parts:

1. before Freud: Karl Abraham;
2. "Mourning and Melancholia" and Freud's subsequent develop-ments;
3. a selected post-Freudian contribution: the Kleinian approach;
4. a seminar on the chronological reading of Freud's texts.

I.   BEFORE FREUD: KARL ABRAHAM (1877–1925)

A pioneer of psychoanalytic research on depression

The hypotheses that Freud presents in "Mourning and Melancholia" owe much to the pioneering work of Karl Abraham, who was an important figure in the early history of psychoanalysis. Born in Germany, Abraham trained as a psychiatrist in Berlin before travelling to Zurich in 1907 in order to have further training under Eugen Bleuler, director of the Burghölzli Clinic, where Jung was senior registrar. It was while he was in Switzerland that Abraham first learned of Freud's work.

Abraham immediately embraced Freud's ideas, though he opened up new paths and did sometimes have disagreements with his mentor. The hallmark of his many papers is their cogency and clarity of expression. I would like to draw attention in particular to Abraham's seminal work on manic-depressive disorders and on the stages of libidinal development. He was the first psychoanalyst to treat manic-depressive patients and, in a paper written in 1911, he showed that depressive patients suffer from a paralysis of their capacity to love because of the violent nature of their sadistic fantasies and the "overstrong sadistic component of [their] libido" (Abraham, 1911 [1988, p. 139]). According to Abraham, depression arises from repression of the patient's sadistic tendency; melancholia and manic states are dominated by the same complexes, and it is only the patient's attitude towards these complexes that is different. He suggested also that depression in adults probably has its roots in a basic depression of childhood; though he was unable to prove this, Melanie Klein did provide him with a clinical demonstration of his hypothesis, and he shared this discovery with Freud (Letter 423A from Abraham to Freud, 7 October 1923, in Falzeder, 2002).

In 1924, Abraham published a wide-ranging synthesis of his points of view, in which he attempted to locate the fixation points of different mental disorders with respect to the stages of libidinal development. He distinguished in particular two sub-stages in the anal-sadistic phase and two in the oral phase of libidinal development. According to Abraham, the anal-sadistic stage can be divided into an *early anal phase* linked to evacuation and destruction of the object—the fixation point of depression and melancholia—and a *later phase* linked to retaining and controlling the object—the fixation point of obsessional neurosis. It may happen in depression that the fixation point is even earlier than the early sadistic sub-stage of expulsion: in such cases, according to Abraham, the fixation point involves the oral stage of libidinal development. Here, too, there are two sub-phases: an *early oral phase* of pre-ambivalent sucking, and a *later oral-sadistic phase,* which corresponds to primary dentition and generates ambivalence between sucking and biting. At the same time, Abraham described the development of feelings of love and hate in terms of object relations up to the time when love for the whole object is established in the course of the genital stage of development: "a complete capacity for love is only achieved when the libido has reached its genital stage" (1924a, p. 425).

II.   FREUD'S "MOURNING AND MELANCHOLIA" AND SUBSEQUENT DEVELOPMENTS

A.   *"Mourning and Melancholia"*

Normal and pathological mourning processes

In "Mourning and Melancholia", Freud explores the individual's reaction to an actual loss or disappointment connected with a loved person, or to the loss of an ideal: why do some people respond with the affect we call mourning, which will be overcome after a certain time, while others sink into depression—a syndrome Freud called "melancholia"?

At this point I would like to stress that what in Freud's day was called "melancholia" would nowadays be called "depression", the term "melancholia" being reserved for the most severe, psychotic form of depression (Bonaparte, Freud, & Kris, 1954; Laplanche, 1980; Strachey, 1957c). This precision in language is essential because there are psychoanalysts who, following Lacan, still consider "Mourning and Melancholia" as describing an incurable psychiatric condition—limiting the notion of "melancholia" and situating it outside the field of psychoanalysis.

Freud notes that, unlike normal mourning in which the process involves consciousness, pathological mourning has more to do with the unconscious because the depressed patient "cannot consciously perceive what he has lost" (1917e [1915], p. 245). In normal and pathological mourning, the inhibition and loss of interest common to both can be accounted for by the work of mourning in which the ego is absorbed. In melancholia, however, there is an additional element: an extraordinary diminution in self-esteem. "In mourning it is the world which has become poor and empty; in melancholia it is the ego itself" (p. 246). In pathological mourning, the loss of self-regard is uppermost, expressed as self-reproaches and self-abasement. How are we to explain these accusations against the self—accusations that may lead to a delusional expectation of punishment?

In melancholia, "*I* am incapable!" really means "*You* are incapable!"

It took me many years' reading and re-reading Freud's "Mourning and Melancholia" to understand what he meant when he described in minute detail the origin of the depressive state. Finally, I really started to deeply understand Freud's complex hypotheses when I observed them functioning in my patients in the course of the psychoanalytic cure. Now I would like to discuss Freud's text using clinical vignettes coming from my clinical experience.

Freud's ingenious idea was the realization that the self-accusations of the depressive individual are in fact reproaches against some important person who has been "lost", usually someone in the patient's immediate circle. Thus, he says, "the woman who loudly pities her husband for being tied to such an incapable wife as herself is really accusing her husband of being incapable, in whatever sense she may mean this" (1917e [1915], p. 248). In other words, when this woman blames herself, saying "*I* am incapable!" this self-reproach is in fact an accusation unconsciously directed towards her husband: "*You* are incapable!" As Freud puts it so succinctly in German, talking of such patients: "*Ihre Klagen sind Anklagen*"—that is, "Their complaints are really 'plaints' in the old sense of the word" (p. 248)—there is a condensation here between *Klagen* ["complaints" in the sense of "to complain"] and *Anklagen* ["complaints" in the judicial sense of "to lodge a complaint against someone": accusations].

Following his intuition, Freud realizes that the words used by the melancholic patient when expressing self-accusations—when, for example, the patient says "I am incapable!"—are an accurate description of his or her inner conflict. "The point must rather be that he is giving a correct description of his psychological situation" (p. 247).

Given that the actual linguistic structure of these self-accusations derives from the organization of the melancholic's inner conflict, Freud makes a systematic exploration of the different elements involved, breaking each step down into its component parts: he describes in turn the oral introjection of the lost object, the identification with this object via regression from object love to narcissism, the turning back upon the subject of the hate originally aimed at the object, and so forth. I shall examine these concepts one by one: for a proper understanding of these processes, the reader will have to pay close attention to my description, especially since the clinical material on which Freud bases his theorizations remains more implicit than explicit. I shall, however, attempt an overview of all these aspects.

The break with the outside world and narcissistic withdrawal

Freud begins by explaining the process that underlies the "You"/"I" substitution in the melancholic's explicit self-accusation "*I* am incapable!" when what is really—implicitly—meant is "*You* are incapable!" What mental processes correspond to the transformations that are given verbal expression in this way? Freud explains that when the object is lost, there is a fundamental difference between normal and pathological mourning—one that originates in the change of direction taken by libidinal cathexes. In normal mourning, the individual is able to give up the "lost" object and withdraw libido from it, so that this libido, now free, can attach itself to a new object. In melancholia, however, the individual does not withdraw libido from the lost object: the ego "devours" the object in fantasy in order not to separate from it, in order to be as one with it—this is the path to narcissistic identification. "Thus the shadow of the object fell upon the ego, and the latter could henceforth be judged by a special agency, as though it were an object, the forsaken object. In this way an object loss was transformed into an ego-loss and the conflict between the ego and the loved person into a cleavage between the critical activity of the ego and the ego as altered by identification" (1917e [1915], p. 249). It is this change of direction from object cathexis to cathexis of the ego amalgamated with the object that explains the melancholic's loss of interest in those who belong to his or her immediate circle and the consequent "narcissistic" withdrawal onto the self: melancholic patients are so preoccupied with themselves that it is as though they are sucked into a whirlwind of self-reproaches. In addition, the turning back of accusations onto the individual implies a split in the ego: one part merges with the lost object while the other criticizes the patient and sets itself up as an agency which Freud calls "conscience". "We see how in him one part of the ego sets itself over against the other, judges it critically, and, as it were, takes it as its object" (p. 247). This criticizing agency is the forerunner of what would later become the superego.

Love regresses to narcissistic identification and hate turns back against the subject

The depressive patient's powerful self-destructive tendency, writes Freud, is the result of an intensification of the ambivalence between love and hate as regards both the object and the ego; these affects then separate, with each following its own path. On the one hand, the subject continues to love the object, but at the cost of a return to a primitive form of love—identification—in which "loving" the object implics "being" that object. "The narcissistic identification with the object then becomes a substitute for the erotic cathexis, the result of which is that in spite of the conflict with the loved person the love-relation need not be given up" (1917e [1915], p. 249). The libido regresses to the cannibalistic oral phase of development in which the ego incorporates the object into itself by devouring it. Also, because of the ego's narcissistic identification with the loved object, the subject's hate aimed at the object in the external world is henceforth turned against the ego, now merged with that object. "If the love for the object—a love which cannot be given up though the object itself is given up—takes refuge in narcissistic identification, then the hate comes into operation on this substitutive object, abusing it, debasing it, making it suffer and deriving sadistic satisfaction from its suffering" (p. 251).

Manifest self-reproaches are latent reproaches against other people

Freud notes a further decisive element when he points out that the melancholic's self-accusations are at the same time an attack on the object—in other words, the patient's narcissistic withdrawal does not exclude the fact that an unconscious object relation still exists. He shows that, like the obsessional patient, the melancholic finds it "enjoyable" to exercise the sadistic and hate-filled tendencies simultaneously both against him- or herself and against some other person—usually someone in the patient's immediate circle. "In both disorders the patients usually still succeed, by the circuitous path of self-punishment, in taking revenge on the original object and in tormenting their loved one through their illness, having resorted to it in order to avoid the need to express their hostility to him openly" (1917e [1915], p. 251). In arguing that the melancholic patient's self-criticisms are a way of attacking the object and exacting revenge on it, Freud shows that, in addition to their narcissism, these patients manage nonetheless to maintain an object relation with their immediate circle—one based on hate and aggressiveness. It was probably the fact that he emphasized the narcissistic withdrawal of manic-depressive patients that led him to conclude that these patients were unable to establish a transference relationship and were therefore inaccessible to analysis: hence the designation "narcissistic neuroses". Post-Freudian psychoanalysts have shown that these patients do establish a transference relationship and that this relationship can be analysed, even though, in this kind of transference, hostility towards the analyst is uppermost.

B. Freud's subsequent developments
to "Mourning and Melancholia"

New ideas, new developments

Freud's initial description of the psychological mechanisms underlying depression is easier to understand when we take into account the developments he later brought forward to complete his initial hypotheses. As for other fundamental concepts, like Oedipus complex, Freud never assembled his ideas on pathological mourning in a paper, nor in a book. Consequently, we need to look ourselves into Freud's relevant papers written after 1917 in order to create our own synthesis.

The introduction of the conflict
between life and death drives (1920g)

The crucial role played by self-destructive impulses in depressive patients was one of the factors that led Freud to revise his first theory of the instinctual drives based on the pleasure/unpleasure principle as he had formulated it in 1915. If the aim of every drive is above all to obtain satisfaction, how are we to explain what may lead the

depressive patient to commit suicide? It was in reply to this kind
of question that, in 1920, Freud put forward a new theory of the
instinctual drives, based on the fundamental conflict between life
and death drives; he would apply this conception to several different
psychopathological conditions, including melancholia.

The conflict between ego, id, and superego (1923b)

In 1915, in "Mourning and Melancholia", Freud attributed the melancholic's self-accusations to the "criticism" that one part of the ego
addressed to another: the "conscience" or "voice of one's conscience"
in the moral sense of the term. In 1923 this "criticism" would become
an agency in its own right; he called it the *superego* and described its
close connections with two other newly-defined agencies: the *ego* and
the *id*. Under normal conditions, the superego has a regulatory role
with respect to the ego, and the latter has to cope with the drive-
based demands of the id. In melancholia, however, Freud noted that
the superego is overly sadistic towards the ego, because in this illness,
he writes, the superego

> rages against the ego with merciless violence, as if it had taken
> possession of the whole of the sadism available in the person
> concerned. . . . What is now holding sway in the superego is, as
> it were, a pure culture of the death instinct, and in fact it often
> enough succeeds in driving the ego into death, if the latter does
> not fend off its tyrant in time by the change round into mania.
> [1923b, p. 53]

Splitting of the ego (1927e)

The idea of splitting of the ego was already present in "Mourning
and Melancholia", either expressed explicitly as "cleavage" or as
one part of the ego being "split off" from the rest, when Freud describes in melancholic patients the severity with which "conscience"
criticizes the ego. Subsequently, in his paper on "Fetishism" (1927e),
he went on to complete his ideas on splitting of the ego by arguing
that, in depression, this split is the result of denial of the loss of the
object. He illustrates his argument with the analysis of two brothers
who had "scotomized" the death of their father while they were still
children, yet neither of them had developed a psychosis.

It was only one current in their mental life that had not recognized their father's death; there was another current which took
full account of that fact. The attitude which fitted in with the
wish and the attitude which fitted in with reality existed side by
side. In one of my two cases this split had formed the basis of a
moderately severe obsessional neurosis [1927e, p. 156]

In other words, in pathological mourning, the idea of splitting of the
ego shows how one part of the ego can deny the reality of the loss
while another part can accept it. In some of his last papers, Freud
would attach more and more importance to phenomena such as
denial ("disavowal") of reality and splitting of the ego.

III.   A SELECTED POST-FREUDIAN DEVELOPMENT

Countless contributions

It is not possible to give an extensive account of the post-Freudian contributions to Freud's "Mourning and Melancholia", not only
because of the limits of this chapter, but also because they are so
numerous. For didactic reasons, I have selected to present only the
main ideas of Melanie Klein and of her followers in the field of
object relationships, love and hate, introjection, projection, denial,
splitting, etc. because they are mainly rooted in Freud's "Mourning
and Melancholia".

Kleinian and post-Kleinian developments

Before she introduced her own specific ideas, Melanie Klein based
the developments of her hypotheses on classic Freudian theory.
Among the fundamental Freudian concepts on which she based her
work, several are to be found in Freud's "papers on metapsychology",
in particular in "Mourning and Melancholia" (1917e [1915]). Klein
herself never spoke of "metapsychology", preferring to present her
concepts in clinical terms: she laid particular emphasis on structural
notions such as the paranoid-schizoid and depressive positions, as
well as on projective identification. I shall begin with a quick overview of these concepts.

A structural conception of the workings of the mind and of change

By introducing the idea of "position", Melanie Klein was able not only to identify two distinct and fundamental states of the structure of the mind—the paranoid-schizoid position and the depressive position—but also to account for the structural changes that occur during the psychoanalytic process. The idea of "position" is different from that of a chronological "stage" of libidinal development (such as the oral stage or the phallic stage), because it is a structural concept that aims to reflect the present state of the organization of the mind and the transitions that take place between these two states.

Many factors come into play in the constitution of the paranoid-schizoid and depressive positions, as well as in the shifts from one to the other, such as the degree of cohesiveness of the ego (fragmented or integrated?), the nature of object relations (part-object or whole-object?), the level of defence mechanisms employed (primitive or more advanced?). In other words, with her structural concept of "position", Klein demonstrated that the transition from the paranoid-schizoid to the depressive position represents a fundamental shift from psychotic functioning to one that is psychologically healthy. These new developments made it possible to analyse the transference of depressive and psychotic patients, a kind of patient Freud classified as "narcissistic neuroses", believing that they are not accessible to psychoanalysis.

From the "purified pleasure-ego" to integrating love and hate

Klein took as her model the "purified pleasure-ego" described by Freud in "Instincts and Their Vicissitudes" (1915c), as well as the notions of projection and introjection that are associated with it, in particular in "Mourning and Melancholia". She described the development of affects in very young infants starting with their earliest part-object relations and proceeding through to the relation with a whole-object experienced as separate. Taking that as her basis, Klein went on to describe the infant's early relationships, showing that they are established with a part-object, the mother's breast, which is split into an ideal breast, source of all expectations, and a persecutory one, the object of hate and of fear—the situation she called the "paranoid-schizoid position". She went on to describe the evolution that followed the gradual integration of the ego and its objects, when the infant begins to perceive and to love the mother as a whole person—this change marks what she called the beginning of the "depressive position".

If we read what Freud wrote in 1915 in the light of Klein's conceptions, we can see that Freud felt intuitively that a change did indeed occur in the quality of affects and object relations; he did not, however, explicitly conceptualize that transition in terms of integrating love and hate and moving from a part-object to a whole-object relation. Klein was later to add her own contribution to Freud's picture of the vicissitudes of love and hate, thus making possible their application to clinical practice.

Mourning and manic-depressive states

The ideas that Freud had put forward in "Mourning and Melancholia" were also an inspiration for Klein as she constructed her own theory of manic-depressive states (Klein, 1935). She discovered that the conflicts between aggressiveness and libido, as Freud had described them in 1917 in adult depressive states, were very early in origin and that the fixation point of depression was to be found in early childhood. Developing what Freud had said about the role played by aggressiveness and guilt feelings in depressive affect, Klein argued that the idea of reparation was particularly significant in this context—the wish to restore/repair the object damaged by aggressive and destructive fantasies. She pointed out that there were two kinds of reparation: normal, creative reparation, which arises from the depressive position and is linked to love of and respect for the object, and pathological reparation, which can take several forms—for example, manic reparation based on a triumphant denial of depressive feelings, or obsessional reparation based on the compulsion to eliminate depressive anxiety in a magical way.

Klein was also forced to revise Freud's ideas on repression when she realized that some defence mechanisms were already in operation before repression *stricto sensu* could be set up, as we have seen in "Mourning and Melancholia". She then drew a distinction between primitive defence mechanisms, which affect the structure of the ego by fragmenting it, and repression, which operates on psychical content without altering the structure of the ego. Primitive defence mechanisms have recourse to a form of suppression that has a particularly violent effect on external reality and on psychic reality, as the denial of the loss of the lost object in depression—and in this they are quite different from repression. Five of these primitive defence mechanisms with particular relevance to Klein's theory are denial, splitting, projection, introjection, and omnipotence. In 1946, Klein added to these the mechanism that she called projective identification, thus making this concept one of the central tenets of Kleinian psychoanalysis, as well as in other currents of thought.

IV.   A SEMINAR ON
THE CHRONOLOGICAL READING OF FREUD'S TEXTS

Many ways of teaching Freud

Freud's published work is both impressive and complex in nature. His psychoanalytic papers fill some twenty-four volumes, while his correspondence comprises over one hundred books in all. How can we have a global view of such an imposing body of work? There are many ways of reading and teaching Freud, and though each has its advantages and disadvantages, they are all complementing one another. When in 1988 I started a Seminar devoted to the reading of Freud's major contributions, the usual way of reading and commenting on a text did not appeal to me. I had the idea that all participants should contribute to shedding light on the text that we were studying by looking at it from different perspectives—biographical, the theory of ideas, post-Freudian developments, and so on. I felt that working along these lines would enable us to supplement our reading of Freud's texts thanks to this twofold method: a chronological study of his writings, allied to a correlative, interactive, and non-linear approach.

The active participation of each member

A crucial point was that participants in the seminar should feel directly involved in what was taking place: it would not be a series of *ex cathedra* lectures, and my role would be limited to helping them in their work over a predetermined period of time (15 sessions of two hours per year, over three years). That kind of participation implied both individual work and sharing thoughts and discoveries with the other members. As we travelled together on our journey, I came to realize that the more the group was asked to participate actively in constructing the seminar, the more they appreciated it and benefited from it. This was highlighted by the fact that the level of absenteeism was practically negligible.

The individual work implied the following:

> *reading the chosen text:* before the seminar session, each participant read the scheduled text so as to be able to share with the others his or her own thoughts on it during the discussion period;

> *freedom of choice as far as translation was concerned:* each participant could choose his or her preferred language or translation, some participants reading Freud in the original German. The great variety of translations meant that we could highlight the complex nature of the questions with which Freud's translators have to cope.

> *writing a short commentary:* each participant wrote a short (one-page) commentary of about 300 words relative to one of the following headings:

1. *"biographies and history"*: a short presentation of the life of Freud and of his contemporaries at the time he wrote the paper under discussion, thereby placing it into its historical context.

2. *"chronological evolution of Freud's concepts"*: showing how, in the paper, Freud gradually introduced new ideas, so as to highlight the history of how his thinking developed.

3. *"post-Freudian developments"*: selecting the main post-Freudian developments based on the text being discussed from a historical and international perspective.

4. *"the minutes of the seminar"*: drawing up a summary of what was discussed in the seminar so as to distribute these "Minutes" at the following meeting.

The sharing of each participant's individual work took place during the seminar session itself. Usually a session would begin with the distribution of the commentaries relating to the various headings I have just described. One participant would then read to the others the material relating to Freud's biography; then another the material relating to Freud's concepts, following which the discussion would be thrown open. In the final part of the seminar session, one participant would read out the material concerning post-Freudian contributions, also followed by a general discussion. The fact that sessions lasted for only a very short time was, paradoxically, really quite stimulating, since before the actual meeting each participant had to think about the various issues involved and prepare a brief statement of the ideas he or she wanted to share with the group.

The high standard expected was a dynamic factor

I am well aware that it was asking a great deal of the participants not only to read personally most of Freud's writings, but also to share their own thoughts on these and do any research required in order to write a commentary relating to one of the headings. Preparing for the seminar sessions demanded that they devote quite some time to this activity, even though their workload was usually heavy enough and they were already short of time for their personal and family life. It was possible for them to do this only if, in return, the seminar meetings were an occasion for sharing pleasant moments. The requirement that each participant play an active role proved to be a decisive factor in the group dynamics that gradually became established as the seminar went on. This "additional" participation in the service of constructing the seminar created a friendly momentum during the fixed period of time we spent together: each of us knew from the outset that the seminar would last three years. In fact, the seminar gave us much more than an increase in knowledge, because working together in this way enabled participants to listen to what each person (including him- or herself) was trying to say, and this furthered personal development in all of us. It was a way of being more open both to what Freud was trying to express and to the great variety of possible points of view.

NOTE

I am grateful to David Alcorn, who has wonderfully translated this chapter. I also express my gratitude to the candidates of the Swiss Psychoanalytical Society who participated actively in the successive seminars I am still giving at the Psychoanalytic Center Raymond de Saussure in Geneva.

REFERENCES AND BIBLIOGRAPHY

Abraham, K. (1911). Notes on the psychoanalytic investigation and treatment of manic-depressive insanity and allied conditions. In: *Selected Papers of Karl Abraham*. London: Hogarth Press, 1927 (reprinted London: Karnac, 1988).

Abraham, K. (1916). The first pregenital phase. In: *Selected Papers of Karl Abraham*. London: Hogarth Press, 1927 (reprinted London: Karnac, 1988).

Abraham, K. (1924a). Development of libido. In: *Selected Papers of Karl Abraham*. London: Hogarth Press, 1927 (reprinted London: Karnac, 1988).

Abraham, K. (1924b). A short study of the development of the libido, viewed in the light of mental disorders. In: *Selected Papers of Karl Abraham*. London: Hogarth Press, 1927 (reprinted London: Karnac, 1988).

Alvarez, A. (1992). *Live Company: Psychoanalytic Psychotherapy with Autistic, Borderline, Deprived and Abused Children*. London: Routledge.

Anzieu, D. (1974). Vers une métapsychologie de la création. In: D. Anzieu et al. (Eds.), *Psychanalyse du génie créateur* [Psychoanalysis of the creative genius]. Paris: Dunod.

Aslan, C. M. (1963). "Acerca del objeto interno perseguidor en el duelo patológico." Paper presented to the Asociación Psicoanalítica Argentina. Mimeographed.

Aslan, C. M. (1978a). Un aporte a la metapsicología del duelo. *Revista de Psicoanálisis, 35* (1).

Aslan, C. M. (1978b). Ritualización y fenomenología del duelo. *Revista de Psicoanálisis, 35* (6).

Aslan, C. M. (1997). Tra la vita e la morte. Metapsicología del lutto. *Psicoanalisi 1* (2).

Aslan, C. M. (1999). Acerca de la metapsicología de los objetos internos. In: *Volviendo a pensar con Willy y Madeleine Baranger. Nuevos desarrollos.* Buenos Aires: Grupo Editorial Lumen.

Aslan, C. M. (2003). Psicoanálisis del duelo. *Revista de Psicoanálisis, 60* (3).

Aslan, C. M. (2006). Acerca de la estructura, la repetición, la historia y la temporalidad. In: L. G. Fiorini (Ed.), *Tiempo, historia y estructura.* Buenos Aires: APA Editorial.

Baranger, M. (2004). La teoría del campo. *El otro en la trama intersubjetiva* (pp. 145–169). Buenos Aires: APA Editorial.

Baranger, M., & Baranger, W. (1961–62). La situación analítica como campo dinámico. In: *Problemas del campo psicoanalítico* (pp. 109–164). Buenos Aires: Kargieman, 1969.

Baranger, M., Baranger, W., & Mom, J. (1983). Process and non-process in analytic work. *International Journal of Psychoanalysis, 64*: 1–15.

Baranger, W. (1961). El muerto-vivo. Estructura de los objetos en el duelo y los estados depresivos. In: *Problemas del campo psicoanalítico.* Buenos Aires: Kargieman, 1969.

Baranger, W., Baranger, M., & Mom, J. (1987). The infantile psychic trauma from us to Freud: Pure trauma, retroactivity and reconstruction. *International Journal of Psychoanalysis, 69* (1988, No. 1): 113–128.

Baranger, W., Goldstein, N., & Zak de Goldstein, R. (1989). Acerca de la desidentificación. *Revista de Psicoanálisis, 46* (6): 895–903.

Bergmann, M. S. (1993). Reflections on the history of psychoanalysis. *Journal of the American Psychoanalytic Association, 41*: 929–955.

Bergmann, M. S. (1997). The historical roots of psychoanalytic orthodoxy. *International Journal of Psychoanalysis, 78*: 69–86.

Bergmann, M. S. (2004). *Understanding Dissidence and Controversy in Psychoanalysis.* New York: Other Press.

Bergmann, M. S., & Jucovy, M. E. (Eds.) (1988). *Generations of the Holocaust.* New York: Columbia University Press.

Bibring, E. (1953). *The Mechanism of Depression in Affective Disorders.* New York: International Universities Press.

Bion, W. R. (1957). Differentiation of the psychotic from the non-psychotic personalities. In: *Second Thoughts: Selected Papers on Psycho-Analysis* (pp. 43–64). London: Heinemann, 1967 (reprinted London: Karnac, 1984).

Bion, W. R. (1959). Attacks on linking. In: *Second Thoughts: Selected Papers on Psycho-Analysis* (pp. 93–109). London: Heinemann, 1967 (reprinted London: Karnac, 1984).

Bion, W. R. (1961). *Experiences in Groups.* London: Tavistock.

Bion, W. R. (1962a). *Learning from Experience.* London: Heinemann; New York: Basic Books.

Bion, W. R. (1962b). A theory of thinking. In: *Second Thoughts: Selected Papers on Psycho-Analysis.* London: Heinemann, 1967 (reprinted London: Karnac, 1984).

Bion, W. R. (1965). *Transformations: Change from Learning to Growth.* London: Heinemann.

Blanchot, M. (1962). *L' attente, l'oubli.* Paris: Gallimard.

Bleger J. (1990). *Symbiosis and Ambiguity: The Psychoanalysis of Very Early Development.* London: Free Association Books.

Blos, P. (1979). *The Adolescent Passage: Developmental Issues.* New York: International Universities Press.

Blum, H. (1999). El valor clínico de los sueños diurnos y una nota sobre su papel en el análisis del carácter. In: E. S. Person, P. Fonagy, & S. A. Figueira (Eds.), *En torno a Freud. El poeta y los sueños diurnos.* Madrid: Biblioteca Nueva.

Bonaparte, M. (1951). *La sexualité de la femme.* Paris: Presses Universitaires de France. (English: *Female Sexuality.* New York: International Universities Press, 1953.)

Bonaparte, M., Freud, A., & Kris, E. (Eds.) (1954). *The Origins of Psycho-Analysis: Letters to Wilhelm Fliess, Drafts and Notes: 1887-1902.* London: Imago.

Borges, J. L. (1967–68). *Arte poético.* Barcelona: Ed. Crítica.

Botella, C., & Botella, S. (1990). *La figurabilité psychique.* Paris: Delachaux et Niestlé, 2001.

Braun, J., & Pelento, M. L. (1988). Les vicissitudes de la pulsion de savoir dans certains deuils spéciaux. In: J. Puget & R. Kaës (Eds.), *Violence d'état et psychanalyse.* Paris: Dunod. (Spanish: *Violencia de Estado y Psicoanálisis.* Buenos Aires: Centro Editor de América Latina, 1991.)

Califano, M. (2002/2003). *I desaparecidos nella storia e nella memoria degli Argentini.* Bachelor's Thesis in Contemporary History, Università degli Studi di Bologna.

Campbell, R. (1983). An emotive apart. *Art in America* (May): 150–151.

Caper, R. (1995). On the difficulty of making a mutative interpretation. In: *A Mind of One's Own: A Kleinian View of Self and Object* (pp. 32–43). London: Routledge, 1999.

Cassorla, R. M. S. (2001). Acute enactment as resource in disclosing a collusion between the analytical dyad. *International Journal of Psychoanalysis, 82* (6): 1155–1170.

Cassorla, R. M. S. (2005a). From bastion to enactment: The "non-dream" in the theatre of analysis. *International Journal of Psychoanalysis, 86* (3): 699–719.

Cassorla, R. M. S. (2005b). "Enactment and Trauma." Panel, IPA 44th Congress, Rio de Janeiro.

Chasseguet-Smirgel, J. (1999). Un comentario. In: E. S. Person, P. Fonagy, & S. A. Figueira (Eds.), *En torno a Freud. El poeta y los sueños diurnos* (pp. 124–125). Madrid: Biblioteca Nueva.

Cotard, J. (1882). Du délires des négations. In: *Études sur les maladies cérébrales et mentales.* Paris: Baillière, 1891.

Deutsch, H. (1930). Melancholia. In: *Psycho-Analysis of the Neuroses.* London: Hogarth Press.

Duhalde, E. L. (1997). *El estado terrorista. Quince años después, una mirada crítica.* Buenos Aires: Eudeba.

Ellman, S. J., & Moskovitz, M. (Eds.) (1998). *Enactment: Toward a New Approach to the Therapeutic Relationship.* Northvale, NJ: Jason Aronson.

Emmert, T. A. (1990). *Serbian Golgotha: Kosovo, 1389.* New York: Columbia University Press.

Engel, G. L. (1961). Is grief a disease? A challenge for medical research. *Psychosomatic Medicine, 23* (1): 18.

Engel, G. L. (1962). *Psychological Development in Health and Disease.* Philadelphia/London: Saunders.

Erikson, E. H. (1956). The problem of ego identification. *Journal of the American Psychoanalytic Association, 4*: 56–121.

Fairbairn, W. R. D. (1944). Endopsychic structure considered in terms of object relationships. In: *Psychoanalytic Studies of the Personality* (pp. 82–136). London: Routledge & Kegan Paul, 1981.

Fairbairn, W. R. D. (1952). *Psychoanalytic Studies of the Personality.* London: Routledge & Kegan Paul, 1981.

Falzeder, E. (2002). *The Complete Correspondence of Sigmund Freud and Karl Abraham, 1907–1925.* London: Karnac.

Ferenczi. S. (1909). Introjection and transference. In: *First Contributions to Psychoanalysis.* New York: Brunner-Mazel, 1980 (reprinted London: Karnac, 1994).

Ferro, A. (1992). *The Bi-Personal Field: Experiences in Child Analysis.* Hove: Brunner-Routledge, 1999.

Freud, S. (1895b). On the grounds for detaching a particular syndrome from neurasthenia under the description "anxiety neurosis". *S.E., 3.*

Freud, S. (1900a). *The Interpretation of Dreams. S.E., 4/5.*

Freud, S. (1905d). *Three Essays on the Theory of Sexuality, S.E., 7.*

Freud, S. (1905e [1901]). Fragment of an analysis of a case of hysteria. *S.E., 7.*

Freud, S. (1908e [1907]). Creative writers and day-dreaming. *S.E., 9.*

Freud, S. (1909d). Notes upon a case of obsessional neurosis. *S.E., 10.*

Freud, S. (1910c). *Leonardo da Vinci and a Memory of His Childhood. S.E., 11.*

Freud, S. (1910d). The future prospects of psycho-analytic therapy. *S.E., 11.*

Freud, S. (1910i). The psycho-analytic view of psychogenic disturbance of vision. *S.E., 11.*

Freud, S. (1911b). Formulations on the two principles of mental functioning. *S.E., 12.*

Freud, S. (1911c). Psycho-analytic notes on an autobiographical account of a case of paranoia (dementia paranoides). *S.E., 12.*

Freud, S. (1912–13). *Totem and Taboo, S.E., 13.*

Freud, S. (1914c). On narcissism: An introduction. *S.E., 14.*

Freud, S. (1914d). On the history of the psychoanalytic movement. *S.E., 14.*

Freud, S. (1915b), Thoughts for the times on war and death. *S.E., 14.*

Freud, S. (1915c). *Instincts and Their Vicissitudes. S.E., 14.*

Freud, S. (1915d). Repression. *S.E., 14.*

Freud, S. (1915e). The Unconscious. *S.E., 14.*

Freud, S. (1916a). On transience. *S.E., 14.*

Freud, S. (1916–17). *Introductory Lectures on Psycho-Analysis. S.E., 16.*

Freud, S. (1917d [1915]). A metapsychological supplement to the theory of dreams. *S.E., 14.*

Freud, S. (1917e [1915]). Mourning and melancholia, *S.E., 14.*

Freud, S. (1920g). *Beyond the Pleasure Principle. S.E., 18.*

Freud, S. (1921c). *Group Psychology and the Analysis of the Ego, S.E., 18.*

Freud, S. (1923b). *The Ego and the Id. S.E., 19.*

Freud, S. (1924c). The economic problem of masochism. *S.E., 19.*

Freud, S. (1925h). Negation. *S.E., 19.*

Freud, S. (1926d [1925]). *Inhibitions, Symptoms and Anxiety. S.E., 20.*

Freud, S. (1927c). *The Future of an Illusion. S.E., 23.*

Freud, S. (1927e). Fetishism. *S.E., 21.*

Freud, S. (1930a). *Civilization and Its Discontents. S.E., 21.*

Freud, S. (1933a). *New Introductory Lectures on Psycho-Analysis. S.E., 22.*

Freud, S. (1937d). Constructions in analysis. *S.E., 23.*

Freud, S. (1940a [1938]). *An Outline of Psycho-Analysis. S.E., 23.*

Freud, S. (1940e [1938]). Splitting of the ego in the process of defence. *S.E., 23.*

Freud, S. (1950a). *The Origins of Psycho-Analysis. S.E., 1.*

Freud, S. (1950 [1895]). A project for a scientific psychology. *S.E., 1.*

Gay. P. (1988). *Freud: A Life for Our Time.* New Haven, CT: Yale University Press.

Green, A. (1983a). The dead mother. In: *Private Madness* (pp. 178–206). Madison, CT: International Universities Press, 1987.

Green, A. (1983b). *Narcissisme de vie, narcissisme de mort.* [Narcissism of life, narcissism of death]. Paris: Éditions de Minuit.

Green, A. (2000). *Le temps éclaté* [Exploded time]. Paris: Éditions de Minuit.

Greenacre, P. (1969). The fetish and the transitional object. In: *Emotional Growth, Vol. 1* (pp. 315–334). New York: International Universities Press.

Grinberg, L. (1957). Perturbaciones en la interpretación por la contraidentificación proyectiva. *Revista de Psicoanálisis, 14*: 23–30.

Grotstein, J. S. (1981). *Splitting and Projective Identification*. New York: Jason Aronson.

Grotstein, J. S. (2000). *Who Is the Dreamer Who Dreams the Dream? A Study of Psychic Presences*. Hillsdale, NJ: Analytic Press.

Grotstein, J. S. (2005). Projective transidentification: An extension of the concept of projective identification. *International Journal of Psychoanalysis, 86* (4): 1051–1068.

Guignard, F. (1996). *Au vif de l'infantile. Réflexions sur la situation analytique*. Lausanne: Delachaux & Niestlé, Coll. "Champs psychanalytiques".

Guignard, F. (1997). Généalogie des pulsions. In: *Épître à l'objet* (pp. 26–32). Paris: Presses Universitaires de France, Coll. Épîtres.

Guignard, F. (2001). Le couple mentalisation↔démentalisation, un concept métapsychologique de troisième type. *Revue Française de Psychosomatique, 20*: 115–135.

Heimann, P. (1950). On counter-transference. *International Journal of Psychoanalysis, 31*: 81–84.

Jacobson, E. (1971). *Depression*. New York: International Universities Press.

Jones, E. (1955). *The Life and Work of Sigmund Freud, Vol. 2*. New York: Basic Books.

Jones, E. (1957). *The Life and Work of Sigmund Freud, Vol. 3*. New York: Basic Books.

Joseph, B. (1985). Transference: The total situation. In: E. B. Spillius (Ed.), *Melanie Klein Today*. London: Routledge.

Joseph, B. (1989). Psychic equilibrium and psychic change: *Selected Papers of Betty Joseph*, ed. M. Feldman & E. B. Spillius. London: Routledge.

Junqueira Filho, L. C. U. (1986). Valor psicanalítico do equivalente mental visual. In: *Sismos e acomodações. A clínica psicanalítica como usina de idéias* (pp. 15–42). São Paulo: Rosari, 2003.

Kaës, R. (1988). Rupturas catastróficas y trabajo de la memoria. In: J. Puget & R. Kaës (Eds.), *Violence d'état et psychanalyse*. Paris: Dunod. (Spanish: *Violencia de Estado y Psicoanálisis*. Buenos Aires: Centro Editor de América Latina, 1991.)

Karo, J. (1557). Duelo. In: *Síntesis del Shuljan Aruj*. Buenos Aires: Editorial Sigal, 1956.

Kernberg, O. (2004). *Contemporary Controversies*. New Haven, CT: Yale University Press.

Kijak, M. (1981). "The Sense of Identity in the Extermination Camp Survivors and in Their Children." Paper presented at the Conference of the American Psychoanalytical Association.

Kijak, M. (1998). El sentimiento de identidad en los sobrevivientes de los campos de exterminio y en sus hijos. *Revista de Psicoanálisis, 60* (3).

Kijak, M., & Funtowicz, S. (1982). The syndrome of the survivor of extreme situations-definitions, difficulties, hypotheses. *International Review of Psycho-Analysis*, *9*: 25–33.

Kijak, M., & Pelento, M. L. (1985). El duelo en determinadas situaciones de catástrofe social. *Revista de psicoanálisis*, *42* (4, Part I).

King, P., & Steiner, R. (1991). *The Freud–Klein Controversies 1941–45*. London: Tavistock/Routledge.

Klein, M. (1921). The development of a child. In: *Love, Guilt and Reparation and Other Works 1921–1945: The Writings of Melanie Klein, Vol. 1* (pp. 1–53). London: Hogarth Press, 1975.

Klein, M. (1927). Criminal tendencies in normal children. In: *Love, Guilt and Reparation and Other Works 1921–1945: The Writings of Melanie Klein, Vol. 1* (pp. 170–185). London: Hogarth Press, 1975.

Klein, M. (1930). The importance of symbol formation in the development of the ego. *International Journal of Psychoanalysis*, *11*: 24–39. Also in: *Love, Guilt and Reparation and Other Works 1921–1945: The Writings of Melanie Klein, Vol. 1* (pp. 219–232). London: Hogarth Press, 1975.

Klein, M. (1935). A contribution to the psychogenesis of manic-depressive states. In: *Love, Guilt and Reparation and Other Works 1921–1945: The Writings of Melanie Klein, Vol. 1* (pp. 262–289). Also in: *Contributions to Psychoanalysis, 1921–1945* (pp. 282–310). London: Hogarth Press, 1968.

Klein, M. (1940). Mourning and its relation to manic-depressive states. In: *Love, Guilt and Reparation and Other Works 1921–1945: The Writings of Melanie Klein, Vol. 1* (pp. 370–419). London: Hogarth Press, 1975. Also in: *Contributions to Psycho-Analysis, 1921–1945* (pp. 311–338). London: Hogarth Press, 1968.

Klein, M. (1946). Notes on some schizoid mechanisms. In: *Envy and Gratitude and Other Works: The Writings of Melanie Klein, Vol. 3*. London: Hogarth Press, 1975. Also in: M. Klein, P. Heimann, S. Isaacs, & J. Riviere, *Developments in Psychoanalysis* (pp. 292–320). London: Hogarth Press, 1952.

Klein, M. (1950). The psychogenesis of manic-depressive states. In: *Contributions to Psycho-Analysis*. London: Hogarth Press.

Klein, M. (1952a). The origins of transference. In: *Envy and Gratitude and Other Works: The Writings of Melanie Klein, Vol. 3* (pp. 48–56). London: Hogarth Press, 1975.

Klein, M. (1952b). Some theoretical conclusions regarding the emotional life of the infant. In: *Envy and Gratitude and Other Works, 1946–1963: The Writings of Melanie Klein, Vol. 3* (pp. 61–93). London: Hogarth Press, 1975.

Klein, M. (1955). On identification. In: *Envy and Gratitude and Other Works, 1946–1963: The Writings of Melanie Klein, Vol. 3* (pp. 141–175). London: Hogarth Press.

Klein, M. (1975). *Love, Guilt and Reparation and Other Works 1921–1945: The Writings of Melanie Klein, Vol. 1*. London: Hogarth Press.

Kleinpaul, R. (1898). *Die Lebendigen und die Toten in Volksglauben, Religion und Sage*. Leipzig.

Kristeva, J. (1994). *El tiempo sensible: Proust y la experiencia literaria*. Buenos Aires: Ed. Eudeba, 2005.

Krystal, H. (1976). *Massive Psychic Trauma*. New York: International Universities Press.

Laasonen-Balk, T., Viinamäki, H., Kuikka, J. T., Husso-Saastamoinen, M., Lehtonen, J., & Tiihonen, J. (2004). 123I-beta-CIT binding and recovery from depression: A six-month follow-up study. *European Archives of Psychiatry and Clinical Neurosciences, 254*: 152–155.

Lagache, D. (1956). Le deuil pathologique. *La Psychanalyse, 2*: 45.

Laplanche, J. (1980). *Problématique, I: L'angoisse*. Paris: Presses Universitaires de France.

Laplanche, J. (1992). *La révolution copernicienne inachevée*. Paris: Ed. Aubier.

Laplanche, J. (1990). Duelo y temporalidad. *Revista Trabajo del Psicoanálisis, 4* (10).

Lehmann, H. (1966). A conversation between Freud and Rilke. *Psychoanalytic Quarterly, 35*: 423–427.

Lehtonen, J. (2006). "Body Ego, Vital Affects and Depression: A Framework Studying the Biological Effects of Psychotherapy on Depression." Paper presented at conference, Psikoanaliz ve Sinirbilimleri [Psychoanalysis and Neurosciences], Istanbul (May 28–29).

Lehtonen, J., Kononen, M., Purhonen, M., Partanen, J., Saarikoski, S., & Launiala, K. (2002). The effects of feeding on the electroencephalogram in 3- and 6-month old infants. *Psychophysiology, 39*: 73–79.

Loewald, H. (1978). Primary process, secondary process and language. In: *Papers on Psychoanalysis* (pp. 178–206). New Haven, CT: Yale University Press, 1980.

Mahler, M. S. (1968). *On Human Symbiosis and the Vicissitudes of Individuation*. New York: International Universities Press.

Marucco, N. (1999). De la represión a la desmentida. In: *Cura analítica y transferencia*. Buenos Aires: Ed. Amorrortu.

Melgar, M. C. (1999). El muerto-vivo. Una pasión narcisista. In: *Volviendo a pensar con Willy y Madeleine Baranger. Nuevos desarrollos* (pp. 301–312). Buenos Aires: Grupo Editorial Lumen.

Melgar, M. C. (2005). Trauma y creatividad. Psicoanálisis y arte. *Revista de Psicoanálisis, 62* (3): 591–600.

Melgar, M. C., & López de Gomara, E. (2000). Carpaccio. Melancolía. Conflicto temporal. *Arte y locura* (chap. 7). Buenos Aires: Ed. Lumen.

Mello Franco Filho, O. (2000). Quando o analista é alvo da "magia" do paciente. Considerações sobre a comunicação inconsciente do estado mental do paciente ao analista. *Revista Brasileira de Psicanálise, 34* (4): 687–709.

Meltzer, D. (1984). *Dream-Life: Re-Examination of the Psycho-Analytical Theory and Techniques.* Strath Tay: Clunie Press.

Money-Kyrle R. E. (1956). Normal counter-transference and some of its deviations. *International Journal of Psychoanalysis, 37*: 360–366.

Niederland, E. G. (1968). Clinical observations of the survivor syndrome. *International Journal of Psychoanalysis, 49.*

Ochsner, J. K. (1997). A space of loss: The Vietnam Veterans Memorial. *Journal of Architectural Education, 10*: 156–171.

Ogden, T. (1982). *Projective Identification and Psychotherapeutic Technique.* New York: Jason Aronson

Ogden, T. (1983). The concept of internal object relations. *International Journal of Psychoanalysis, 64*: 181–198.

Ogden, T. (1994). *Subjects on Analysis.* London: Karnac.

Ogden, T. (1995). Analysing forms of aliveness and deadness of the transference countertransference. *International Journal of Psychoanalysis, 76*: 695–709.

Ogden, T. (1997). *Reverie and Interpretation: Sensing Something Human.* Northvale, NJ: Jason Aronson; London: Karnac.

Ogden, T. (2001a). *Conversations at the Frontier of Dreaming.* Northvale, NJ: Jason Aronson; London: Karnac.

Ogden, T. (2001b). Reading Winnicott. *Psychoanalytic Quarterly, 70*: 299–323.

Pollock, G. (1975). Mourning and memorialization through music. In: *The Annual of Psychoanalysis, Vol. 3* (pp. 423–436). New York: International Universities Press. Also in: *Psychoanalytic Explorations in Music* (chap. 10). Madison, CT: International Universities Press, 1990.

Pollock, G. (1989). *The Mourning–Liberation Process, Vols. 1 & 2.* Madison, CT: International Universities Press.

Pontalis, J. B. (2003). *La traversée des ombres.* Paris: Éditions Gallimard.

Puget, J. (1988). Preface. In: J. Puget & R. Kaës (Eds.), *Violence d'état et psychanalyse.* Paris: Dunod. (Spanish: *Violencia de Estado y Psicoanálisis.* Buenos Aires: Centro Editor de América Latina, 1991.)

Quinodoz, J. M. (2004). *Reading Freud: A Chronological Exploration of Freud's Writings,* trans. D. Alcorn. London/New York: Routledge, 2005.

Racker, H. (1948). La neurosis de contratransferência. In: *Estudios sobre técnica analítica* (pp. 182–221). Buenos Aires: Paidós, 1977.

Rocha Barros, E. M. (2000). Affect and pictographic image: The constitution of meaning in mental life. *International Journal of Psychoanalysis, 81*: 1087–1099.

Roheim, E. (1945). Animism and dreams. *Psychoanalytic Review, 32*: 62.

Rosenfeld, H. (1987). *Impasse and Interpretation.* London: Tavistock

Rosolato, G. (1996). *Le porté du désir ou la psychanalyse même*. Paris: Presses Universitaires de France.

Saarinen, P. L., Lehtonen, J., Joensuu, M., Tolmunen, T., Ahola, P., Vanninen, R., Kuikka, J., & Tiihonen, J. (2005). An outcome of psychodynamic psychotherapy: A case study of the change in serotonin transporter binding and the activation of the dream screen. *American Journal of Psychotherapy, 59*: 61–73.

Sandler, J. (1976). Countertransference and role-responsiveness. *International Review of Psychoanalysis, 3*: 43–47.

Sandler, J. (Ed.) (1988). *Projection, Identification, Projective Identification*. London: Karnac.

Sandler, J. (1993). On communication from patient to analyst: Not everything is projective identification. *International Journal of Psychoanalysis, 74*: 1097–1107.

Sandler, J. (1998). A theory of internal object relations. In: *Internal Objects Revisited*. Madison, CT: International Universities Press.

Sandler, J., & Rosenblatt, B. (1962). The concept of the representational world. *Psychoanalytic Study of the Child, 17*.

Scruggs, J., & Swerdlow, J. L. (1985). *To Heal a Nation: The Vietnam Veterans Memorial*. New York: Harper & Row.

Segal, H. (1957). Notes on symbol formation. *International Journal of Psychoanalysis, 38*: 39. Also in: *The Work of Hanna Segal* (pp. 121–130). New York: Jason Aronson.

Smith, J. H. (1975). On the work of mourning. In: B. Schoenberg, I. Gerber, A. Wiener, A. H. Kutscher, D. Peretz, & A. C. Carr (Eds.), *Bereavement: Its Psychological Aspects* (pp. 18–25). New York: Columbia University Press.

Sodré, I. (2005). Notes on Freud's "Mourning and Melancholia". In: R. J. Perelberg, *Freud: A Modern Reader*. London: Whurr.

Steiner, J. (1993). *Psychic Retreats: Pathological Organizations in Psychotic, Neurotic and Borderline Patients*. London: Routledge.

Steiner, J. (1996). The aim of psychoanalysis in theory and in practice. *International Journal of Psychoanalysis, 77*: 1073–1083.

Stern, D. N., Sander, L. W., Nahum, J. P., et al. (1998). Non-interpretative mechanisms in psychoanalytic therapy: The "something more" than interpretation. *International Journal of Psychoanalysis, 79*: 903–921.

Strachey, J. (1934). The nature of the therapeutic action of psycho-analysis. *International Journal of Psychoanalysis, 15*: 127–159.

Strachey, J. (1953). Editor's comment. In: S. Freud, *Three Essays on the Theory of Sexuality* (1905d). *S.E., 7*: 3.

Strachey, J. (1957a). Editor's introduction. In: S. Freud, "Papers on Metapsychology" (1911–15). *S.E., 14*: 105–107.

Strachey, J. (1957b). Editor's note. In: S. Freud, "Instincts and Their Vicissitudes" (1915c). *S.E., 14*: 111.

Strachey, J. (1957c). Editor's note. In: S. Freud, "Mourning and Melancholia" (1917e [1915]). *S.E.*, 14: 237.

Suárez, J. C. (1983). Reflexiones acerca de un sobreviviente de los campos de exterminio. *Revista de Psicoanálisis, 40.*

Tähkä, V. (1984). Dealing with object loss. *Scandinavian Psychoanalytic Review, 7*: 13–33.

Tausk, V. (1913). Compensation as a means of discounting the motive of repression. *International Journal of Psychoanalysis, 5* (1924): 130.

Viñar, M. (2005). Por qué pensar en los desaparecidos? Violencia dictatorial y memoria del terror. *Semanario Brecha.*

Volkan, K. (1992). The Vietnam Memorial. *Mind and Human Interaction, 3*: 73–77.

Volkan, V. D. (1972). The "linking objects" of pathological mourners. *Archives of General Psychiatry, 27*: 215–221.

Volkan, V. D. (1977). Mourning and adaptation after a war. *American Journal of Psychotherapy, 31*: 561–569.

Volkan, V. D. (1981). *Linking Objects and Linking Phenomena: A Study of the Forms, Symptoms, Metapsychology and Therapy of Complicated Mourning*. New York: International Universities Press.

Volkan, V. D. (1985). Complicated mourning. In: *Annual of Chicago Institute of Psychoanalysis* (pp. 323–348). Chicago, IL: University of Chicago Press.

Volkan, V. D. (1991). On "Chosen Trauma." *Mind and Human Interaction, 3*: 13.

Volkan, V. D. (1997). *Bloodlines: From Ethnic Pride to Ethnic Terrorism*. New York: Farrar, Straus & Giroux.

Volkan, V. D. (2004). After the violence: The internal world and linking objects of a refugee family. In: B. Sklarew, S. W. Twemlow, & S. M. Wilkinson (Eds.), *Analysts in the Trenches* (pp. 77–102). Hillside, NJ: Analytic Press.

Volkan, V. D. (2006). *Killing in the Name of Identity: Stories of Bloody Conflicts*. Charlottesville, VA: Pitchstone.

Volkan, V. D., & Ast, G. (1997). *Siblings in the Unconscious and Psychopathology*. Madison, CT: International Universities Press.

Volkan, V. D., Ast, G., & Greer, W. (2001). *The Third Reich in the Unconscious: Transgenerational Transmission and its Consequences*. New York: Brunner-Routledge.

Volkan, V. D., Cilluffo, A. F., & Sarvay, T. L. (1975). Re-grief therapy and the function of the linking object as a key to stimulate emotionality. In: P. Olsen (Ed.), *Emotional Flooding* (pp. 179–224). New York: Behavioral Publications.

Volkan, V. D., & Josephthal, D. (1980). The treatment of established psychological mourners. In: R. V. Frankiel (Ed.), *Essential Papers on Object Loss* (pp. 299–324). New York: University Press.

Volkan, V. D., & Zintl, E. (1993). *Life after Loss: Lessons of Grief.* New York: Charles Scribner's Sons.

Winnicott, D. W. (1945). Primitive emotional development. In: *Through Paediatrics to Psychoanalysis* (pp. 145–56). London: Hogarth Press, 1958.

Winnicott, D. W. (1953). Transitional objects and transitional phenomena. *International Journal of Psycho-Analysis, 3*: 89–97.

Winnicott, D. W. (1971). The place where we live. In: *Playing and Reality* (pp. 104–110). London: Routledge.

Wolfenstein, M. (1966). How mourning is possible. *Psychoanalytic Study of the Child, 21*: 93–123.

Wolfenstein, M. (1969). Loss, rage and repetition. *Psychoanalytic Study of the Child, 24*: 432–460.

Young, J. E. (1993). *The Texture of Memory: Memorials and Meaning.* New Haven, CT: Yale University Press.

Zuckerman, R., & Volkan, V. D. (1989). Complicated mourning over a body defect: The making of a "living linking object". In: D. Dietrich & P. Shabad (Eds.), *The Problem of Loss and Mourning: New Psychoanalytic Perspective.* New York: International Universities Press.

INDEX